Now & Then, The Movies Get It Right

A Dozen Films that Dazzle, Delight... and *Say* Something

by **NEAL STANNARD**

"Now and then, movie critics and historians do get it right, which is happily the case this time for Neal Stannard's new book, Now and Then, The Movies Get It Right, which is nothing short of a tour de force of twelve fabulous films from the Silver Age, 1951 to the present. Hat's off!"

David Hagberg, New York Times bestselling author of
The Expediter, Burned, Mutiny, and *Soldier of God*

"I am most impressed, not only with Neal's approach to the subject, but also with his choice of films to support his thesis. I find it provocative; I find it stimulating; and I see it as a course in upper grad work for a university program in Philosophy."

Lawrence Montaigne, film and TV actor, dancer, educator best known as "Stonn" and "Decius" in *Star Trek* and "Haynes" in *The Great Escape*

"A fascinating read for people who like to think beyond the confines of the box; for people who seek the message behind the marquis; and for people who open their minds and hearts to unusual perspectives of human drama, in and out of the movies. Be prepared for a stimulating ride. Neal Stannard has definitely produced a winner."

Marshall Frank, author of *Criminal Injustice in America, From Violins to Violence, Militant Islam in America* and *The Latent*

Now and Then, The Movies Get It Right
© 2010 Neal Stannard. All Rights Reserved.

No part of this book may be reproduced in any form or by any means, electronic, mechanical, digital, photocopying or recording, except for the inclusion in a review, without permission in writing from the publisher or copyright holder. However, excerpts of up to 500 words may be reproduced online if they include the following information, "This is an excerpt from *Now and Then, the Movies Get It Right* by Neal Stannard."

Published in the USA by:
BearManor Media
PO Box 1129
Duncan, Oklahoma 73534-1129
www.bearmanormedia.com

ISBN 978-1-59393-614-3

Printed in the United States of America.
Edited by David W. Menefee.
Book design by Brian Pearce | Red Jacket Press.

Dedication
For Linda Schiffer, who turned a dream into reality.

Stand by your convictions
With a mellow tone.
— Gemini Joe Fuccino
from Gemini Joe *by Janet Sierzant*

The man he was had been taken from him,
and I hope deposited in some good place for safekeeping.
—*from* Paul and Me: 53 Years of Adventures
and Misadventures with My Pal Paul Newman *by A.E. Hotchner*

Be kind whenever possible. It is always possible.
— *13th Dalai Lama*

Table of Contents

Introduction by Gene Colan 11

Acknowledgments 15

Overture: Twelve Courageous Stands 19

STUDY I: ROCK HUDSON 25
1. *Giant.* Rock Hudson is the Texas cattle baron gently nudged by his imported wife, Virginia belle Elizabeth Taylor, to gradually overcome the prejudices he'd never have otherwise questioned. 27

2. *The Spiral Road.* Hudson, always underrated as a dramatic actor, has another all-too-rare chance to show his dramatic mettle, as a jungle physician whose greatest enemy isn't his environment, but rather his own ambition, arrogance, atheism, and alcoholism. 41

STUDY II: JIMMY STEWART 63
3. *Shenandoah.* Jimmy Stewart shines as a Civil War farmer who resembles, more than a little, Ayn Rand's Howard Roark in *The Fountainhead:* a strong-willed man who firmly believes his own integrity and stubbornness can shield his family from the devastation around them — and, in making his Stand, learns differently. 66

4. *Flight of the Phoenix.* Elleston Trevor's novel of plane-crash survivors who, "...faced with the choice of dying or doing the impossible, elect to live," spotlights Jimmy Stewart and an all-star cast, who will make their Stand by building a new aircraft from the wreckage of the old, if they can overcome not only the heat and the thirst, but each other, and their own inner demons. 87

STUDY III: *STAR TREK* *121*

5. *Star Trek:* "Arena." It's not the first time, and certainly not the last, that a *Star Trek* commander will represent all of humanity, but it's one of the best, as William Shatner's iconic Captain James T. Kirk, ordered by seemingly omnipotent beings to kill his alien enemy, makes his Stand, telling them "I won't do it — you'll have to get your entertainment somewhere else!" *122*

6. *Star Trek:* "The Doomsday Machine." William Windom bestrides the grand, operatic stage of *Star Trek* as a starship captain who has lost everything, his crew and his ship, to the title device, and whose Stand is a grand, if suicidal, gesture of defiance that paves the way for victory. *137*

STUDY IV: ERROL FLYNN *159*

7. *Too Much, Too Soon.* Meant to be tragedy, Diana Barrymore's account of her own self-destruction descends all too often into self-pity — but this uneven film achieves a certain radiance in Errol Flynn's loving but unsparing portrayal of his idol, John Barrymore — who, in Diana's words, "…fulfilled his promise as few men have, yet always felt himself a fraud and a failure." *162*

8. *The Roots of Heaven.* Predating the popularity of environmentalism, *The Roots of Heaven* found little audience for its wry and witty story of a bad-tempered ex-p.o.w. (Trevor Howard) who makes his Stand fighting to preserve the African elephant, and inspires a cast of colorful characters to follow him: Orson Welles, Juliette Greco, Eddie Albert, Paul Lukas, Friedrich Ledebur, and Flynn again, finding a level of personal redemption in his last big-screen role. *180*

STUDY V: THE REAL-LIFE HEROES *199*

9. *MacArthur.* Gregory Peck straightforwardly portrays the many virtues, and the myriad flaws, of the flamboyant General who made his greatest Stand not in helping to win the Pacific war, but in almost single-handedly winning the peace afterward. *200*

10. *Schindler's List.* Often avoided because of its setting amidst the real-life horrors of the Holocaust, Steven Spielberg's film biography of the German manufacturer (Liam Neeson) who, while 6 million were perishing, saved 1,100, is a highly entertaining account of a man whose Stand celebrates the victory of common decency over overwhelming evil. *226*

**STUDY VI: *TREK* EL GRANDE
OR *TREK* PURE SPIRIT?** *273*
11. and 12. *Star Trek* (2009) and *Star Trek: Of Gods and Men*. Two remarkable versions of Gene Roddenberry's vision appeared late in the 2000s: J. J. Abrams' *Star Trek* hit movie screens in a big-budget, high-energy effort to jumpstart a stalled franchise, recasting roles and updating technology, while on the Internet, an independently produced feature quietly emerged, aimed more at longtime fans than potential new viewers. *275*

Finale: Three Prescriptions..*301*

Bibliography...*311*

INTRODUCTION by Gene Colan

A book about films and the Silver Age? That sure sounded like *my* cup of tea, so I started reading Neal Stannard's *Now and Then the Movies Get It Right,* and boy, am I glad I did!

I can't speak for other artists, but the biggest influence on my storytelling was film. I just love film, and part of me wishes I'd gone into that industry instead of comics. But the grass is always greener!

I'll never forget when my father took me to see *Frankenstein* in 1931. I was five. My father took me to see it up in the Bronx. I still remember the theatre up on a big hill. I was never the same after that film!

I've spent sixty years drawing comics, but really, I've always been making movies in my own mind. I try to capture on page for a reader what a viewer would see on the screen. I set up my own storyboards and then use light and shadow to add the drama to every panel. Sometimes I even surprise myself.

There's something about movies that inspires all of us. For me, there's nothing better than a film like *It's A Wonderful Life* or *The Treasure of the Sierra Madre*. We all have our favorites, the movies that inspire us and change us. In this wonderful little book, Neal Stannard has found thirteen films that do both of those things, or try to, and he shows us how they did it. What fun!

Most of the films that Neal looks at come from the early 1960s. Boy, was that a magical time in comics. I was still leading a double-life as Adam Austin and Gene Colan (it's a long story, and maybe someone will make a film about it one day!). The 1960s seemed to be a time of change for everything politically and socially, and comics and film certainly reflected those changes. I'll tell you this: nobody wanted to be preached to anymore, so if you had something to say you had to say it straight. For me, it meant drawing the most exciting and interesting stories that I could — and I was lucky because I had a boss like Stan Lee who was willing to push the envelope. Marvel Comics was part of what was happening in the 190s. It really was. Somewhere between the lines, we were able to communicate our own ideas about what was right and wrong, about behaving properly. As Spider-Man learned very early, with great power comes great responsibility.

Today's fans refer to the 1960s as the Silver Age of Comics. I've never really understood what that term means. To me, the Golden Age is when you were a child, so I guess the Silver Age is when you are an adolescent! But it was certainly a magical age, and I guess it makes sense to consider that time a Silver Age of Movies, too. To fit that framework, films from that time would have to meet that certain standard of "getting it right" in the stories they told and the values they imparted.

The thirteen films in this book do exactly that, and that's why they remind me of the stories we were turning out during those same days. At the very least, reading them entertained you. At the very best, you were a better person for having read them.

So here are thirteen films that reach for the same brass ring we were going for in those days — films that try to do something important. The stories of the films and the people who made them are important and inspiring, too. Enjoy!

ACKNOWLEDGEMENTS AND SUCH

This book is blessed by contributions from two of the twentieth century's premiere American artists: the introduction by Gene Colan, and the illustration (on page 198) by Joe Sinnott. The fact that both worked in the medium of comic books — sequential storytelling, to those who take it seriously — should in no way diminish the importance of their work. In an era where Manga-influenced cartoon caricatures are all the rage, "Gentleman Gene" and "Joltin' Joe" have spent more than half a century bringing an extraordinary photographic realism to their illustrations.

Comic art is usually, though not always, a two-step collaboration, with the artwork laid down in pencil by the initial artist, and then rendered in India ink by the inker, or finisher. Though Colan and Sinnott are adept in both media, Sinnott earned the bulk of his reputation as an inker, considered the best of the best by his peers, and best-known for highly-regarded runs on the *Fantastic Four, Thor, Captain America,* and other Marvel titles. Colan literally transformed pencil art, evolving a magical mix of light and shadow that came to be known as "Painting With a Pencil," honing his craft on a wide variety of Marvel characters such as *Sub-Mariner, Iron Man, Daredevil, Dracula* and *Howard the Duck*, and other company features including *Batman, Archie, Teenage Mutant Ninja Turtles,* and *Buffy the Vampire Slayer!*

Heavily influenced by cinema, Colan has more than returned the favor: Blade, featured in three films and on television, was created for *Tomb of Dracula* by Colan and writer Marv Wolfman, while Whiplash, the villain of *Iron Man II* (2010), was introduced by Colan and Stan Lee — in 1968!

Both Colan and Sinnott are well into their eighties, and both are, coincidentally, recuperating from serious arm injuries. Colan, who seldom pencils full-length stories these days, won rave reviews last year for a double-sized, forty page *Captain America* special — and Sinnott, as of this writing, keeps the Silver Age alive by inking the weekly *Spider-Man* newspaper strip. Amazingly, both continue to produce the best work of their careers, raising the bar for writers, filmmakers, artists, and craftsmen in all media.

Others without whom this book would not be possible:

Ben Ohmart, the publisher who believed in a first-time author. Ben's BearManor Media occupies a publishing niche that is huge not in size, nor in revenue, but in passion: people love the movies, TV shows, and radio programs that have touched them with a heartfelt fervor found nowhere else.

David W. Menefee, editor, who cleaned up the awkwardness and digressions in this book, and whose own published titles, including *Sarah Bernhardt in the Theater of Films and Sound Recordings*, *The First Female Stars: Women of the Silent Era*, *The First Male Stars: Men of the Silent Era*, *George O'Brien: A Man's Man in Hollywood*, *Richard Barthelmess: A Life in Pictures*, *"Otay!" The Billy "Buckwheat" Thomas Story*, and *Wally: The True Wallace Reid Story*, reveal a deep love and knowledge of film history and lore.

Mark Sinnott, who maintains the website that celebrates the life and career of his famous father, and arranged for the use of the *MacArthur* still-life illustration.

Harry Langdon, photographer extraordinaire, who allowed the use of his photo of Rock Hudson and one of his dogs. That photo may say more about Hudson than all our words.

Sky Conway, Ethan Calk, and Jack Treviño, whose amazing *Star Trek: Of Gods and Men* celebrates an incredible legacy, and who have been incredibly generous with time, information, and resources.

Clifford Meth, whose career as a writer of dark and "self-consciously Jewish" fiction is seriously jeopardized by two things: first, in the words of Harlan Ellison, "the demented titles he puts on" his stories (*Crib Death & Other Bedtime Stories; This Bastard Planet; Crawling From the Wreckage: The White Man Limping; Wagging the Rebbe; Perverts, Pedophiles & Other Theologians*), and second, the increasing amount of time he spends helping friends and colleagues who have fallen onto hard times.

Joyce Levi, proofreader of eagle-eye and infinite patience.

Finally, authors tend to conclude these acknowledgements by saying that the credit for whatever the book gets right should go to those named above, while blame for all errors and omissions should be laid at the author's feet. This is a cliché; it is also the unvarnished truth.

Neal Stannard
June 2010

OVERTURE:
TWELVE COURAGEOUS STANDS

Films are for people. To entertain. To instruct. And, ever so rarely, to inspire. How odd, then, that those who do the entertaining, the instructing, and the inspiring — the actors — are so seldom treated as people. Especially in the heyday of the Hollywood studio system, they were brand-name products, commodities, and audiences tended to identify them with the parts they played.

One of the greatest of Hollywood film legends and actresses, Miss Bette Davis, summed it up succinctly for an interviewer: "The more successful an actor, the less he or she gets to act…People come to expect a personality, and that's the kind of parts you get offered, ones to suit audience expectations of your star's persona."

Bette Davis knew about Stands and how to take them. She also knew about the costs of making and taking those Stands. The actors in this book, as well as the real people presented herein, recognized the truth in Miss Davis's statement, for they, too, had their own Stands to make, on and off stage.

Courage is not a commodity — and it can often break the will and spirit of those who express it. Hollywood was good at that!

So is the world we live in.

ARKADIN

And now I'm going to tell you about a scorpion. A scorpion wanted to cross a river, so he asked a frog to carry him. "No," said the frog. "No, thank you. If I let you on my back you may sting me, and the sting of the scorpion means death." "Now, where," asked the scorpion, "is the logic in that? No scorpion could be judged illogical. If I sting you, you will die — I will drown." The frog was convinced and allowed the scorpion on his back, but just in the middle of the river felt a terrible pain and realized that after all the scorpion had stung him. "Logic!" cried the dying frog.

"There is no logic in this!" "I know," said the scorpion, "but I can't help it — it's my character." Let's drink to character!

— from Mr. Arkadin *(1955) Screenplay by Orson Welles.*

If this book has anything to say to anybody, it is this: yes, damn it, the scorpion *can* help it. So can we. If we choose to.

One thing we have chosen to do, here, is to spotlight the word "Stand." If "Stand" makes you think of Stephen King, go to the head of the class. Much like the new preacher who is taken to task by the church Board for preaching the same sermon each Sunday for his first seven weeks, and responds "Ayup, an' I'm gonna keep a-preachin' it until y'all start a'-*doin'* it," many writers are often trying to convey the same message, over and over again, until some one *hears* and, more importantly, some one *heeds*.

Carrie, Christine, most especially, *The Tommyknockers,* and to a lesser extent, *The Stand,* are all about making a Stand — just as other King stories, most notably *The Shining,* are about characters who fail to make a Stand, and the consequences that ensue.

To paraphrase, King's definition of a Stand seems to run something like this: This far have I been pushed, but no further. Here I Stand. No more retreats, no more temporizing, no more compromises. Here I Stand and I will not be moved. You may destroy me. But you will not defeat me. Here I Stand!

ORSON WELLES
I expected more from you, Mank.

HERMAN MANCKIEWICZ
Me, too. But I got used to it.

— from RKO 281: The Battle Over Citizen Kane *(1999) Screenplay by John Logan*

Is Humanity perfectible? That's one of the weighty questions that all of man's religions have wrestled with — and with the exception of a few diehard Humanists, all have answered unanimously — *no!*

But if it's not perfectible, it can bloody well be *improved*. If you seek the answer to a treatise that includes *Star Trek* and *Schindler's List* ("There is no logic in this!" said the frog), here is the logic: in each and every one of these twelve, the character or characters triumph over themselves. Often they triumph over circumstances as well, but not always. The triumph that is achieved is that of the individual over him — or herself. In the darkening shadows of a person's life, that may be the only triumph that matters.

Certainly, it may be the one we have to settle for.

That is the index of true character.

When it's done right — and how incredibly seldom that happens — the ideal medium for telling the story of the Stand, of triumph over self, is film. The written word has been cited, correctly, as the ideal medium for transmitting a complex idea from one mind to another. The Stand, at least as defined here, is not just an idea, it's an experience — an emotional experience — and that is best transmitted by film, preferably film watched in a darkened room without distractions.

So, here are twelve such films, six of them from the fifties and sixties, featuring actors who may surprise you: Rock Hudson, Errol Flynn, and James Stewart — none of them in the roles, or type of roles. they became famous for, but bringing all their talent and power to characters who make just the sort of Stand described here; then, two visions of the future by one of the greatest visionaries of them all, Gene Roddenberry, who saw, and created, a better world and a grander universe than we could ever hope for; followed by the life stories of two very real men who lived their Stands: Douglas MacArthur and Oskar Schindler, whose heroism stems from the defiance of others' expectations; and finally, back to the grand operatic showcase called *Star Trek* for two recent offerings, as different in their creation and execution as two films with one theme can possibly be.

So, here is a journey, a trek — through a series of cinematic Stands. Actually, it's best enjoyed as a sort of "Cliffs Notes" accompaniment to the films described. However, if you want it to read on its own merits, don't let us stop you!

If we're going to examine twelve films while asking deep and profound questions, the question properly arises: Why this book? By this author? Now?

Andre Brink wrote a magnificent story called "A Dry White Season," which was made, as magnificent stories often are, into an indifferent film, with Donald Sutherland and Marlon Brando, which offers an answer to that question:

> "I have the feeling that deep inside every man there's something he is "meant" to do. Something no one but he can achieve. And then it's a matter of discovering what your own personal something is. Some find it quite

early in life. Others drive themselves to distraction trying to find it. And still others learn to be patient and prepare themselves for the day when, suddenly, they'll recognize it. Like an actor waiting for his cue... So there must be something no one but me can do; not because it is 'important' or 'effective,' but because only I can do it."

Donald Sutherland and Marlon Brando in A Dry White Season. *It shoulda been a contender.*

Later, as if sensing an overweening nobility in that answer, as well as a tad too much self-importance, Brink circles back to his own theory a few pages later and brings it back down to earth:

"Never aspire to save the world. Your own soul and one or two others are more than enough... There are only two kinds of madness one should guard against, Ben. One is the belief that we can do everything. The other is the belief that we can do nothing."

Finally, this book is for all those who share the belief that all men and all women, everywhere, of all colors and all traditions and all intellects, are worthy of respect, and that anything one does to any one of them, one also does to God — whatever one chooses to call Him or Her.

As for those who persevere in their provincialism, who continue to fly in the face of universal brotherhood and bellow hysterically, "Kill 'em all and let God sort it out," this book is not for them.

It is intended for living minds, not dead ones.

Roy Fitzgerald and friend. PHOTO BY HARRY LANGDON.

STUDY I
Rock Hudson

He was the #1 box-office draw in the United States for six years in a row, in the top ten for ten years, yet Rock Hudson has never really been appreciated as an actor, during his lifetime, or since. In his early years of fame, he appeared without his shirt more often than not, a sort of "male Marilyn Monroe" syndrome in which he was expected to look beautiful and "move well to direction" (his words) and not much else. A 1959 pairing with Doris Day in *Pillow Talk* revealed a natural flair for light romantic comedy, defining the stereotype that enriched him, and dogged him for the rest of his career.

Few noticed that, after requiring thirty-eight takes to get a single line right in his first film, *Fighter Squadron* (1948), Hudson had learned his craft quickly and thoroughly as a Universal contract player. As is the case with all artists of consequence, training and experience freed and augmented what was already there: a natural gift for the craft, to "hold the mirror to reality," as Shakespeare put it.

If anything unites the actors spotlighted here — Hudson, Errol Flynn, James Stewart, William Shatner, Gregory Peck, Ben Kingsley, Liam Neeson — it is this: the ability to convey emotion beyond dialogue, through the eyes, through expression, through posture. Technique can be taught, but the art of conveying the character's thoughts, emotions, experiences — you have it or you don't. Hudson had it in spades.

Yet his acting career was, and is, eclipsed by his off-screen life — or the public perception of that life, which, because he was an intensely private man, has largely been a fiction. Legend has it that he was named "Rock" by his notorious agent, Henry Willson, and legend, as usual, is wrong; nevertheless, he was part of the Willson "stable" of similarly-named stars that included Tab Hunter, Rory Calhoun, and Rip Torn, and the name helped fix the image of the handsome hunk, the desirable male. The name boosted the image yet circumscribed the career. When casting an American President, which actor do you choose — "Charlton" or "Rock"?

Presidential roles came to Hudson late in his career, but seldom the respect of his peers in film, at least in his native land. He was honored with five Bambis, the German equivalent of the Oscar, two Venetian Film Festival Awards, other awards from Britain and elsewhere, but none from the Motion Picture Academy or the American Film Institute. When the fact that he had or may have had AIDS was revealed not long before his death in 1985, the image of Rock the Dashing Lover was replaced by another: Rock the Closet Homosexual. Though his posthumous role as The Poster Boy for AIDS research has raised a great deal of badly-needed money, the image of Rock as an exclusive homosexual is no more accurate than his previous image as an exclusive heterosexual — and the preoccupation with his sex life, which continues to this day, obscures the fact that the man was a linguist, a musician, a painter, and an actor of rare ability. Roy Harold Fitzgerald — his real name — was uniquely and magnificently equipped to portray the kind of character this essay is all about: the man who triumphs over himself, who makes a Stand.

Three times in his career, Hudson was cast in roles that allowed him to fully demonstrate that talent: in *Giant* (1956), *The Spiral Road* (1962), and *Seconds* (1966). The first was probably the closest he came to actual recognition — an Academy Award nomination — but the attention went to fellow nominee James Dean, who died immediately after filming so that his legend "lives on, unhampered now by his existence," which was a phrase originally used by Ernest Hemingway to describe Theodore Roosevelt. The second failed at the box-office and sank into the oblivion of late-night television, only achieving DVD release in 2006. The third, a dark, harrowing science fiction tale of resurrection gone horribly wrong, failed at the time, but gradually gained the status of a cult classic. Thankfully, Hudson lived to enjoy satisfaction over that status.

Seconds is not a part of this collection, because the central character *doesn't* triumph over himself, which is the whole point of the film, but the characters in the first two films do exactly that. Meet them now: Bick Benedict and Anton Drager, two men whose Stands shine as glowing examples of the human spirit — and serve as the enduring legacy of a fine actor, and an even finer *man*.

STAND ONE: *GIANT*

(11/24/1956: Warner Bros.) Directed by George Stevens; Written by Fred Guiol & Ivan Moffat, from Edna Ferber's novel; Music by Dimitri Tiomkin; Photographed by William C. Mellor; Edited by William Hornbeck.

JORDY
Oh, look, Papa, if I'm concerned it has to do with the people that oughtta know better — like my own father. Oh, Good Lord, I don't care about Jett Rink! But you, Papa, that's different!

BICK
Now, you look here, Jordy... There's ways of livin' and there's ways of doin' things that folks abide by, when they wanna live right and happily in comfort with their own people. An' I always say Juana's a mighty fine little gal, but...

JORDY
Don't sit there and prove what I say, please, I don't like to hear you do it! Now stop it!

That's the central conflict of the film, though this scene between Jordan "Bick" Benedict (Rock Hudson) and his son Jordy (Dennis Hopper) marks the first time it is put into overt words. Texans remember this 1956 epic of epics as a paean to their "country," while film fans and appreciation societies mark it as the third and last starring role for James Dean before his early death. Both of these views miss the point.

Many Texans had taken novelist Edna Ferber to task, having wined and dined her and then found her novel to be something between a biting satire and an outright condemnation of their land and their lifestyle. Actually, it's an allegory, with Texas representing any human society — nation, religion, or group — whose inordinate pride renders them blind to their own failings and injustices. And Bick Benedict, the central character, represents Everyman in such a society: the good-hearted, brave, decent man who, in the normal course of events, will never realize his own potential for goodness, because of that very blindness. Ninety-nine men out of a hundred will never overcome that blindness of pride, and most will never even see why they should *want* to do so, or would perceive such an ambition as a sign of weakness. Bick Benedict is the one-in-a-hundred who is strong enough to outgrow his limitations — but he would never do so, or want to do so, without both the prodding and example of his wife.

Ferber's novel starts with the Benedicts, married for a quarter-century, attending the opening of Jett Rink's airport and hotel, the latest and greatest self-aggrandizing project of that megalomaniac oilman (James Dean), and then reverts to flashback to show how Bick courted and married his wife. Screenwriters Fred Guiol and Ivan Moffat eliminate the flashback, starting the story in 1920s Maryland, where Bick has gone to buy the beautiful black stallion, War Winds, from the prominent physician Dr. Horace Lynnton (Paul Fix) — and winds up smitten with Lynnton's headstrong daughter, Leslie. In casting the gorgeous Elizabeth Taylor, George Stevens ignored Ferber's description of Leslie as not beautiful but rather possessing a unique glow or aura, perhaps the only particular in which Taylor doesn't fit the character with precision.

The flashback was scrapped, says Moffat on the DVD commentary, "to show our first glimpse of Texas after Maryland, as Leslie would see it — having come from the charming green, open setting of Maryland she'd always known. We wanted to jar the audience the same way the first sight of Texas jars Leslie. Contrast is the theme here: contrast of culture, contrast of nature, contrast of surroundings and attitudes, the contrast between Texan and Mexican, the contrast between Leslie and Bick — that's the machine that drives the movie, right from the start and right up to the end."

The visual contrast is certainly a vivid one, as Leslie steps from the train onto the arid Texas plain, then endures a fifty-mile ride across the Reata ranch to the Benedict "house" — a gothic mansion in the middle of nowhere — but it's nevertheless a contrast she's prepared to accept and even savor. What she's not prepared to accept, not for a moment, is the condescending attitude of her husband and his compatriots to the Mexicans who live with them — in the role of servants and employees.

BICK
Take it easy, Leslie. Down here, we don't make a fuss over these people. You're a Texan now.

LESLIE
Is that a state of mind? I still have a mind of my own. Elsewhere, being gracious is acceptable.

Quickly, Leslie comes into conflict with Bick's somewhat brusque and mannish sister Luz (Mercedes McCambridge), who runs the house and perhaps even the ranch, as Bick acknowledges. While the other Texas women have succumbed to their roles with meekness and docility, Luz has compensated by becoming rough and domineering — and at first, she attempts to dominate the newcomer, even assigning Bick and Leslie separate bedrooms. Leslie responds by beginning to manage domestic affairs, telling Luz "I don't want to take your place, but I can't have you taking my place, either. I can't be just a guest in my husband's house." This bids fair to escalate into a major conflict, but this element of the story is quickly cut short when Luz attempts to express her authority by riding War Winds in an especially

vicious manner — "I suppose you came out here to show me how to run things, too" — only to be thrown and killed by the spirited animal.

Luz's death has cleared the way for Leslie to assume her role as Lady of the Manor, but it hasn't changed her need to treat the Mexican workers with humanity, as she commandeers the physician who had come to treat the dying Luz:

LESLIE

Dr. Walker…Mrs. Obregon's baby is very sick. His temperature must be over 105. I'll go with you myself, Doctor.

BICK

Leslie, you can't do that. He can't go there. He's our doctor. He don't tend those people. They have a way of doin' things by themselves.

LESLIE

Jordan, darling, I don't think you quite understand. There's a child who is very sick. I must take Doctor Walker.

This is another point where the story can go off the rails into overt conflict, but doesn't. Such is Bick's strength of character — and love for his wife — that, when she returns, he simply asks her how the child is

doing. This will be a recurrent theme in the film: Leslie will continue to proceed according to her own lights, usually with the concurrence of her chief ally in the Benedict family, Uncle Bawley (Chill Wills, whose gentle folksiness masks a shrewd and perceptive character), and as a rule, Bick will come, gradually, to buy into his wife's values.

There is one notable exception, and the one time that the relationship threatens to erupt into violence: Bick is discussing politics with family and friends — *male* family and friends — all of whom fall deathly silent at Leslie's approach. Her gently humorous attempts to persuade them to continue fail to move any of them, even Uncle Bawley ("You too, Uncle Brutus?"), prompting a tirade:

LESLIE
Men's stuff? Lord have mercy! Set up my spinning wheel, girls, I'll join the harem section in a minute. If I may say so before retiring, you gentlemen date back one hundred thousand years. You oughtta be wearing leopard skins and carrying clubs! Politics! Business! What is so masculine about a conversation that a woman can't enter into it?

Bick is incensed and ready to spend the night in a separate bedroom, but it doesn't happen. At one point, they do undergo a trial separation, with Leslie returning to Maryland with their three children, but Bick soon follows, and the pattern is set for their marriage:

LESLIE
Jordan, I — I'm no different than I was when I left.

BICK
We Texans like a little vinegar in our greens, honey — gives 'em flavor.

Neither Ferber nor Stevens is inclined to cross the line into outright conflict, or for that matter, into the soap opera territory later explored so profitably by *Dallas* and *Dynasty* (ironically, Rock Hudson's last acting assignment). A good example of the soap opera that threatens to happen, but doesn't, involves James Dean's character, Jett Rink.

The contribution of Jimmy Dean (as all his colleagues on the film called him) has been blown out of all proportion because, in the words of the Warner Bros. press book, Dean "...was killed in an auto tragedy even before the film was released and became the object of an adoration cult, classing him among film immortals like Rudolph Valentino, Jean

Harlow and Marilyn Monroe." Dean and Hudson were both nominated for Best Actor Oscars, but Dean's part is distinctly supporting and, in terms of the aging of the characters over a quarter-century, not nearly as well-acted as the characters of Hudson, Taylor, or even supporting players such as Wills and Jane Withers (a breezy presence as the Benedicts' neighbor, Vashti Snyth).

Jett Rink is a ne'er-do-well, jack-of-all-trades working as a ranch hand at Reata, who has found favor in some strange way with Luz. Upon her death, he learns that she has left him a small piece of the ranch, which Bick immediately offers to buy from him at twice the market value — but Rink declines, deciding it's "…a pretty good idea to gamble along with old Madama…Just gamble on, just keep what she give me."

Rink is not especially bright, but he's *cunning*, and the cunning pays off when the "worthless" land yields oil, in staggering amounts. Rink tweaks the noses of the rich ranchers he has always resented, in what amounts to Dean's tour-de-force scene:

JETT
My well came in, Bick. Ever'body thought I had a duster? Y'all thought ol' Spindletop an' old Burkburnett was all the oil there was, din'ya? Well, I'm here ta tell ya it ain't, boy! It's here, an' there ain't a dang thing you

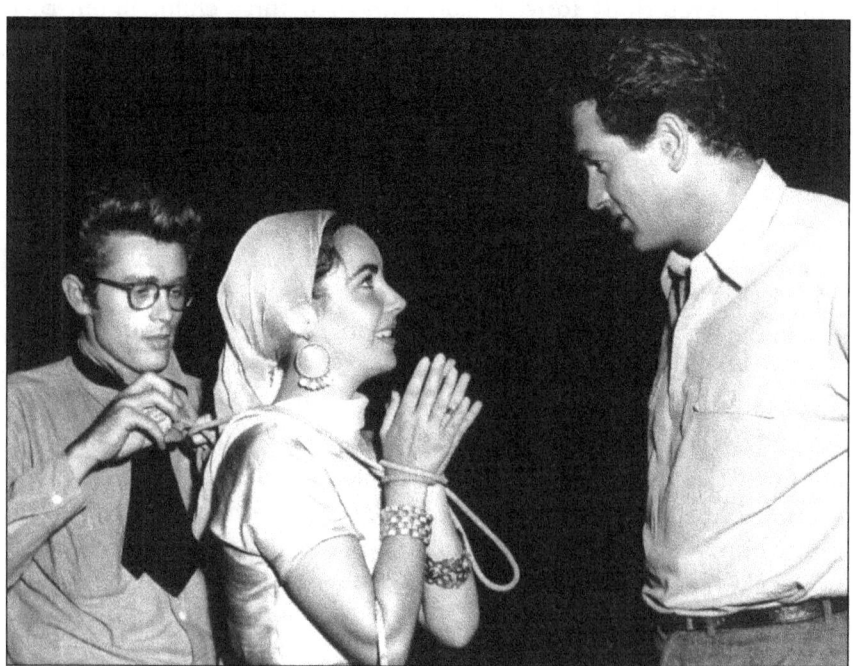

gonna do about it. My well came in big, so big, Bick, an' there's more down there an' there's bigger wells — I'm rich, Bick! I'm a rich 'un. I'm a rich boy. Me, I'm gonna have more money'n you ever thought you could have — you 'n' all the rest'a you stinkin' sons of Benedicts!

Uncle Bawley sums up the influence Rink's fortune will have on the land and the people:

BAWLEY
Bick, you shoulda shot that fella a long time ago. Now he's too rich to kill!

The film moves rather quickly through the next two decades, as Rink amasses wealth and the Benedicts watch with disgust. Bick resists the temptation to sell oil concessions on his own land for many years, but he eventually realizes — in the midst of a well-played Christmas morning drinking binge — that no one wants the massive ranch he's fought so long and hard to preserve: his son, Jordy, wants to be a doctor, not a rancher, and his son-in-law, Bob Dace (Earl Holliman), who *is* a rancher, wants his own, smaller place — "Big stuff is old stuff now!" Bick finally gives in and does business with his one-time employee — to his great profit, since this is December 1941, and the USA has just entered World War II.

BICK
Y'know, all this oil 'round here hasn't made a lotta difference. We live pretty much the way we always have here at Reata.

BAWLEY
Mm-hmm. Just like we Benedicts found it. Bick, the Lord was good to you to set that concrete pool right down in y'own front yard, though.

The relationship between Rink and the Benedicts is another area where the story could degenerate into outright soap, but never does. Rink pines after Leslie, and later, after her daughter, Luz the II (Carroll Baker), but Leslie never reciprocates, and Luz II merely flirts with the idea.

Eventually, the film reaches the point where the book began: the opening of the Jett Rink airport, and the associated hotel, the last word in opulence. Here, the culture clash erupts yet again: to his father's chagrin, young Jordy Benedict has not only chosen medicine over ranching, but has married a beautiful Mexican girl, Juana (Elsa Cardenas). At the Rink soirée,

Juana is refused service at the hotel's beauty salon because of her ethnicity. This leads Jordy to smash the salon window (in the book, he shoots up the place), and he storms into the banquet honoring Rink, calling the tycoon out. The later dialogue between father and son sums up the action:

BICK

When that ruckus started down there tonight, who went after Rink? Your ol' man! An' who took him to account? Your ol' man!

JORDY

And why? Because of my wife? No! No, because your son, Jordan Benedict, descendant of the long, proud line of Reata, got knocked right flat on his back in front of all Texas — that's why!

Actually, when Bick confronts Rink behind closed doors, the long-anticipated fisticuffs never come, because Rink is too drunk to even form a decent fist — "You ain't even worth hittin'," a disgusted Bick tells him. Bick stalks off, and Rink staggers into his own banquet, up to the microphones set up to broadcast his speech from coast to coast, and passes out cold.

To this point, young Luz feels a real sympathy for Rink and resentment of her own family: "It seems that my family just can't tolerate his success!"

But Bawley takes her to see how low her hero has sunk, as Rink addresses the now-empty room in a grotesque parody of his prepared speech:

JETT

Ladies 'n' gennlemun, distinguished guests. Tonight, I just wanna count the blessings that this great domain has bestowed upon her humble son... Old Mother Texas! Wha'd she give ta me? Not a Goddamn thing! Ya gotta work 'n' sweat 'n' steal it from her. But I got mine — right outta the ground! Poor Jett — fightin' for what is good. Flunky! Flunky for Bick Benedict...her husband...Pretty Leslie. Wonderful, beautiful girl bride...Rich, rich Mrs. Benedict. She's beautiful. Lovely. The woman a man wants! The woman a man's gotta have, too!

It should be another crowning moment for Dean in the film; it *isn't*, because unlike Hudson and Taylor, Dean has not mastered the older version of his character, beyond outward physical manifestations. In fact, *the voice in this scene is not even Dean's* — he had played the drunkenness so far over the top that the words were unintelligible, so the dialogue was re-voiced after his death by actor Nick Adams.

In story terms, though, the pathetic, self-pitying speech makes its point: *Jett Rink is a loser.* He has attained the outward trappings of power and success, but he has failed to overcome his own prejudices and his own limitations. Jett Rink is an empty shell of a man, neatly summed up in Ferber's book in an especially well-turned phrase: "Jett Rink...walked, not as a man who has authority and power, but as a man who boasts of these."

The contrast with Bick Benedict is glaringly obvious. Bick has been gradually emerging as a genuinely fine man; at the conclusion of the war, he is seen presenting his personal Texas state flag to the parents of a Mexican ranch hand who came home in a coffin: Angel Obregon, Junior (Sal Mineo) — poignantly, the same Obregon, whose fever, as an infant, had prompted Leslie to challenge local taboos.

Bick has come a long way since then, but, as his son pointed out, his basic thinking still hasn't changed. That will come in the penultimate scene in the film, the moment when Bick surprises those around him, and even himself — the moment when...

BICK BENEDICT MAKES HIS STAND

Returning from the fiasco of the Rink hotel bash, Bick is traveling with his wife, Leslie, Luz, Juana, and grandson Jordan IV, an infant who has inherited the Hispanic looks of his mother — when the four stop for a quick bite at a roadside café called Sarge's Diner.

Sarge (played by Mickey Simpson, one of the few character actors big enough to fight Rock Hudson) is a grizzled veteran with a typical Texas attitude toward "wetbacks." After initially objecting to the two Hispanics in the party — "That there papoose down there, his name

Bick Benedict makes his Stand: "On the floor, on your back, in the middle of the salad, you were at last my hero!"

Benedict, too?" — he relents and allows Bick's party to eat in peace, only to take his wrath out on the next family to enter the eatery, an elderly Hispanic couple and their daughter: "This bunch here's gonna eat somewheres else!"

The night before, Bick Benedict challenged Jett Rink, more out of a sense of wounded pride. This time, there's no temporizing, no evasions, no excuses: Bick takes on the burly restaurateur in one of the most realistic fistfights ever filmed — realistic enough that Bick, being older and heavier than the other man, loses.

Back at home, he laments that this latest failure is the last in a long line — until, once again and for good, his wife sets him straight:

BICK
I'm a failure. Nothin's turned out like I planned. I just feel like my saddle's turnin' right out from under me.

LESLIE
Do you want to know something, Jordan? I think you're great! You know all that fine riding you used to do and all that fancy roping and all that glamour stuff you did to dazzle me? Oh, it was impressive — but none of it ever made you quite as big a man to me as you were on the floor of Sarge's hamburger joint. When you tumbled rearward and landed crashing into that pile of dirty dishes, you were at last my hero — ooh, what a fight! It was glorious! Before we went into that place, I was feeling like you are now. I was thinking to myself: Well, Jordan and I, and the others behind us, have been failures. And then it happened! You wound up on the floor, on your back, in the middle of the salad. And I said to myself: Well, after a hundred years, the Benedict family is a real big success!

And there the film ends, on a close-up of the eyes of the two Benedict grandchildren, the blue-eyed Anglo and the brown-eyed Hispanic, as the soundtrack segues into "The Eyes of Texas Are Upon You." So they are — and they have beheld their Grandpa, the man who overcame himself to make his Stand.

The analogy is complete. There is greatness in Bick Benedict, just as there is greatness in Texas.

Greatness is not measured in boasting and swaggering and breast-beating. Greatness is measured in doing right when it is least expected.

Greatness is as greatness does.

THE BALANCE SHEET

Oddly enough, Ferber did not even include Bick in the diner scene in her book — thus, the full-circle redemption of the cattle baron's character is an invention of the filmmakers, rather than the author — which is as it should be, since filmmaking is more of a collaboration than almost any other art.

Says George Stevens, Jr. in the DVD commentary: "Often credited, as we do, as 'A George Stevens Film,' *Giant* simply could not exist without Edna Ferber: she wrote a novel that was the whole platform for this movie. Yet there is a whole additional layer, or layers, that are imposed upon her script, y'know, the personal insights of and observations that come from Ivan (Moffat) and (Fred) Guiol, and Dad, who worked on the screenplay, and Ferber herself, who worked in certain aspects on the screenplay."

Rock Hudson, who struck up a deep and long-lasting friendship with "the little lady who wrote the big book," later reported that Ferber approved many of the changes made in the movie, even regarding some as "corrections." One of the most poignant scenes *not* originating with Ferber occurs about midway through the film, when Leslie has taken the three young children, barely old enough to talk, to visit her parents in Maryland. The three youngsters are allowed to feed and befriend the Lynntons' turkey, "Pedro," an idea that backfires on Thanksgiving Day. Confronted with the centerpiece of the holiday feast, the children react with recognition, asking *"Is that Pedro?"* — after which they break into screaming and bawling and refuse to eat.

Could you eat a hamburger if you were on a first-name basis with the cow?

It is such humanity that informs the film, that never allows it to disintegrate into an epic ramble. Nor is that humanity limited to what shows on-screen. Filming in the small town of Marfa, Texas, George Stevens used many of the townspeople as extras, and invited everyone to the rushes, shown each night in a local theatre. Just as much through his own personality as with his adroit filmmaking, he enlisted the support of the natives. The same folks who had resented Ferber's often sarcastic, acerbic book embraced the film, as George Stevens, Jr., explains: "The people in Texas were very frightened of this movie, and I remember before it came out, a man named Bob O'Donnell, who was the biggest exhibitor in Texas, had threatened not to show it in Texas, because the book had really made Texans uncomfortable, it was very unkind. I think my father's nature as a storyteller and a person — he didn't like blacks and whites, in terms of characters that were simple — and this becomes a much more complex story. And when the film opened, the Texans loved it...though it made fun of them in some respects...it's a film with such humanity, and the conflicts were so real, that they couldn't but respect and feel proud of it. So, this book that was the bane of Texans' existence for a while became a film which is probably the proudest cultural document of Texas."

So many of the young actors cast by Stevens in *Giant* went on to notable careers in film and/or television: Dennis Hopper, Carroll Baker, Earl Holliman, Sal Mineo. The English nobleman who marries Leslie's sister is played by a young Australian called Rodney Taylor — later, and better, known as Rod Taylor (in wedding photo, above).

As for the leads, two of the great performances on film were almost totally overshadowed by that of the supporting player who died so suddenly, and became such a cult figure of obsessive fascination and even worship. Donald Spoto explains in *Rebel: The Life and Legend of James Dean:*

> Elizabeth Taylor and Rock Hudson, who were required to do much more with their roles, acted with remarkable subtlety and to far more emotional effect. They could not have been happy to read that critics wrote almost exclusively of the supporting player... James Dean died before he could fail, before he lost his hair or his boyish figure, before he grew up."

Such was not the fate of Taylor or Hudson, whose careers and lives endured the frequent shakes and shocks of changing audience tastes, their off-screen reputations, and finally, devastating illness. Taylor's many marriages (two of them to Richard Burton) often overpowered the public's appreciation of her talent, which found few further suitable outlets — for instance, her razor-sharp work in *Who's Afraid of Virginia Woolf?* (1966).

As was the case with many studio contract players, Rock Hudson returned home to a studio that never seemed to appreciate what he had accomplished during his loan-out. Universal continued to exploit him as a handsome hunk — and, after *Pillow Talk* (1959), in a number of romantic comedies. Universal did not give their #1 box office draw a chance to really act until 1962...

STAND TWO: *THE SPIRAL ROAD*

(8/3/1962: Universal) Directed by Robert Mulligan; Written by John Lee Mahin and Neil Paterson, from Jan de Hartog's novel; Music by Jerry Goldsmith; Photographed by Russell Harlan; Edited by Russell F. Schoengarth.

> JANSEN
> *Back in so-called civilization, you can ignore God and get away with it. But out here in the jungle, God takes people who say He doesn't exist, pokes 'em with His finger and makes 'em squirm a little. There are times out here when you can almost hear the Old Boy humming.*

The idea of a hero who is made to squirm — whether by an almighty God, or by his own hubris — is a hard sell for audiences, then and now. Maybe that's one reason that a film that had everything going for it — hot director, hot star, hot property — died at the box office and languished in obscurity for over forty-four years, until Universal almost *sneaked* it into release on the tail-end of a five-DVD collection of oddly selected Hudson films in 2006. Perhaps they had heard from the small but vocal minority who felt the full power of this compelling story — including this writer. *The Spiral Road* grabbed my ten-year-old soul as a "late, late movie" in the summer of 1967, and has never let it go, a condition testified to by several others writing on the Internet Movie Database website over the years.

Film press books, especially vintage examples, are a treasure trove for the true aficionado. Whether the film in question is *Gone With the Wind* or *Amazon Women of Zenn-La*, it is presented as the greatest artistic achievement since Pope Julius II made Michelangelo paint a ceiling. Even so, *The Spiral Road* press book offers a contemporary peek at the hopes and expectations for the movie:

> "Rock Hudson, the number-one box office star of the motion picture screen, zooms his triumphant career even farther into the golden orbit of international popularity with the most intensely dramatic role he has ever essayed in Universal's powerfully absorbing *The Spiral Road*...the great literary achievement by the noted Dutch novelist, Jan de Hartog...the adventure story of a doctor's tormented journey through the hell of his temptations...a brilliant appraisal of civilized man's struggle against the jungle, combining the jungle's brutal dangers with the constant battle of the human spirit against the lures of depravity and degradation, was partly filmed on location deep into the jungles of Surinam (Dutch Guiana)..."

Not mentioned is the fact that director Robert Mulligan was coming off the success of *To Kill A Mockingbird* with Gregory Peck; that film had yet to achieve its status as a timeless favorite. To expect this movie to do the same was not unrealistic, just inaccurate. And that's a shame, because the story of Anton Drager, and the Stand he makes, is a valuable and important one with ramifications for those who discover it.

Anton Drager (Hudson) is the man every parent wishes a daughter would bring home, at least superficially. He's a doctor, he's bright and hardworking, the winner of Gold Medals, and, as we'll see, gifted with a rare, instinctive capacity for the practice of medicine. Apparently he has worked his way up from poverty: in this year of 1936, five years before Japanese bombs began to fall on this portion of the proposed "Greater East Asia Co-Prosperity Sphere," this young Dutchman has turned up in Batavia (now Jakarta, Indonesia) under terms of a contract: "In consideration of the monies expended by the Government in your behalf, you will, upon graduation, report to the Netherlands East Indies Health Service for a period of not less than five years."

As he loses no time in informing his immediate superior, Dr. Piet Kramer (Larry Gates), he has very definite plans: to work with the legendary Dr. Brits Jansen (played with appropriate physical and psychological bulk by Burl Ives).

DRAGER
Because he's top man out here in tropical medicine — and certainly the world's foremost authority on leprosy. But isn't it true, sir, that except for a few tracts written almost twenty years ago, he hasn't recorded anything about his work — his successes, his failures, methods of diagnosis, proposals for future research? Then let me work out my five years with him, sir! Let me get to know what he knows and I'll see that it's done. I'll do it with him!

Kramer points out that Drager has chosen a less-than-lucrative field.

DRAGER
But in research, sir? If a man like Brits Jansen were in Holland right now, he'd be offered millions for research.

KRAMER
And the same is also possible for a young man who stepped off the boat wrapped in the aura of Brits Jansen's knowledge.

DRAGER
Dr. Kramer, I don't intend to get off that boat with just a wrinkled white suit, and the hope of getting over malaria. Is there anything wrong with that?

Impressed — or bemused — Kramer tells his Field Service supervisor, Dr. Martens (Robert F. Simon), to send the new man to the village three weeks upriver where Jansen is fighting a plague epidemic:

KRAMER
Marty, our Gold Medal winner wants to win some more medals. If he can get along with Brits, I'll pin one on him myself. If not, he'll come running back, ready to work and behave himself.

Dispatched to the frontier town of Rokul to be outfitted for his trip, Drager meets two men who will figure dramatically in his future: Harry Frolick (Philip Abbott), a Beethoven-loving, alcoholic river master, and the local Salvation Army representative, Captain Willem Wattereus (Geoffrey Keen). At dinner, a sozzled Frolick taunts the "illustrious prescriber," apparently part of a long-standing antagonism, but a dryly disgusted Drager puts an end to it. When Wattereus attempts to explain, we first glimpse Drager's religious convictions — or lack of same.

WATTEREUS

Poor Harry. He's going through a hell all his own, trying to prove that God doesn't exist. For if God doesn't exist, then Harry's sins don't exist. That's why he's so violent and unhappy, you understand.

DRAGER

I'm afraid not, Captain. To me, Harry Frolick is just a poor idiot who can't hold his liquor.

Equipped by hotelier Krasser (Leslie Brandt) with everything he needs for the trip — including a broad-brimmed hat he is loath to wear, until the pounding sun changes his mind — Drager sets off in command of two canoes manned by native bearers. They are reluctant to accept his commands, since he is a "Totuk" ("Take no offense," Kramer had told him. "It simply means 'newcomer.'") The term seems to also carry connotations of "greenhorn" and "wet behind the ears." Nevertheless, an impressively bearded Drager arrives at the village of Rauwatta, with his cargo of anti-plague venom and "P.G." He is mystified when The Great Man opens a tin of the latter and takes a great, satisfying swig.

DRAGER

What is that, Doctor? They didn't tell me.

JANSEN
Gin. P.G. Pure Gin! If you're gonna faint on me, ya better have some!

The Great Man treats the "Totuk" with evident condescension: at one point he tosses Drager a stick of dynamite, and in answer to "What'll I do with it?" retorts "Son, don't tempt me or I'll tell ya!" The smart-ass routine meets unexpected resistance when the two men are cleaning up:

JANSEN
I'm an authority on Totuks. I've wet-nursed a half-a hundred in my time. Which reminds me: you haven't asked the one big question yet... Doctor, do you think I'm suited to this work?" Well, go on, ask it.

DRAGER
I don't give a damn whether you think I'm suited to this work or not!

JANSEN
Well said. Well said! There's some hope for you, my boy! Now, don't boil over this early. You'll run outta steam!

Nurturing the beginnings of respect, Jansen takes Drager to meet the native ruler of the region, The Sultan (Edgar Stehli, who plays an Oriental in that time when white actors were accepted in such roles):

JANSEN
I've hated his guts and he's hated mine for the past thirty years — and that makes us pretty close. Y'know, Totuk, as you get older it's the relationship that counts, not the nature of it — just the fact that it exists.

Told that his village — and his palace — must be set to the torch, the cagey native challenges the giant medical man to a game of billiards: Thirty years earlier, Jansen had won just such a game, the stakes of which were the Sultan's acceptance of the Government Health Service. Jansen agrees to the rematch as a sop to the old man's vanity, only to find himself unexpectedly losing — until Drager's younger, sharper eyes spot a number of imperfections in the table's surface — "little manufactured bumps!" Jansen thunders. The two doctors then proceed with the dramatic burning of the village, forcing the plague-carrying rats into a gasoline-filled trench, which Drager sets alight.

Shortly afterward, Drager finds the old Sultan sitting regally in Jansen's tent, and ritually serves him tea from Jansen's own cup — noticing, in the process, the beginnings of a leprous lesion on the old man's hand. When he reports this to the "world's foremost authority on leprosy," the result is predictable:

JANSEN

Listen, Totuk, you can diagnose fallen arches, head colds, athlete's foot, bumps on billiard tables, anything you like, except leprosy! Is that clear?

Of course, it comes as a surprise to the crusty old veteran — but not to the audience — that Drager's assessment is absolutely correct.

JANSEN

All right, Totuk, how'd you know? What made you so certain it was leprosy...an intuitive diagnosis, hmm?

DRAGER

Call it what you like.

JANSEN
Very well. I'll say you made an intuitive diagnosis. That's a rare gift —
Doctor *Drager.*

Now that Drager's role as a subordinate of promise has been established, the two take the Sultan to the Manpuko leper colony, run by Jansen's "closest friends," Willem and Betsy Wattereus. Greeted with fondness by the Captain, Drager is taken aback to learn that the man's wife, gorgeous in a photo, is a far-gone, speechless leper, victim of the disease she spent her life fighting. This leads to another religious confrontation between the two physicians:

DRAGER
You ever thought of putting her out of her misery? I'll do it, if you like.

JANSEN
I think you mean it. Well, let me tell you why I couldn't go through with it. It was three years ago. She could still talk a little then. She opened her eyes and looked at me — and she knew. Then she asked God to forgive me — even for the thought of it, to forgive me. Y'see, she reminded me of something that, 'til that moment, I had almost forgotten: the Lord giveth, and the Lord taketh away, and I had no right to play God.

Religious convictions aside, the master and the pupil continue to work well together. Old Brits has only one fear, and that is that "…every Totuk has his Honey Lamb" waiting back home, and Jansen doesn't want his protégé distracted. When "Honey Lamb," the very Nordic and very naïve Els Van Diem (Gena Rowlands), wangles a visit to the frontier outpost Labuan Redjo, in the company of a colonial official (Parley Baer) and his wife, Jansen swings into action, organizing a drunken, riotous welcoming party designed to frighten the three visitors out of their wits.

While the VIP couple is successfully distracted, Els is not, slipping outside into Anton's arms — and shortly thereafter, into the office of a Justice of the Peace who marries them. Confronted with the fact that his plan has backfired, a drunken Jansen quickly sobers up and dismisses the newlyweds:

JANSEN
I had plans for your continuing to work with me. No, it wouldn't work out at all. It — it never has. A man in the field has to be of one mind. He can't be worried about a wife back in Batavia. He can't have any ties,

with the work that I have planned for him. He must be a man alone — and I somehow got the feeling that you were. That's why I thought that perhaps, some day, you could — well, but that's that, I guess.

In the ensuing months, Anton spends more time attending to Jansen's disorganized notes at Manpuko than to his new wife. Finally, Els intercepts the older physician at the Batavia airport and makes a Stand of her own:

ELS

Dr. Jansen, I want you to take Anton back. It just isn't working out, our marriage, I mean. He came down here with just one thought in mind, that was to work with you, that's all he ever talked about. You didn't take the trouble to know me, and to know that I could do what I said, and that Anton could go on working with you, because you're stubborn and you're bullheaded and you know it. Now, I'll make a bargain with you. You take Anton back, and I'll stay here, and I swear I won't make any trouble — and if it doesn't work out, you tell me, and I'll leave — I'll go back home, if I have to. Just take him back, that's all. I love him — and I want to see him happy — and I mean every word I say!

Getting a little drunk to do it, Doctor Bullhead relents, and Anton rejoins him, spending all his spare time on his laboriously hand-printed project — which, after four months, he presents to the Old Man. Titled *"Jansen On Leprosy, Edited by Anton Drager, M.D.,"* it is an obvious compilation of Jansen's Manpuko notes, which first infuriates, then impresses the old man. Anton Drager has achieved what he came for, but he overplays his hand, boasting that he will be in a position to demand additional staff, space and financing when the book is published, and he returns home to Holland. Jansen is shocked and disappointed:

JANSEN
This is what you came for! This is all you wanted — this, and what it'll bring you! Isn't it? You don't give a damn about what we're tryin' to do out here!

DRAGER
I don't intend to bury myself out here forever, sweating my life away here in these islands. For what? Killing yourself for people who can't even say your name?

JANSEN
I — know — my — name, but I'm beginning to forget yours fast, because I don't know what you care about or who you care about. Willem said you had a cross to bear. And you do. And sooner or later, it's gonna break ya, boy. But not here! I can't afford it. I'll get a replacement as quick as I can.

Drager is crushed; he responds by taking comfort in the arms of a gorgeous native girl (Judy Dan) and the ever-present P.G. But his dismissal has set the stage for the central confrontation of the film: the three-part struggle with the crafty witch doctor, Burubi (Reggie Nalder).

Taking his leave of the native girl Laja, Drager is replaced by the Totuk Schutters (David Frankham) and departs with the district constable, Inspector Bevers (Karl Swenson). En route, Drager accompanies Bevers on his search for the missing rivermaster of Kokoto. Entering the deserted village, Drager hears the strains of Beethoven and realizes the man in question is his old acquaintance, Harry Frolick.

Finding Frolick's quarters in an advanced state of dilapidation, Anton shuts off the record player, which produces a frightening apparition: wildly bearded, disheveled, clad in rags, Frolick has clearly gone "mataglap" — jungle-mad.

The crazed "ape-man" charges Anton with a machete, and Anton has to pump six shots into his attacker to bring him down.

Back in Batavia, Anton reports that Frolick had succumbed to alcoholic psychosis, as evidenced by the many empty bottles of Holland Dry Gin scattered about his quarters. Bevers disagrees: the place was also littered with the accoutrements of "guna-guna" — black magic — and the gin bottles date from a shipment lost in the jungle twenty years before, and employed, Bevers believes, by "somebody clever enough to use it to drive a man mad." That man, Kramer realizes, is Burubi, the "witch doctor" who rules the remote area known as Mamawi — where Kramer's Javanese associate, Dr. Sordjano, has recently set up a clinic.

Anton returns to his home with Els, but, in Rock Hudson's own words, "disillusionment and frustration are becoming dark veils dropping over him, changing him from the man Els recognizes and loves to one she cannot comprehend and who frightens her."

The two encounter Captain Wattereus at the club, who commiserates over the shooting of Frolick and attempts to make sense of it:

WATTEREUS

Don't you see? They tortured him out there — with silence. They forced him to stand alone — and he had nothing to fight them with. Nothing. He'd cut himself off from God, and from people — at least the love of people — the only sources of strength a man can call on. And he was

defenseless against the wilderness. We began in the wilderness, all of us. But with a choice: to take the Spiral Road upward, leading to God — or to remain in the wilderness and degenerate back to the animal.

Anton's response is, as Els later puts it, "cruel and offensive and embarrassing." Anton then declares that Wattereus is preaching "spiritual gibberish," the "same stuff" that his own hypocritical father did:

DRAGER
I've heard stuff like that since I was a kid, only now it doesn't scare me. I stopped that a long time ago. I was ten years old and I stopped it, for once and for all, I stopped it! I knelt in that church of his, with him up in the pulpit screaming at us, and I dared God to kill me, to strike me dead. I said, "I don't love you, God, you hear me? So kill me. I hate you, I'm afraid of you and I hate you. So, go ahead, burn me, crush me, hit me, go ahead, but I won't love you. And so I knelt there, and I stuck my tongue out behind my hands, and I said, "Go ahead, do it, now, go ahead, kill me!" And I waited, and I got so frightened I started to cry. And I waited, and nothing happened — nothing. I kept that up every Sunday for a month. And then — I knew. I knew God couldn't touch me, he couldn't hurt me — and if he couldn't hurt me, he couldn't help

me. *Nobody* could. So I knew then I'd have to take care of myself, help myself, and I did, I didn't need anybody!*

ELS
You don't need anyone. You don't need me, do you?

DRAGER
Go back home to Holland. You never should've come down here in the first place — because you're right. I don't need you — or anybody! So, for both our sakes, go! Go home!

Anton returns to the bar, where his serious drinking is interrupted by a phone call from Kramer: weak, fading radio signals indicate that Sordjano is in trouble at Mamawi station. Realizing that "it's more of this Burubi business," Kramer dispatches Bevers and Anton to rescue Sordjano, and close the station.

Ten days upriver, the rescue party arrives at Mamawi station, a narrow-gauge railroad car left over from an earlier attempt to build a railroad. Inside, they find Burubi's second victim: Sordjano, nearly comatose and hemorrhaging. He, too, is surrounded by gin bottles, but these are unopened: "Jano never touched 'em."

Jano is barely able to gasp out what happened to him: he and his retainers were enticed by "friendly" natives to accompany them inland to

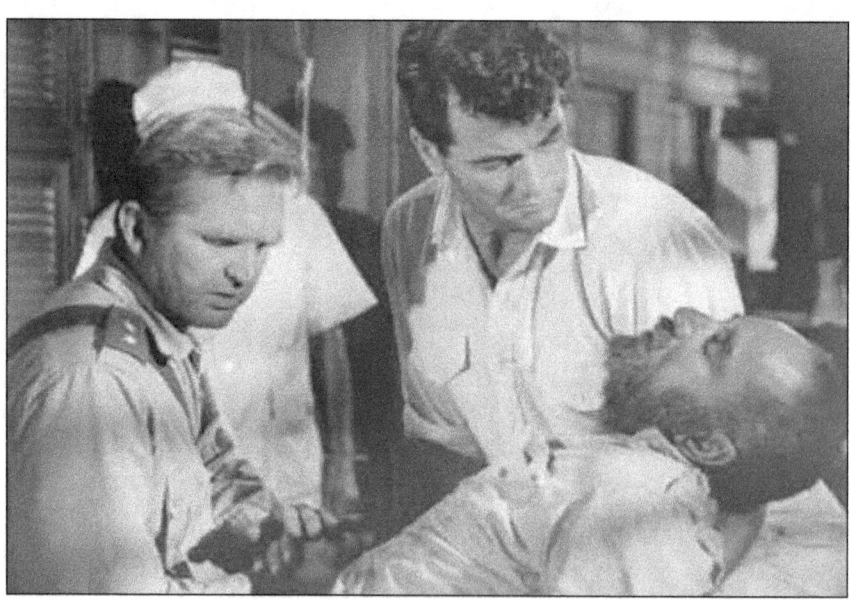

their village — only to have bamboo shaved into their food. "It works like ground glass, only slower," explains Bevers — "cuts your insides to ribbons."

A blood transfusion from Anton himself briefly revives Sordjano, who talks about how he must go outside to give thanks to Allah, then stay to help the natives, who fear Burubi. But help has come too late, and Jano dies — whereupon Anton decides to take over the station himself.

>BEVERS
>
>*You are asking for trouble! Why? You've seen what can happen. You saw Frolick — and now Sordjano.*

>DRAGER
>
>*I'm not Frolick, and I'm not Sordjano. I don't need liquor, or a prayer rug, or the Bible! I can handle this, and my way!*

Grumbling, Bevers leaves Drager to his fate. Soon Anton's isolation is complete: the constant clattering of Burubi's "jungle drums" scares off the native retainers, and shorted-out batteries have disabled the radio. Nevertheless, Anton seems to be winning the battle: he dumps the gin bottles and, deducing that they are lowered into the railway carriage through the skylight, fashions a trap that catches the next native to try it.

This is when Burubi (Reggie Nalder) himself appears. Cool, composed, and deceptively docile, the witch doctor bows before Drager and entreats

him to bring his medicines to the village. Feeling victorious, Anton warns Burubi, "I don't get careless. I eat what you eat."

Brave words, but the jungle is Burubi's home, not Anton's. After a certain amount of travel, Burubi and the other native melt into the jungle, leaving Anton well and truly lost.

Weeks pass. Bevers returns with fresh batteries for the radio, but finds the camp "deserted, apparently for some time." Anton, meantime, is stumbling through the jungle — now bearded, tattered, clearly going the way of Frolick. The constant clattering of the jungle drums keeps him from sleeping for days at a time, so that, when it finally ceases, he falls into an exhausted slumber, and is easily relieved of rifle and backpack.

Finding and following the river, Drager makes his way back to Mamawi, and drags himself into the carriage — where he discovers the radio is working, and begins to key the only message his disordered mind can focus on: his own name, repeated again and again. (This approximates the scene in the book where a feverish Drager fills page after page with the answers to the great questions of existence, only to later find that he has written his own name over and over again.)

Collapsing into sleep, Drager is awakened by the clatter of the drums — and lured from the relative safety of the carriage in a childishly simple manner: Burubi shows himself at the edge of the jungle. Mumbling, "I'll kill you. I'll kill you," Anton charges back into the bush — and back into Hell.

His friends, having received his radio message, are on the way — Bevers, Jansen, Wattereus, even Els (which is fairly unbelievable; the scripted scene that explains her presence has been deleted). Anton Drager shows, in this respect, an astonishing similarity to the real-life Errol Flynn, the featured actor in Study 4 of this book: he could treat his friends and loved ones in a cavalier, even cruel manner, yet their affection remained undiminished. It's almost too late, though: Drager is, like Frolick, disintegrating into a subhuman. All is not lost, though, because this is when....

ANTON DRAGER MAKES HIS STAND

Seeing a heavily bearded, haggard face reflected in a waterhole, Anton is convinced he's being pursued by Harry Frolick, and flees madly, aimlessly, through the underbrush, and finally circling back to the same waterhole. Here, he sees the reflection again and the truth dawns: "it's — me," he's barely able to gasp.

As is the case of all the heroes of this collection, Drager makes a totally unexpected Stand: earlier, he had reacted with derision, when Willem

Wattereus declared that Harry Frolick had succumbed because "He'd cut himself off from God, and from people — at least the love of people — the only sources of strength a man can call on." Now, however, Anton looks skyward, overcomes himself, and says the words that set him free: "God, help me" — then he stumbles out of the waterhole, calling the name of his wife.

The end is quick in coming, and almost anti-climactic: slipping into a coma, Anton is nursed for days on end by his wife, and when he finally regains consciousness, Jansen and Wattereus are amazed and gratified by his words: "Els…oh, thank God."

Anton Drager has reached out for "the only sources of strength a man can call on," and saved himself. The film ends on the image of Anton and company in their canoes, returning to civilization, over which is superimposed a Bible verse:

"No man hath seen God. But if we love one another, God dwelleth in us, and His love is perfected in us." I John IV, 12

Thus ends the story. And thus ends the lesson, largely unseen and unappreciated. Why?

BOOK VS. FILM

The press book stated that this film was Rock Hudson's "most intensely dramatic role." What it didn't say was that he had fought tooth-and-nail to play the part, telling his closest friends, "This is the one that will crack the comedy shit and let me be an actor again." He couldn't say that in public; he'd have looked like an ingrate after three wildly successful comedies — *Pillow Talk, Come September,* and *Lover Come Back* — had made him richer and more popular than ever before. And even after the studio agreed to make *Spiral* with him as the lead, he had to fight constantly against their efforts to remold the part of Anton Drager into "Rock Hudson, Romantic Star."

Other remolding was taking place. Like most great novels adapted into films, *The Spiral Road* is choc-a-bloc with color and richness of detail, much of which is inevitably lost in translation. The question is what can afford to be lost? And because Universal was in a state of flux, that answer kept changing. So much was cut, chopped, and mutilated that it was never the same script twice. Writers were changed, worked, original writers brought back, collaborated, and collided to the point that the final shooting script became a mass of blue, pink, yellow, and white pages. Ives' character of Brits Jansen remained irascible throughout, strong and determined, yet with a soft underside, but the same consistency never applied in the case of Hudson's protagonist. Anton Drager is a man in a state of transition — and the script never was cohesive enough to create a flow in that transition. Audiences were thus robbed of much of their identification with the character.

Just one example of a nuance lost: in the book, Drager is haunted by the fact that he had to shoot the degenerated Frolick. When Jansen finds Drager in the same condition, he hits him, and Drager experiences a moment of clarity — and epiphany: "I should have knocked Frolick down. I am a murderer."

Being one of de Hartog's earlier works, the book is very Dutch is setting and tone, and this was predictably softened in the film: Dr. Anton

Zorgdrager becomes Dr. Anton Drager; Dr. Brzhezinska-Jansen becomes Dr. Brits Jansen; Manpukochu is simplified to Manpuko; and on and on. But perhaps the cruelest emasculation of all is that of Geoffrey Keen's character, Captain Willem Wattereus.

The book presents a very seamy back-story for the captain and his wife: before their "salvation," she is a whore in an Amsterdam brothel,

Hitting their marks: Ives, Hudson, and Geoffrey Keen as Wattereus on the Manpuko Leper Colony set.

and he a petty thief. More pointedly, when Anton and Brits arrive at the leper colony, Wattereus is secretly tormented by erotic dreams and fantasies. Again Anton diagnoses what his mentor has missed: the erotomania is an unfortunate side effect of hormone injections the Captain has been receiving for chronic prostatitis. At this point, Wattereus makes a Stand of his own: offered a surgical solution, he refuses to leave his dying wife for the required three-week convalescence, preferring to continue the injection treatment — now that he knows what he is fighting.

This situation made it to late drafts of the script, but is completely missing from the film. Because Anton needs the "chemical conversion" theory to thwart Wattereus' "Spiral Road" theory, the incident is reclassified as a story from Anton's past, a classic idea of how one scene involving one actor can be re-shot to create wholesale revisions in the story.

                    DRAGER
      (to Wattereus, as originally written)

No, wait a minute. I have something that might interest the Captain. You see, I've been thinking about those injections you were taking. Remember? Well, they had the effect of turning a saint into a sinner, didn't they? Consider that now. If a simple injection can produce that kind of transformation, then the reverse must also be true. It's quite possible that somewhere, waiting to be discovered, there must be a particular combination of chemicals that can turn a sinner into a saint. Think of it! It would be the first bio-chemical explanation of faith: like putting God into a test-tube.

                    DRAGER
      (to Wattereus, in the finished film)

No, wait a minute. I have something that might interest the Captain. Back home, just before I came out, a gentle, God-fearing little shopkeeper committed a brutal sex crime. It seems he'd been taking hormone treatments for chronic prostatitis and an accidental overdose was apparently responsible. Now, if a simple injection can change a saintly man into a sinner, then the reverse should also be true. Consider that. It's quite possible that somewhere, waiting to be discovered, there must be a particular combination of chemicals that can change a sinner into a saint. Think of it! It would be the first bio-chemical explanation of faith: like putting God into a test-tube.

With that simple rewrite, several time-consuming scenes revolving around Wattereus could be conveniently eliminated, taking with them a huge chunk of the character's richness. Much of what contributed to the story's strength disappears between shooting script and finished film in a similar manner. In particular, two steamy sex scenes were filmed but excised: one in which the native girl, Laja, performs fellatio on Drager, the other where a distraught and frustrated Drager rapes his wife. This last scene actually made it into theatres, briefly, but the prints were quickly recalled and replaced, victims of the incredibly restrictive Production Code still in effect, if only for a few more years.

In the final analysis, it is amazing that this film turned out as well as it did, after what was done to it through interference by studio heads, director's cuts, writing staff changes, et cetera. Certain potent subtleties remain intact, for instance, the language of the natives: whenever it is spoken by a white man, it is spoken in a rude and condescending tone, except by Brits Jansen — and, because he learned from Jansen, by Anton Drager.

THE BALANCE SHEET

Needless to say, *The Spiral Road* did not "zoom Rock Hudson's triumphant career even farther into the golden orbit of international popularity." In fact, it marked the beginning of a gradual decline. Universal slapped him back into comedies, but they were not nearly as funny as the earlier ones — some, such as *Man's Favorite Sport* and *A Very Special Favor,* were decidedly mean in tone.

Rock Hudson tried once more to "crack the glass ceiling" and make himself known as a serious actor — and once more he failed. In 1967, he starred for John Frankenheimer in *Seconds,* the dark story of a sixty-something banker (John Randolph) who is surgically restructured into a leaner, younger man (Hudson) — but whose stodgy banker's soul cannot make the transition. Audiences at the Cannes Film Festival were typical: they cheered Hudson himself for his body of past work, but booed the movie. The film was not truly appreciated until much later. As Frankenheimer noted, "It became a classic without ever having been a success."

In the late 1960s and early 1970s, Hudson largely escaped the "romantic comedy" pigeonhole by a appearing as a military man in a number of films: *Tobruk* (1966), *Ice Station Zebra* (1968, his last big-screen hit), *The Undefeated* with John Wayne (1969), and *Hornet's Nest* (1970). Yet newer venues of success were to open for him: starring with Susan Saint

James in *McMillan and Wife*, he became television's most successful and highest-paid detective up to that time. When his old friend, Carol Burnett, brought him to the stage for the first time in *I Do! I Do!* (1973), it ushered in a series of stage roles that *finally* allowed him to display the breadth and range of his talent that had barely been glimpsed on film. An incredible irony was that *I Do! I Do!* was a musical adaptation of *The*

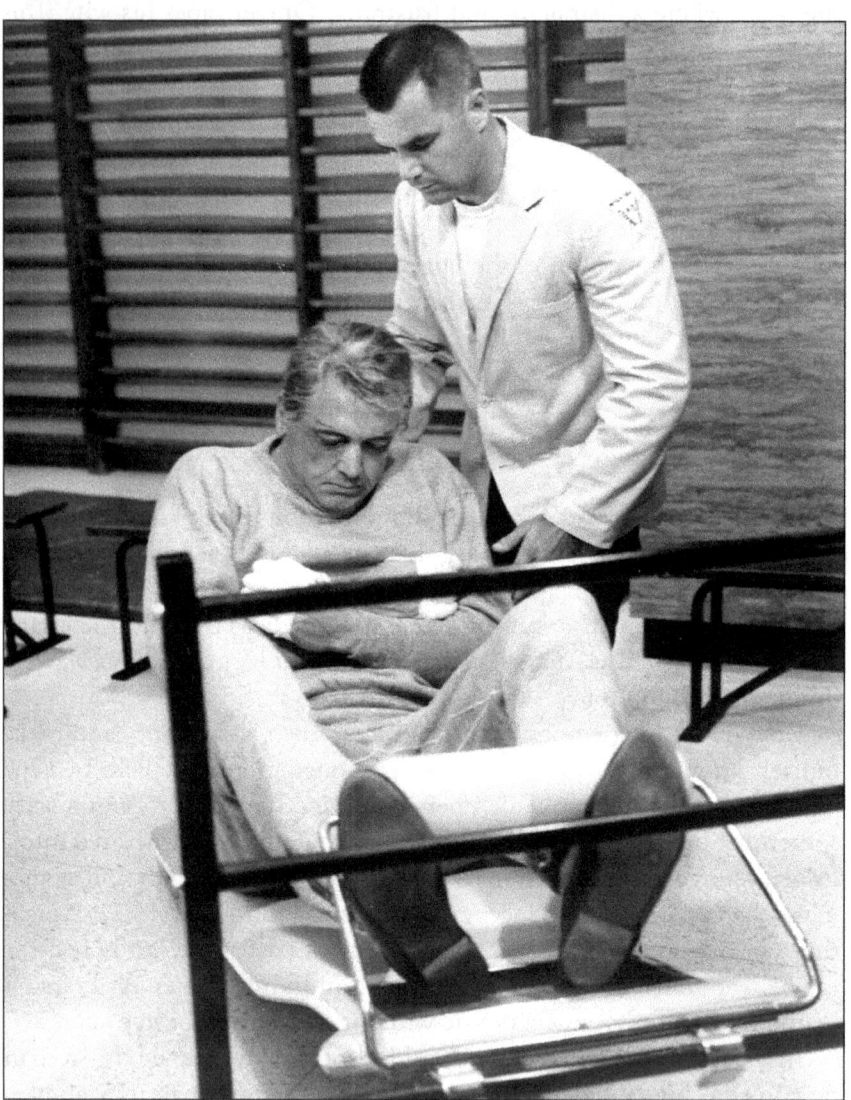

Physical therapy completes the transformation of John Randolph into Rock Hudson in Seconds.

Fourposter, by, of all people, Jan de Hartog. Finally, the author and star *of The Spiral Road* had achieved a successful collaboration!

The all too well-known end of Rock Hudson's story often has the unfortunate effect of eclipsing the accomplishments of his career: the revelation in 1985 that the obviously dying man had been diagnosed with HIV led to his posthumous role as a poster boy for AIDS. It was a part he took on with courage and deliberation, largely to help the efforts spearheaded by his *Giant* co-star Elizabeth Taylor to raise money for AIDS research. Yet few realize that he may not have died of that dread disease at all: after initial treatments in Paris, he had actually tested *negative* for HIV — but was by that time being eaten alive by liver cancer. Because Hudson and those closest to him decided that his sadly wasted corpse would not be subjected to the further indignity of an autopsy (the records of which would probably have shown up for sale online), no one will ever know exactly what killed him — not that it matters. The tragedy is that this man, with so much yet to offer, died scant weeks short of his sixtieth birthday.

In the final weeks of his life, Hudson had authorized Sara Davidson to produce his "official" biography, *Rock Hudson: My Story*, which did little more than perpetuate the lies of his "exclusive" homosexuality produced by the AIDS revelation. This portrait was no truer than the studio-generated fantasies of "Rock the Ultimate Ladies' Man" pushed by the fan magazines of the 1950s and 1960s. In point of fact, this intensely private man was aggressively — and enthusiastically — *bisexual*. This is best illustrated by an exchange between Hudson and his close friend, actor George Nader: "Rock, just because it wiggles you don't have to fuck it." "Oh, yes, I do!" But in death, as in life, the outsized and mostly fictionalized focus on Rock Hudson's sexuality continued to cast his talents as an actor — and his qualities as a man — far into the background.

Like everything else written about him, *Rock Hudson: My Story* tended to portray him as a furtive and desperate man. Living his last days with his typically zany humor (which the public seldom saw), Hudson had suggested several terribly tasteless — but riotously funny — titles for the Davidson book: *Cleaning My Closet, Backing Out Carefully*, and the one that had his friends rolling on the floor, *Rock Hudson's Fairy Tails!* Had the publishers had the gumption to go with this one, perhaps the public image of Rock Hudson would be a bit closer to reality: in all ways, his talent, his work ethic, his kindness, even his sex drive, Roy Fitzgerald — "Rock Hudson" — was the most *life-affirming* of men.

STUDY II
JAMES STEWART

He was too good to be true — superficially, at least.

"Jimmy" Stewart was dogged by neither the beefcake preoccupation nor the sex scandals, true or fabricated, that plagued Rock Hudson and Errol Flynn. His forty-five-year marriage to Gloria Hatrick McLean, which lasted up to her death, set a record for longevity and devotion that would impress anywhere, let alone Hollywood.

He earned professional accolades and public affection early on, and aged his way gracefully through a career full of entertaining and provocative roles in quality films, surviving to become a revered and folksy elder statesman of the film community.

But he, too, fought the battle of stereotyping. And his biggest hurdle was returning after World War II to the make-believe world of picture-making; not only returning, but making it meaningful.

Jimmy Stewart had gone to war secure in the firmament of film stars with his Oscar for *The Philadelphia Story* (1941) fresh under his belt. But between the Japanese attack on Pearl Harbor in December 1941, and the German surrender on Victory in Europe (VE) Day in May, 1945, Stewart had progressed from corporal to full colonel in the Army Air Corps. He had flown twenty bombing missions over Nazi-occupied Europe in Consolidated B-24 Liberators, and risen to command the 2nd Bomb Wing of the 453rd Bomb Group in the legendary Eighth Air Force. He had taken human life, and he had written the letters to the widows of his own men.

Stewart, the man, had changed, and so had public taste. The escapist expectations of the wartime and pre-war filmgoers had given way to an appetite for grittier fare, and while the essential decency of Jimmy Stewart, the man, had never changed (and never would), the gangling, "aw-shucks" naïveté had long been outgrown. So, the first thing Stewart did with this long-established persona — was to kill it.

Forsaking his long-time studio home, MGM, Stewart had entered into independent production with Frank Capra (they had scored big-time with *Mr. Smith Goes to Washington* in 1939) in the oddball tale of a stolid Midwesterner, whose kind heart and guilelessness had led him into what he perceived as total failure, and a swan dive into a snowy river, a final exit forestalled by a somewhat inept guardian angel. *It's A Wonderful Life* grew in time into a treasured Christmas perennial, and the favorite film of both Stewart and Capra, but in 1946, it sold precious little popcorn.

Stewart's salvation came, oddly enough, in the saddle. More than anyone else, director Anthony Mann saw in the eyes of this gentle man of quiet courage not only a depth of character but a smoldering rage, an explosive violence ready to burst forth in sudden, savage fury. Films such as *Winchester '73* (1950), *Bend of the River* (1952), and *The Naked Spur* (1953) heralded the metamorphosis of Jimmy Stewart into James Stewart: still the man with an inner core of dignity, but sometimes now a man of intense frustrations and even neuroses, just waiting to be set off by the proper spark. One scene in one Western exemplifies the essence of meaningful acting. When he is shot point-blank in his gun hand by Alex Nicol in *The Man from Laramie* (1955), Stewart cannot fall back upon profanity, as would actors of later decades. Nor does he permit himself to flail about in a wild outburst of scenery-chewing agony. Instead, he clutches his pain to him as a man does, allowing only eyes, expression, and posture to reveal the extent of his anguish.

Stewart's output through the 1950s and into the 1960s rivals that of any other film actor in terms of quantity and quality. Fans have their favorites, of course: the charmingly eccentric Elwood P. Dowd, friend of *Harvey* (1950), the beloved big-band leader in *The Glenn Miller Story* (1954), the immobilized witness to murder in *Rear Window* (1954), the beleaguered policeman in *Vertigo* (1958), and the sharp-witted Michigan lawyer of *Anatomy of a Murder* (1959). Relatively few such lists, however, include the Stewart characters spotlighted in this collection: Charlie Anderson in *Shenandoah* (1965), and Frank Towns in *The Flight of the Phoenix* (1966).

Arguably, these two roles represent the zenith of Stewart's acting career. Lead roles continued to come his way, but *Shenandoah* and *The Flight of the Phoenix* represented the last truly big-scale productions dominated by this living legend, and Stewart, still in good health as he neared sixty, brought his thirty years of strengths and subtleties to these two intense characterizations. Neither the Civil War patriarch nor the burned-out pilot was considered easygoing or affable; both, in fact, were outwardly inflexible and unapproachable. But at the moment of crisis, each finds it within himself to behave contrary to his own nature, to surprise those around him — and himself, as well. These portrayals represent two of the finest moments in the long and honored career of James Stewart, and two of the most remarkable Stands in this collection.

STAND THREE: *SHENANDOAH*

(6/3/1965: Universal) Directed by Andrew V. McLaglen; Written by James Lee Barrett; Music by Frank Skinner; Photographed by William H. Clothier; Edited by Otho Lovering.

CHARLIE
Lord, we cleared this land. We plowed it, sowed it and harvested. We cooked the harvest. It wouldn't be here, we wouldn't be eatin' it if we hadn't done it all ourselves. We worked dog-bone hard for every crumb and morsel, but we thank you just the same anyway, Lord, for this food we're about to eat, amen.

That cleverly-written "grace" sums up the character of Charlie Anderson to a "t." As the father of six sons, a daughter, and a daughter-in-law, Charlie Anderson is a Biblical patriarch who has rejected the Bible. "Your mother wanted you all raised as good Christians," he says, going through the motions, but making it painfully obvious that he's doing precisely that, to the point that his pastor (Denver Pyle) asks him outright:

PASTOR BJOERLING
Charlie Anderson, I wonder if you'd be good enough to tell me exactly why d'ya bother to come to services. Meaning no disrespect, of course.

CHARLIE
It was my wife's last request, Pastor Bjoerling — meanin' no disrespect, a'course.

In his heart of hearts, Charlie Anderson is in full charge of his family, his farm, and his future. If the man is guilty of a sin, it is the sin of pride. Before the film is over, he'll be called upon to pay the wages of that particular sin — and by then, when he tries to speak that same grace, the words will stick in his throat. But at the same time he learns a lesson in humility, and he'll make a Stand that will shine as a glowing example of what a man can do, and what a man can be.

It would be instructive to know just how familiar the story's author, James Lee Barrett, was with the work of author Ayn Rand, because the character of Charlie Anderson could easily have stepped directly from the pages of *The Fountainhead* or *Atlas Shrugged*. Charlie is especially

reminiscent of Rand's signature hero, Howard Roark, in *The Fountainhead*: Proud, self-sufficient, and uncompromising to a fault. In his insistence on boycotting the Civil War thundering all around him, Charlie recalls the aggressive determination of architect Roark to build his buildings as he and he alone sees fit, with no regard for the opinions or preferences of anyone else, the very essence of Rand's Objectivist philosophy. In fact, Stewart's Anderson, who is capable of both wry amusement and intelligent self-questioning, comes closer to the Howard Roark of Rand's book than does the performance of Gary Cooper in *The Fountainhead* (1949), whose film version of Roark expresses the character's dogged determinism through the trademark Cooper stoniness — effective as far as it goes, but greatly reducing the emotional range of the role. The book begins with the words "Howard Roark laughed," but it's almost impossible to picture Cooper's Roark doing that. By contrast, Stewart, whether softly chuckling, roaring with rage, or quietly addressing the grave of his long-dead wife, gives full expression to the colorings and complexities of a hard-headed but soft-hearted man, who at film's end, has grown in wisdom through his sorrowing — and humbling — experiences.

JACOB

They come closer every day, Pa.

CHARLIE

They on our land?

JACOB

No, sir.

CHARLIE

Then it doesn't concern us. Does it?

Following the opening credits of the film, this exchange between Charlie and his eldest son, Jacob (Glenn Corbett), has the feeling of having been gone through by them many times, as does the ensuing dinner table conversation in which Jacob proclaims "Anything that concerns Virginia concerns us." Charlie then questions his sons as to whether they'd like to own slaves. The answer is a resounding "No," and it is the second oldest, James (Patrick Wayne), who articulates his reasons: "If I can't do my own work, with my own hands, it'll never get done." (Taking after the patriarch, the Andersons tend to speak in absolutes. That, too, will change.)

The first half of the film is episodic and often whimsical, as the family attempts to pursue its day-to-day activities in the midst of the encroaching battle. James and Ann (Katharine Ross) are expecting their first child. Jennie (Rosemary Forsyth) is being courted by the shy but sincere Confederate Lieutenant, Sam (Doug McClure), and the youngest son, a sixteen-year-old simply called "The Boy" (Philip Alford), spends his time hunting and fishing, usually in the company of a teenage slave called "Gabriel" (Gene Jackson). The difference in their status means, of course, nothing to the boys. It's on one of these outings that The Boy finds a battered Confederate cap floating in a stream, and impulsively begins wearing it — which will led to disastrous (though predictable) consequences.

Almost to spite Charlie's "They on our land?" criteria, the war comes riding into the Andersons' front yard in the form of both sides. First, a Confederate patrol, led by Lieutenant Johnson (Tom Simcox) comes seeking to enlist the Anderson boys, but runs into a brick wall in the form of the Charlie:

CHARLIE
Now let me tell you somethin', Johnson, before you get on my wrong side. My corn I take serious, because it's my corn. And my potatoes and my tomatoes and fences I take note of because they're mine. But this war is not mine and I take no note of it...I've got five hundred acres of good, rich dirt here. As long as the rains come and the sun shines, it'll grow anything I've got a mind to plant. And we pulled every stump, we cleared every field, and we've done it ourselves, without the sweat of one

slave. So, can you give me one good reason why I should send my family that took me a lifetime to raise down that road like a buncha damn fools to do somebody else's fightin'?

> LIEUTENANT JOHNSON
> Virginia needs all of her sons, Mister Anderson.

> CHARLIE
> That might be so, Johnson, but these are my sons! They don't belong to the state. When they were babies I never saw the state comin' around with a spare tit! We never asked anything of the state and never expected anything. We do our own livin' an' thanks to no man for the right!

> LIEUTENANT JOHNSON
> Mr. Anderson, you can sit in the middle of this war and not get touched, I congratulate you.

With that, Johnson and his party ride off straight into an ambush. Charlie is shaken, but still adamantly defiant. Next, a local ne'er-do-well (Lane Bradford) leads a group of Federal Purchasing Agents onto the farm to buy — or confiscate — horses for the Cavalry. When The Boy asks what 'confiscate' means, Charlie tells him: 'Steal!' — which provokes a confrontation:

> AGENT CARROLL
> I think what Mr. Tinkham means is that, uh, he sorta figured that anybody's too, uh — too yellow to fight — wouldn't mind makin' a couple dollars off the war?

> JACOB
> Yellow?

> CHARLIE
> I apologize for my son's manners, Mr. Carroll; he's taught to have more respect for his elders...Jacob, I don't know what gets into you every once in a while. You know you shouldn't hit this gentleman — long as I'm around to do it!

With that, a lusty free-for-all ensues between the Andersons and the agents in which the former easily prevail. (The fight very much resembles the brawl in *McLintock*, the John Wayne film that director Andrew McLaglen had just completed!) When Tinkham ups the ante by pulling a pistol, Jennie shoots it out of his hand with her rifle, and ushers "you and these other animals" off the farm.

Charlie's not about to surrender any of his horses, but his daughter is another matter, as he tells The Boy, "Your sister's ripe and the pickers are here." Jennie's picker of choice is a young Confederate Lieutenant named Sam Stephens (the surname "Stephens" appears in the press book, but never in the film), and his request to Charlie for "your daughter's hand" is a classic rendering of the nervous suitor approaching the authoritarian father, although Sam is somewhat startled by the question Charlie asks:

CHARLIE
D'ya like her?...No, no, you said ya loved her. There's some difference between lovin' and likin'...Y'see, Sam, when you love a woman without likin' her, the night can be long and cold and contempt comes up with the sun...Well?

SAM
I like Jennie, sir. I've always liked her.

> CHARLIE
>
> *All right, then, you be good to her. 'Cause if you don't, it's between you and me, boy.*

When Sam exclaims "Well, then, you have no objections, sir?" Charlie's answer is an honest "I didn't say that," but it's accompanied by a handshake of congratulations. In the days that follow, it's clear that he enjoys having a prospective son-in-law around, to whom he can pass along his own ideas on how men should treat women.

> CHARLIE
>
> *It's no easy job, Sam, takin' care of a woman... They expect things they never ask for. And, when they don't get them, they ask you why. Sometimes they don't ask, and they just go ahead and punish you for not doin' somethin' you didn't know you were supposed to do in the first place... Suppose Jennie started to cry one day, you don't know what she's cryin' about, so you ask her why... you ask her, and she won't tell ya. And that's when you ask her what it was you did that caused her to cry. She still won't tell ya. And that's when you start to get angry — but don't get angry, Sam. She won't tell you why she's cryin' 'cause she doesn't know. Women are like that, Sam... and it's exasperatin', it's, it's — mmmmmppff! But don't let it make ya angry. When she's like that, just walk up and hug her a little bit. 'Cause that's all they really want when they're like that, Sam — a little lovin'.*

Jennie, meantime, is getting her own coaching from the only woman around, her sister-in-law Ann.

> ANN
>
> *Husbands like to be alone once in a while... You never know why. But I can always tell when James wants to be alone. A mood comes over him; I can always see it in his eyes before it really gets there. I don't know where the mood comes from, or why, but that's when I leave him alone. It seems, sometimes, things get so thick around a man that he comes to feel that everything is closin' in on him, and that's when he wants to be left alone.*

The day of the wedding brings mixed blessings. After a genuinely moving ceremony, Sam is accosted by a corporal with a message that he must return to the front: "It's the Yankees; they have broken through at Winchester, sir." Charlie brought his daughter down the aisle. Now, he must escort her back, as her husband rides off.

Charlie has another concern: Ann has just doubled over with labor pains. Before the day is out, there will be a new Anderson (to everyone's surprise, a girl) delivered by old Doc Witherspoon (Paul Fix). Despite his show of indifference to the war, Charlie can't resist the opportunity to ask his old friend how he feels about what's happening:

DOC WITHERSPOON
I was born in Virginia, lived here all my life, raised three sons and two daughters under her flag. My oldest son, Paul, lies buried somewhere in Pennsylvania... They said Gettysburg is where he fell, at a place called Little Round Top. My youngest boy came home last week with

tuberculosis. He won't see another Christmas. My third son rides with General Forrest; I don't know where they are…you were asking me how I feel about it all. That's the only way I know how to answer you.

The Andersons' isolation is about to come to an end, however. Shortly after his niece's birth, The Boy is out hunting raccoons with Gabriel when the two stumble into a Union-Confederate skirmish. The Boy is still wearing his battered Confederate cap, and that is his downfall:

BOY

I'm *no soldier*.

YANKEE SERGEANT

I don't look that ignorant, do I? We seen enough'a them Johnny Reb caps to last us a lifetime.

Taken prisoner, The Boy asks Gabriel to "Go tell my pa." That's not necessary, according to one of the other soldiers, a black man: "You don't have to tell his pa nothin'. You're free." Nevertheless, Gabriel runs through the fields to the Anderson farm, where he gasps out his story, finally evoking from Charlie the long-delayed but inevitable reaction:

> CHARLIE
> Now *it concerns us.*

Charlie Anderson and sons prepare to ride out in search of their missing member. Meantime, Jennie has asked Gabriel if it isn't time for him to return to his field boss. But the young black man has other ideas:

> GABRIEL
> *Ol' Jethro don't care nothin' about me. When my momma died, he even took our cabin. I don't gotta go back, do I, Missy? Man say I'm free. Don't that mean I don't gotta go back?*

> JENNIE
> *Well, man said you're free, Gabriel, I guess that means you can go anywhere in the world you wanna go.*

> GABRIEL
> *You mean I can just walk on down that road — and keep on' walkin'?*

> JENNIE
> *You can run if you like, Gabriel.*

Charlie has announced that he will ride out in search of The Boy, leaving James to look after the farm, his wife Ann, and his daughter, who they've just named "Martha" in honor of her late grandmother. Charlie intends to take the rest of the boys with him, but draws the line when daughter Jennie mounts up also — curtly instructing her to "…unstrap, unhook, get outta your brothers' clothes — you're a woman!"

> JENNIE
> *Yes, I'm a woman — but I don't see anybody here I can't outrun, outride and outshoot. I'll unstrap for ya, Papa, and unhook, and I'll even sit here and watch you ride out of sight…and then I'll follow.*

Knowing when he's licked, Charlie sets out for the nearest Union camp, where he accosts the commander (George Kennedy):

> CHARLIE
> *You the leader'a this band of fools?*

COLONEL FAIRCHILD
Colonel Fairchild is my name. Whether or not I am the leader of fools is a question which has often entered my mind.

Fearing that Charlie is embarked on a fool's errand, Fairchild nonetheless writes out a note to the commanding officer of the nearest prison train:

COLONEL FAIRCHILD
If I had him, Mr. Anderson, I'd give him to you, but I don't have any prisoners here. We sent them all to the railroad for shipment north...I do wish you good luck, Mr. Anderson. I have a sixteen-year-old son, too. He's in school in Boston — thank God.

Charlie and family proceed to the railroad depot at Ivy Glen, where bedraggled Rebel prisoners are being loaded into cattle cars. But they receive no help there, as the commanding officer (Berkeley Harris) tells them: "If your son is among these prisoners, you're too late. There's a war going on, Mr. Anderson...We have schedules to meet."

Charlie Anderson is not so easily deterred. Late that night, the prison train is stopped by a flaming barricade, atop which sits Charlie. He is rapidly surrounded by the handful of Union guards — who are themselves then surrounded by the Anderson sons.

CAPTAIN RICHARDS
Now I remember. Anderson! Your name is Anderson...You're the man who's lookin' for his son.

CHARLIE
And you're the man that's got schedules to keep!

Proceeding to search the train, Charlie is accosted by the engineer (Strother Martin), who wants to know how long his train will be held up.

CHARLIE
Now I'm glad you asked me that, 'cause I believe in a man knowin' all there is to know about his business. First I'm gonna empty your train, and then I'm gonna burn it...It's not the kind of a train I favor.

ENGINEER
Sir, I've been the engineer on this train for ten years. She's been a good train all that time an', well, it ain't right to burn her just 'cause she come onto hard times.

CHARLIE
Now, you run a sad kind of a train, mister. It takes people away when they don't want to go and won't bring 'em back when they're ready.

The Boy is not aboard the train, but another familiar figure is: Lieutenant Sam. He is reunited with his wife and, telling the other troops, "Go home. The War is lost," and then he rides off with the Andersons.

The Boy, meanwhile, is in a Union holding pen, where he has been befriended by a Rebel soldier named Carter (James Best):

CARTER
You can have yer chance tonight, boy...to run. They don't waste many men on prisoner duty; they're usually the worst of the lot. They plan on herdin' us on that sternwheeler. Some of us don't fancy no sightseein' trip up north. When they open that gate tonight, you stick as close to me as a flea on a hound dog. Sum'pin else: When we get goin', you're on your own. I gotta forget you ain't nothin' but a lap baby.

That night a torrential rain begins to fall. The Andersons take shelter in a deserted farmhouse, where Charlie mystifies the others with his noisy movements behind the closed doors of the bedroom. Finally he emerges, beckoning Sam and Jennie: he has arranged the bedroom into a snug little nest for their long-delayed wedding night:

CHARLIE
Your mother and I had it a little better'n this; it's not very comfortable, but when you've lived together for a dozen years, you'll realize that comfort's not what counts. Now it's customary for a gentleman to carry his bride across the threshold, so if ya wanna — ya wanna —

The same torrential rainfall provides cover for the escape of Carter, The Boy and several other Rebels. Despite the fact that his farm lies to the north, The Boy is reluctant to abandon his newfound friends, and flees south with them, where they join up with a beleaguered Confederate regiment — just in time to be attacked by vastly superior Union forces.

Fighting furiously, Carter is killed by a bullet in the forehead. The Boy is felled by a bullet in the leg, and finds himself about to be bayoneted by a Yankee soldier. His death seems imminent. Then, he sees just who it is standing over him. It is the kind of coincidence that strains credibility in fiction, but happens with alarming frequency in real life. The man with the bayonet is actually a boy no older than The Boy. It is, in fact, Gabriel. He has made his post-slavery way in the world by joining the Union army.

And now he makes his own Stand.

Tenderly lifting The Boy in his arms, he carries his childhood friend into the bushes, out of harm's way, and then returns to the battle.

The Andersons, of course, know nothing of this, nor that a tragic scene has occurred back at their own farmhouse. As they make camp for the night, contemplating their dwindling supplies and the futility of their quest, Charlie makes a pronouncement:

CHARLIE
I've known since the train that we weren't liable to find him [the Boy], it's just a hair of a chance that we got Sam back…mebbe I knew before we even left home. But, somehow, I just had to try. And if we don't try, we don't do. And if we don't do, why are we here on this Earth?

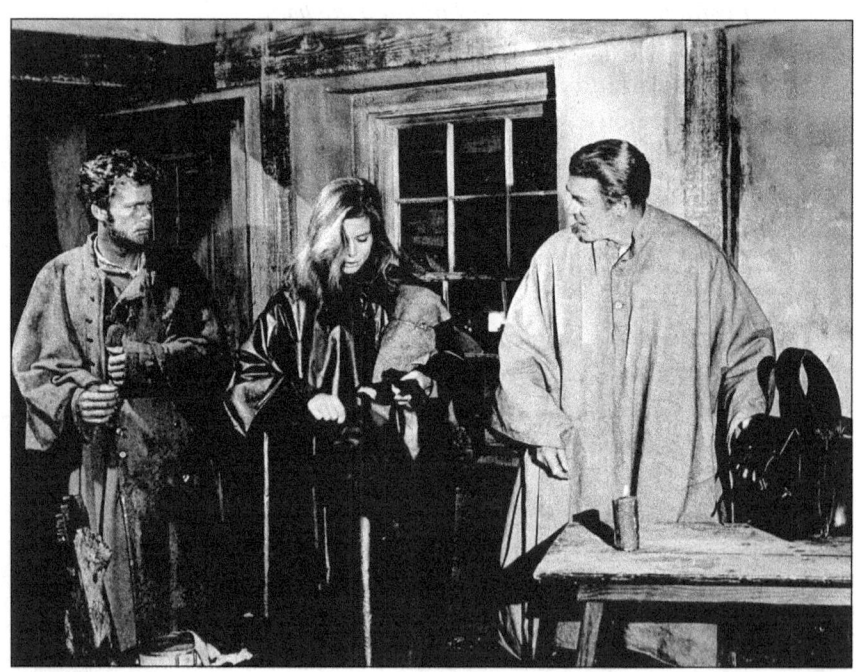

It is Jacob who speaks for the other Andersons, when he tells Charlie that they're all with him — but Charlie has decided to return home, hoping to find The Boy there.

Now comes the central moment of the film, the moment when....

CHARLIE ANDERSON MAKES HIS STAND

A young Confederate picket (James Heneghan, Junior) is all but asleep at his post at a wooden bridge as the Anderson clan approaches. Belatedly alerted by the sound, he raises his rifle and fires, blowing Jacob out of the saddle. Charlie bends over his son and learns the awful truth.

His face suffused with the inexpressible rage of hopeless grief, he advances on his son's killer. Howling the one word that expresses the tragedy — "Dead!" — he knocks the boy to the ground, locks hands around the boy's neck, begins to strangle him, and then, incredibly, astonishingly, stops.

CHARLIE
How old are you? How old?... Sixteen. I'm not gonna kill you. I want you to live! I want you to live to be an old man, and I want you to have many, many, many children. And I want you to feel about your children then the way I feel about mine now! And someday, when some man comes along and kills one of 'em, I want you to remember! I — I want you to remember.

That's it. That's Charlie Anderson's Stand.

And it's utterly remarkable and absolutely unique.

The standard for Stands in this study has been that they must be so unexpected, so contrary to the nature of the person making them that they astound and surprise not only those around him, but himself as well.

Charlie Anderson's stand is contrary not only to his own nature but, indeed, to basic *human* nature. Charlie Anderson loves his children with all his heart and all his soul. He has just seen his eldest snuffed out in the blink of eye. Even for a man who does not acknowledge the authority of the Bible, the dictum of 'an eye for an eye' is rooted deep in the human psyche. There must be revenge. There must be atonement. There must be justice. There must be an accounting! *The scales must be balanced!* But revenge produces no balance. Revenge but compounds the crime. And in his mind, in his heart, in the core of his being, Charlie Anderson knows this.

If he killed the sentry who had killed his son, many would cheer. Most who didn't would understand and commiserate. Charlie Anderson would get away with it in any court in the land, but he would never get away with it in the court of his own soul. The white-hot rage and blinding grief of parental bereavement are not enough to blind Charlie Anderson. His eyes are still open to the truth. His eyes are open to the point that he can see his son — in the face of his son's killer, and he can see himself there, as well.

Human history is built on an achingly endless wheel of offense followed by revenge, followed by revenge, followed by revenge, followed by revenge, followed by revenge, followed by revenge, followed by revenge, until one remarkable man says, '*Enough*. This wrong I will *not* avenge. *The cycle — stops — here.*'

Such a man is Charlie Anderson, which is damned scant comfort as Charlie and family bear Jacob's body home. Now, the grief piles on thick and fast, as they are met at the gate by Doctor Witherspoon, who informs them that, though baby Martha is quite all right, James and Ann are dead, killed by scavengers.

Now, we see what war has done to the Andersons. The family at the dinner table is dramatically diminished; though Sam seems to have slid right into place, he can't take the place of three. Charlie attempts the rather arrogant 'grace' that began the film, the "Oh, Lord, we did it all ourselves but thank you anyway" speech, and can't say it. It's crap, and well he knows it. He leaves the table and goes to the family graveyard, where his Martha, sixteen years gone, has been joined by three new graves:

CHARLIE

I don't even know what to say to you any more, Martha. There's nothin' much I can tell you about this war. It's like all wars, I suppose: the undertakers are winnin' it. Oh, the politicians'll talk a lot about the glory of it. And the old men'll talk about the need of it. The soldiers — they just wanna go home. I guess you're not so lonely any more, with Ann and James and Jacob — and mebbe The Boy. You didn't know Ann, did you? Well, you'll like her. You'll like her a lot, Martha. Why, she and James are so much alike, they're just like — no. No, we were never that much alike, were we, Martha? We just sorta — we just sorta grew alike through the years. But I wish — I wish I could just know what you're thinkin' about it all, Martha. Then mebbe it wouldn't look so bad to me — if I only knew what you thought. (He hears the church bells ringing.) Aah, you never give up, do ya?

Charlie's bowed, but he's not beaten. He gathers the family together to attend services. Life will go on, promises will be kept. Again, the Anderson clan disrupts services by arriving late. This time, there's a new irritation: baby Martha will not stop bawling. The long-suffering Pastor Bjoerling perseveres: "With God's help, we will turn to Hymn — "

Then the door opens, and Bjoerling sees who is limping in on a crude crutch.

" — 137," he amends. "Shall we all rise and sing?"

It's The Boy. Wounded, but alive, he limps into his father's embrace. The hymn is the Doxology, "Praise God, From Whom All Blessings Flow."

The boy sings it with full heart. So does the father. He has learned, finally, "From Whom All Blessings Flow."

On this note ends a remarkable film.

THE BALANCE SHEET

In terms of reaching an audience *Shenandoah* may well be the most successful film in this collection. It scored well both at the box office and with contemporary critics, and remains well-regarded forty years later, recently re-released on DVD in a James Stewart Collection. It did not rack up a slew of Academy and other awards, as did *Schindler's List,* but neither of those two is often rented by parents to show to their kids, although, God knows, they should be.

Shenandoah is a family film, in the best sense of that phrase: safe for consumption by all ages, yet in no way insipid. Yes, the characters are idealized; yes, they speak in noble phrases that may ring falsely on modern ears. The fact that they do so says more about the erosion of civility in day-to-day life than it does about the movie. But they do come into conflict with the real world, and not all emerge triumphant: Jacob dies suddenly and senselessly, James is brutally murdered, while Ann is raped and murdered. The rape is never referred to as such, but unmistakably implied, in a lesson for present and future filmmakers from screenwriter James Lee Barrett and director Andrew V. McLaglen.

McLaglen, who is often — and unjustly — criticized as a director with "no personal style," has skillfully set up the scene where James (Patrick Wayne) is drawing water from the well, when he is accosted by the rebel scavenger Mule (chillingly portrayed by Kevin Hagen). Asked for water, James/Wayne delivers an uncanny impression of his famous father when he drawls, "Yer welcome ta all ya c'n drink an' all ya c'n carry."

McLaglen does not show the actual plunging of the bayonet into James' guts, but his facial expression, and the quick cut to Mule's ice-cold eyes, effectively renders *horror without gore*. Conveying horrific events by way of reaction shots is a hallmark of McLaglen's supposedly non-existent style.

Even more effective is the manner in which he communicates the assault on Ann (Katharine Ross). Spying Mule and his two associates, Ann screams and runs up the stairs. The three men follow unhurriedly, with the sword tied to a cord around Mule's waist clanking menacingly against each step. To viewers old enough to understand what a phallic symbol is, the implication is inescapable; to those too young for that comprehension, the dread sense of menace still comes through. Screenwriter Barrett echoes the indirect method of storytelling: When Charlie Anderson and family arrive home, Doc Witherspoon tells them, "From what I could tell, James died instantly…Ann had — she was dead, too."

Earlier in the film, Charlie arranges the bedroom of a deserted farmhouse so that Sam and Jennie can have their long-delayed wedding night. What they're going to do in that double bed is glaringly obvious; it doesn't need to be shown, and it isn't. Hemingway called this sort of thing "storytelling by omission." Many modern filmmakers have yet to grasp the concept, or choose not to.

The film is constructed entirely around Jimmy Stewart, and the other parts seem to have been cast with the thought of supporting him. With television making significant inroads into film revenue, Universal sought to retrieve some of the audience by featuring two popular television stars in top-billed roles: Doug McClure from *The Virginian* as son-in-law Sam and *Route 66*'s Glenn Corbett as eldest son Jacob. (A couple years later, Corbett was memorably cast as Zefram Cochrane, whose invention of Warp Drive made possible all the interstellar trekking on *Star Trek*.) Two future stars of *The Dukes of Hazzard* are on view here: James Best as The Boy's Rebel friend, Carter, and Denver Pyle chewing his way through a Swedish accent as Pastor Bjoerling.

Much was made of the fact that several of the cast members are sons of the famous: John Wayne's son, Pat, and John McIntyre's son, Tim, play two of the other Anderson boys. Harry Carey, Jr. has a bit part as a Rebel soldier, while Bob Steele, son of director Robert N. Bradbury, has a similar small part as a Union Guard. Gene Jackson, son of *Our Gang*'s Eugene Jackson, plays his only film role as Gabriel, and quite movingly, too. He's billed as Eugene Jackson, Junior; switching to Gene Jackson, he embarked on a still-flourishing career as a camera operator. And, of course, director McLaglen is the son of the beloved character actor Victor McLaglen.

Several equally memorable character actors score in small parts: Paul Fix (Elizabeth Taylor's father in our Stand One, *Giant*) literally inhabits the sorrow-filled figure of the town doctor, Tom Witherspoon. Strother Martin, true to form, steals all his scenes as the prison train engineer. And George Kennedy, who normally plays hardboiled types, is unusually soft-spoken as Colonel Fairchild, the sympathetic commander who tries to aid Charlie Anderson in his search.

Two actresses make their film debuts in *Shenandoah*: In terms of screen time, Rosemary Forsyth, as daughter Jennie, is the closest thing Stewart has to a "co-star." Universal pushed the fact that they had carefully schooled her for two years, and it shows. Her Jennie displays the strength of character that informed all of her best roles.

In this film, she's a much better actress than Katharine Ross, who brings to the part of James's wife Ann a sometimes wooden delivery ("You-understand-don't-you?") and little self-confidence. Her star-making turns in *The Graduate* and *Butch Cassidy and the Sundance Kid* were still to come, but she does project a certain luminous beauty. In a clumsy convention of the time, she emerges elegantly coifed and perfectly composed immediately after giving birth!

And finally, Philip Alford, fresh from his success as the son of Gregory Peck (see Stand Nine, *MacArthur*) in *To Kill a Mockingbird*, carries long stretches of the picture as The Boy. For whatever reason, he never made the transition from child to adult actor.

Shenandoah endures. Charlton Heston wrote in *The Actor's Life* that *Shenandoah* was not his idea of a Civil War film; he then proceeded to make *Major Dundee* with director Sam Peckinpah, a muddle of a movie that achieved neither the contemporary nor the lasting triumph of *Shenandoah*, which was made into a Broadway musical in 1975 and since revived.

Not that *Shenandoah* is without its faults. Historically, it stumbles from time to time: Doc Witherspoon laments that his eldest son fell at Gettysburg, where no Virginia troops actually fought; Carter says "I hear in Vicksburg they're eatin' rats," whereas Vicksburg had surrendered a day before Gettysburg fell. Gabriel and other Black soldiers are shown fighting alongside White troops, whereas they'd have been assigned to all-Black units; and the Andersons ride out on the Quixotic search bearing rifles of a later historic design. The Anderson boys, by the way, are all in violation of mandatory conscription laws, though Lieutenant Johnson fails to point this out to them. The rich Virginia farmland portrayed in *Shenandoah* was actually shot twelve miles outside of Eugene, Oregon. And critics with an insistent nit to pick complain that the film has the "look" of a contemporary television Western such as *Bonanza* or *Gunsmoke* (McLaglen directed episodes of each, especially the latter.)

So what? Again, *Shenandoah* endures. If it presents initially as quaint, simple-minded family fare, that image is quickly dispelled: Rosemary Forsyth's Jennie is an inspiration to all feminists. Some critics questioned the fact that Jennie is a crack shot. What's to prevent her, having periods? Gene Jackson's Gabriel starts out as a "yassuh, Massa" type of slave, but evolves into his own man, who makes his own Stand.

There are those who wonder why The Boy is welcomed with tears and open arms in the finale, instead of being roundly chastised for causing the deaths of two brothers and a sister-in-law. Such critics betray an excellent understanding of pure logic and a poor understanding of human nature.

Shenandoah is a celebration of that very human nature. It portrays men and woman who demonstrate just what human beings are capable of becoming and achieving when they continue to do right, even when their world is coming down around their ears. "If we don't *try*, we don't *do*. And if we don't *do*, why are we here on this Earth?" Charlie Anderson himself embodies a truth that continues to elude most of the world, and most of the world's leaders: *Revenge is not a right, nor is it an entitlement.*

Some admirers of James Stewart would choose his portrayal of Michigan attorney Paul Biegler in *Anatomy of a Murder* (1959) as the signature of his long career, the part in which he fused the folksiness and shy charm of his "Jimmy" Stewart years with the toughness and potential ferocity of the James Stewart films. One could say the same about Charlie Anderson.

After sixty-seven film roles, Stewart had hit yet another one "out of the park" in *Shenandoah*. The years of character cameos and elder statesmen roles were quickly approaching.

But he had one more "larger than life" role to come…

STAND FOUR:
THE FLIGHT OF THE PHOENIX

(12/15/1965: 20th Century-Fox) Directed by Robert Aldrich; Written by Lukas Heller, from Elleston Trevor's novel; Music by Frank DeVol; Photographed by Joseph Biroc; Edited by Michael Luciano.

TOWNS
I've lost five men, Lew. Gabrieli in there, he's on the way, that'll be six. Are you asking me to try to kill the rest of them trying to get a deathtrap off the ground? I don't know — I don't know, Lew. It won't work — it just can't work.

MORAN
All right, then, it can't. Maybe it can't and we'll all be killed. But if there's just one chance in a thousand that he's got something — boy, I'd rather take it than just sit around here waiting to die!

Richard Attenborough's statement to Stewart is the logical next step up from Stewart's statement to his own children in *Shenandoah:* "If we don't *try*, we don't *do*. And if we don't *do*, why are we here on this Earth?" This time, "to do" is defined as "to do in the face of all but impossible odds." It is what the aircraft designer in *Flight of the Phoenix* —Dorfman in the movie, Stringer in Elleston Trevor's book — would call a "serviceable" definition of heroism. So is the quote with which Trevor opens the novel: "There are certain men who, when faced with the choice of dying or doing the impossible, elect to live. This story is written in honor of their kind."

That dedication to the heroic in the spirit of man springs neither from the imagination of novelist Trevor nor that of producer/director Robert Aldrich, but rather from the kind of unique, real-life event that fires the admiration and the imagination of men.

In May 1958, oil prospectors flying over the Central Libyan Desert in a Dakota DC-3 spotted a derelict lying literally in the middle of nowhere: a four-engine B-24 Liberator bomber, of the type flown by the Allied air forces in World War II. This one, bearing American insignia, lay on the desert floor some 380 miles directly south of Tobruk, in an area no sane man visits — unless he's looking for oil, the lifeblood of modern civilization.

Not until February of the following year did the prospectors actually approach the derelict plane on the ground. They found a ship frozen in time — filled with live ammunition, functional equipment, canteens and thermoses full of potable water and coffee — but no bodies.

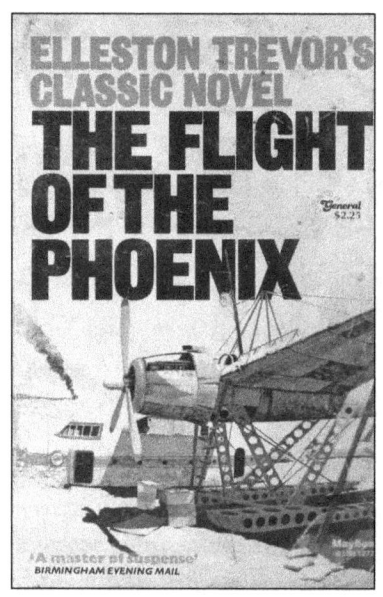

Months of research revealed the grim irony — the *Lady Be Good* (its name still emblazoned on the nose) had crashed after its initial mission to bomb Naples, Italy on the night of April 4, 1943. The green crew, under the command of First Lieutenant William J. Hatton, had over-flown their base near Benghazi on the Libyan coast and continued on into the desert — indistinguishable from the water in the pitch-darkness of night — until lack of fuel forced them to parachute from the *Lady Be Good*, still flying on one engine, which then continued on to execute an all but-textbook-landing on the desert floor.

Predictably, the "ghost bomber of the desert" captured the imagination of the American public, which demanded that the bodies of the crew be found and shipped home for honorable burial. A special detail from Wheelus Air Base in Tripoli set out to do just that, and completely failed. Acting on accepted rules of desert survival, the searchers assumed that the American airmen, already mentally and physically exhausted at the time of their bailout, could not have lived more than a day or two, and would be found within a few miles of their plane. The searchers returned home, empty-handed. It was almost a full year before oil explorers, again, stumbled upon the remains of a pitiful camp, including the skeletons of five men, sixty-five miles from their crashed plane.

The five skeletons still bore their dog tags and private papers, identifying them as members of the *Lady Be Good's* crew — and in the pocket of Second Lieutenant Robert F. Toner, the co-pilot, was a diary detailing how the men had walked for five days, not two, on little more than a few capfuls of water and an energy bar or two. Not only that, but one entry showed that others *kept* walking: On Friday the 9th, Toner wrote, "Shelley, Rip, Moore separate and try to go for help, rest of us very weak, eyes bad. Not any travel, all want to die." The body of Staff Sergeant Vernon Moore has never been found. The remains of the other two were located, again, by the oil prospectors. Sergeant

Lady Be Good *after fifteen years in the Central Libyan Desert.*

Ripslinger's body was found on the side of a sand dune, twenty-six miles further into the desert, and Sergeant Shelley's remains a mile-and-a-half beyond that. The amazing Guy Shelley had walked 115-and-a-half miles!

This is the kind of story that writers, artists, and filmmakers find irresistible, for good reason. The first filmed variation on the story of the *Lady Be Good* was presented as the second season opener of television's classic *Twilight Zone* on September 30, 1960. Charles Beaumont's teleplay, entitled "King Nine Will Not Return," cast Bob Cummings, then the star of his own popular television show, as the pilot who wakes up in the desert next to his crashed plane, and spends the balance of the episode searching for his crew.

Significantly, the filmmakers substituted for the four-engine B-24 Liberator a two-engine B-25 Mitchell, a smaller bomber more easily procured by the props department. (The B-25 used in "King Nine" still exists, in storage!).

The same substitution in models was made, although the B-25 was made to look amazingly like the *Lady Be Good*, in the 1970 television movie *Sole Survivor*, which became a trivia question for fans of the original *Star Trek* (Stands Five and Six in this collection): The derelict is discovered by pilot John Winston (Chief Kyle) and investigated by William Shatner (Captain Kirk). This adaptation introduces a totally fictional twist in the form of the title character, the plane's navigator (Richard Basehart), who bails out over the Mediterranean, thereby causing his crewmates to miss their base in the dark. He survives to become a Brigadier General, joining the investigators (Shatner and Vince Edwards) at the crash site, where he is confronted by the ghosts of his dead comrades, led by the plane's pilot, Patrick Wayne (from *Shenandoah*, our Stand Three).

The best line in the movie is spoken by a ghost crewman (Brad David), who has been listening on the investigators' transistor radio to Vin Scully's call of a Dodger baseball game, and tries to explain to his buddies, "Things must have changed a lot back home — I don't know how they worked it, but Brooklyn is now in Los Angeles!"

Despite their physical and metaphysical deviations, both of these adaptations followed the historical record in portraying a crashed bomber discovered after almost two decades. Conversely, in *Flight of the Phoenix*, Elleston Trevor, to quote Jan de Hartog (author of *The Spiral Road*, Stand Two) "...used the novelist's prerogative of being inspired by historical facts rather than governed by them..."

Rather than following, even partially, the historical outline of the *Lady Be Good* saga, Trevor invented a set of fictional characters, set his novel in the then-present 1963, and placed his crash victims in the exact section of the Central Libyan Desert where the *Lady* crashed, aboard a twin-boom aircraft — the only type of airplane that could conceivably be rebuilt into a smaller reincarnation of itself — into a *Phoenix*. He exercised "the novelist's prerogative" to give his characters the "one in a million" chance that Bill Hatton's crew deserved but never got — the chance to "do the impossible" and thereby "elect to live."

"It's much more than an adventure story," said the man who produced and directed the film, the tough-minded Robert Aldrich, "but it has all the wonderful entertainment ingredients of an adventure story; superimposed on that is the survival dilemma of what men will and will not do to stay alive under pressurized conditions; third is the twist that I don't think has even been done in film before, which makes the surprise ending not just a gimmick. There are no parallels. You can't say it's like some other kind of picture, and you hope it isn't."

It wasn't, then or now. A long story, with a middle-aged male cast (except for one sequence with a hallucinatory dancing girl), the film was no success at the box office — Stewart biographer Howard Thompson dismissed it as "a Fox misfire," yet the uniform excellence of the all-star cast ensured its eventual enshrinement as a classic, to the point that it was remade by Fox almost forty years later.

The extra length was unavoidable, according to Aldrich. "You end up with a film that is a little longer than you would normally want, and probably a little fuller than you originally expected. Because you *do* improvise. The screenwriter, Lukas Heller, takes liberties with the book that help the film, and you take liberties with the screenplay that you think help the film, and to that degree a great deal has been added since the original conception."

Aldrich had one major competitor for the screen rights: the man who'd eventually star in the film. "I have a guy in England who reads galleys for me; he told me about it...Then, about a month later, *Life* came out with a rave review of the book: the price skyrocketed...No sooner had we signed the contract than I got a call from Jimmy Stewart's agent: 'Is it really true that you own *Flight of the Phoenix?*' I said, 'Yes, why?' He said, 'Well, I've been trying to buy it for the past two weeks for Jimmy Stewart.' I said, 'Well, I presume he wanted to buy it because he wanted to play it. He could play it; he'd be marvelous, he'd be just wonderful....' Once we knew he was doing it, we certainly wrote the part for what Stewart *seems* to be. We took his characteristics as an actor into account."

Despite his claim to have taken liberties, the fact is that Aldrich and Heller almost slavishly follow the outline of Trevor's novel. The major change is in the nationality of the characters. According to Aldrich, "In the book they were all British, and we changed that to predominantly American with a sprinkling of others. That kind of snowballed...the key to the casting of the whole picture was an idea that the young, intelligent engineer-type be German. And there was a great deal of resistance in my own little group whether this was wise or not, because you take on many things people will read in — more than anything the script may refer to — by this man being German; you take on many problems of political and social theory. Then, having thought about that for a long time, I didn't think the worries were valid. Having decided on the idea, we agreed only two guys could play the part, maybe three. I thought the ideal was Krüger and we were lucky enough to get him. Having gotten Krüger and having gotten Stewart — that already changed the complexion of the kind of picture it could be. Then I said — having been a fan of Attenborough's for a long time — wouldn't it be sensational if we got Attenborough for the other big, big part. And we were lucky enough to get Attenborough. Now, having gotten Stewart, Attenborough and Krüger, then, gee, why not have a much broader-based film? A picture with more international aspects."

It's worth considering in detail the changes that were made:

Five Englishmen — pilot Towns (James Stewart), accountant Standish (Dan Duryea), drillers Trucker Cobb (Ernest Borgnine), Mike Bellamy (George Kennedy) and Bill Lawson (William Aldrich) — become Americans.

The one American in the book — driller Loomis, a Texan — becomes the French Doctor Renaud (Christian Marquand).

Three British men retain their nationality: navigator Lew Moran (Attenborough) and the two British Army men, Captain Harris (Peter Finch) and Sergeant Watson (Ronald Fraser).

Two other British drillers are changed to a Mexican (Alex Montoya) and a Greek (Peter Bravos).

The caustic Cockney, Crow, morphs into an acerbic Irishman (Ian Bannen).

As mentioned, the British aeronautical engineer, Stringer, becomes the German Heinrich Dorfman (Krüger), so the critically injured boy, Otto Kepel in the book, becomes the Italian, Gabriele Scarnati (Gabriele Tinti).

Many, many films lay claim to "all-star," but consider the stellar cast of *The Flight of the Phoenix*: Attenborough, Krüger, Finch, Borgnine, and Duryea, all had carried films on their own, Kennedy did so later, while Marquand and Montoya commanded star power in their respective countries. "I've never been on a picture that there wasn't a beef. This picture, which is a tragic tale, is without one single, personal abrasion," marveled Aldrich. "Because these guys are terribly individualistic and they couldn't be more un-alike. I was prepared, just by the nature of things, that there would be unpleasant days — maybe quite a few of them. And I don't know what happened. They just had an enormous regard and respect for each other…it was pleasant together; everybody got the same kind of treatment; nobody was favored."

Some reports alleged that Stewart was intimidated by some of his Continental co-stars — but only at the beginning, because, according to Aldrich, "They have a different set of standards concerning what are good films, what constitutes a good film, than probably Stewart does and I thought there could be a variety of collisions. Being more film-conscious than most major American actors, these guys all have known every single one of his pictures, and seen them, and just honestly flattered him as opposed to kissing his ass. He couldn't believe *that* many people knew that *much* about his own pictures and other pictures. And they just got along wonderfully well."

Robert Aldrich rehearses his actors in a chalked outline of the plane. Notice the actors, still in "civvies," have not yet assumed the physical stances of their characters. Aldrich's son, Bill, in upper left.

And so a one-of-a-kind story, based on the exploits of Americans, fictionalized as an adventure involving Brits, becomes a story of courage involving — and applicable to — everyone.

The film opens with a shot of the blazing sun, and taking off into it, a World War II vintage passenger-freighter, a twin-boom Salmon-Rees Skytruck. We are introduced quickly to pilot Towns, navigator Moran, and the passengers, with whom Moran shares his blasé assessment of their plane: "Never yet taken off in one of Arabco's old tubs without something being wrong. This time we've got faulty regulators and a duff radio."

(It's worth pausing here, for two observations: Moran is the navigator. Most casual synopses of this film call him the co-pilot, but it is vital to the plot that there *is* no co-pilot: the title device, the *Phoenix*, will be

flown by Frank Towns or no one. Other equally casual accounts fault author Trevor because the Skytruck aircraft has certain characteristics, like engines cooled by anti-freeze, not actually reflected in this type of plane. What they miss is that the Skytruck is an entirely fictional invention of Elleston Trevor, with its own fictional peculiarities. The actual plane shown in the film is a C-82 Packet, serial number N6887C, for completists.)

The faulty regulators are no big deal, but the radio is. The rules state that in the "absence of radio contact, a pilot shall immediately turn for his alternate airport." Towns and Moran have reasons not to do so: their alternate amounts to little more than what Moran calls "Three stinkin' mud huts and a poisoned well." There is a sandstorm on the horizon, but it's not enough to worry the pilot, at least not yet.

TOWNS
We're bigger than a little local sandstorm...A pilot is supposed to use his own judgment, don'tcha think? Gee, if it weren't for that — I dunno, Lew. I suppose pilots are just as good now as they ever were, but they sure don't live the way we did. I — I can tell you that there were times when you took real pride in just getting there. Flying used to be fun. It really did, Lew. It used to be fun.

Trevor's book goes into some detail regarding the career of Frank Towns, a "seat of the pants" flier, who has resisted upgrading to more complicated aircraft, thus gradually reducing his own assignments from mainline, trans-oceanic routes to "fringe" operations: jungles, arctic tundra — and deserts. The film viewer is left to infer this, as much from Stewart's manner as from his dialogue.

While Moran is concerned enough to sneak a nip from a bottle, signifying his incipient alcoholism, the passengers are blithely passing about a bottle of ouzo. Only one of them senses their growing peril, a youngish man in a suit (Hardy Krüger), who is obviously not an oilman, but he cannot communicate his concerns to the hulking driller (Ernest Borgnine) beside him:

DORFMAN
I must say, without a radio I would've expected them to turn for their alternate airport by now. Wouldn't you?

COBB
I don't know you, do I, boy? Are — Are you from the oil fields?

                    DORFMAN
My brother is there — Dorfmann. I went to visit him on my holiday…
He's chief analytical geophysicist for the Arabco Oil Company.

                    COBB
That sand's a bastard, you know that? A real bastard!

And it is, too — the storm has escalated to the point that it chokes the starboard engine, forcing Towns to feather the prop.

                    TOWNS
That right engine didn't make it. The other'n probably won't either. We're just gonna have to put her down before this one quits too.

MORAN

We going in with our wheels down?

TOWNS

I'd give anything not to, but we'll never get up again if I don't!

Things happen quickly, now. The remaining engine packs up, forcing the plane into a plummeting dive. The restraints on the cargo of worn-out drilling equipment give way, exposing the passengers to lethal projectiles.

Now comes one of the most effective opening-credits sequences in films: with all of the actors gathered together in one place, Aldrich can freeze-frame them individually, including the two examples of blatant nepotism, his son, William, and his son-in-law, Peter Bravos. Not to worry, these two will be crushed to death before the credits end with the plane skidding to a stop on the desert floor.

Also immobilized — by guilt — is Frank Towns; apparently, in his 40,000 hours of flying, he has never lost passengers to bad judgment. His shock and bitterness are evident as the two casualties are buried:

STANDISH

Do you want to say something?

TOWNS

Like what? Sorry?

In the face of Towns' ennui, it is the British Army Captain, Harris (Peter Finch), who steps forward to take charge:

HARRIS
How much longer do you estimate, uh, we'll have to be here? I mean, uh — I take it there will be an air search before long.

MORAN
Um — yes. Well, uh — we're not due in Benghazi till, uh, well, now.

Harris' efforts are not met with universal acclaim — especially by his less-than-worshipful subordinate, Sergeant Watson, a career soldier by default: "I was what they called a boy soldier. Me dad joined me," and the largely aimless man has remained in the service for lack of anything better to do — but he has nursed a simmering resentment against superiors in general, and Harris in particular, that will have tragic consequences later, as will the derangement of Trucker Cobb, which the crash has only worsened. Meantime, in the cockpit, Frank Towns has scribbled a detailed rationale for the accident in his log, which he then scratches out and replaces with a two-word merciless verdict:

"16:00 hours, March 17th…Cause of crash: pilot error."

By the next day, Captain Harris' rationing plan is in effect: one pint of water per person, per day — the bare minimum requirement — will give them ten to eleven days. As for food, there's an almost unlimited supply of pressed dates on board. "They're being sent back from Jebel," Crow notes sourly, "because no one'd eat them!"

Now, Trucker Cobb breaks out his transistor radio, which Towns grabs, trying to find news of their crash. He dials up and down the band, searching, but the sound is obliterated by a high-pitched whine. It's coming from the plane, where the young man, Dorfman, is shaving with an electric razor.

TOWNS
Hey! Shut that damn thing off! What are you trying to prove?

DORFMAN
I'm trying to remain reasonably clean.

TOWNS
You think this is some kind of a picnic?

After which Towns' mouth continues working in an old man's tremble (a brilliantly subtle bit of acting from Stewart). This has been his first clash with Dorfman, but not his last.

That night, another sandstorm forces the men to shelter inside the fuselage, where Towns, in a rare moment of warmth, persuades Cobb to loan his radio to the injured Gabriele. The disturbed Cobb moves quickly from pique to delight as he watches the bedridden boy clutching the radio.

So pass the days and nights, with nothing to break the monotony except the sighting of one airplane, far too high to have seen them. Eventually, it is again Captain Harris who proposes action:

> HARRIS
> *It's time we tried to march out of here…It's five days; we've had two sandstorms; we're not sure if they're even looking for us anymore.*

Moran and Towns break out the charts to show Harris their estimated position, and the impossibility of marching out. Their nearest water point is Marada, 106 miles to the north, "London to Birmingham," as Moran says.

> MORAN
> *Look, I don't know what your practical navigation's like. Mine's n-not bad. I wouldn't march ten paces from here. In the daytime, it's hitting 120 in the shade. And out there, there is n-no shade. If you could take as much as four pints a day with you, you'd still be sweating ten… Now, look where Marada is. Just look…If you miss this glorious little bunch of trees…there's nothing between you and the coast. And that's 500 miles.*

Towns and Moran continue to point out the rational objections — the magnetic rock in the surrounding mountains will confound the compass, navigation by the stars will be insufficiently precise to locate the isolated oasis — but, as Moran admits to Towns, "he goes by the book, and you can't rewrite it for him."

While Harris prepares to depart, taking his sergeant and whoever else wants to go, Dorfman approached with an alternate idea, which no one takes seriously.

                    DORFMAN

Gentlemen, I've been examining this aeroplane... We have everything here that we need to build a new one and fly it out! Now, if you would like to have a look at my calculations — I don't know whether you can read my handwriting—

                     TOWNS

Are you trying to be funny?

                    DORFMAN

That is precisely the reaction I would have expected from a man of your obvious limitations.

Now another man makes his move: Sergeant Watson "trips" in the doorway "spraining" his ankle. Harris is phlegmatic: "Ah, looks as if you're for the sick parade, Sergeant."

(From Trevor's book: "Watson decided to play it the way he'd often played it, the way these pipsqueaks liked it. They never saw through it, because they never wanted to.")

"Just my luck, eh, sir? I suppose, sir, I'd only be a burden to you...Perhaps if, uh, if I could rest it tonight, uh, I'll be all right tomorrow."

Harris tells him not to worry. Towns rejoins with, "What do you mean, don't worry? You don't think you're going out there on your own?" which prompts the mentally disturbed Cobb to pipe up:

COBB

Oh, no. No, he's not. He's not gonna go alone. I'm goin' with him, huh! Isn't that right, Captain?

HARRIS

I'm afraid not, old chap You're in no condition to come with me. Sorry, but it's better that you stay here.

COBB

Well, I toldja I was going! I toldja — I toldja—

Berserk, Cobb knocks the man down, and the others descend on him, trying to bring him under control. His protests finally disintegrate into childish sobbing, leading Crow to speculate, "We'll all end up like him, I'm thinkin'."

Meantime, Carlos (Alex Montoya), the Mexican driller carrying a monkey, has asked Bellamy (George Kennedy) to "look after Chucho for a few days. I'm gonna go along with Captain Harris." When Bellamy scoffs at the idea, Carlos rejoins, "Who knows, Mike? Maybe after a few days' walking and — we'll be better off than you are." Scathing comments from the sarcastic Crow can't mask his affection for his Mexican friend, or the general sadness as the two men march off at sunset.

The next morning, Watson has stepped outside to urinate, and sees another set of tracks following those of Harris and Carlos: Cobb has followed them. Watson comes *running* around the fuselage to tell the others — only when he encounters Captain Towns does he remember to resume limping on his "injured" leg. The look on Towns' face is priceless, another great moment from James Stewart.

Guilt-ridden ("I should'a *watched* him. I'm gonna bring him back, Lew.") Towns follows Cobb's tracks into the desert, where he spots a vulture descending on the man's collapsed form. Towns frightens the bird away and hurries to Cobb's side, but the man is already dead of heatstroke. In the film's most poignant scene, Cobb's last action has been to draw his name in the sand above his head — "E. COBB" — as though marking, however temporarily, his last resting place. (In the original shooting script, he has written his full name: EDWARD COBB. Apparently, in shooting, the shorter name was found to be easier, or more effective.)

After Towns staggers back into camp, he confides to Moran, "We're stuck here, Lew. You know that, dontcha?" Moran, however, has been questioning young Dorfman in Towns' absence and learned that the man is, indeed, an aircraft designer — so he urges Towns to "just talk to him." Dorfman's grand design sounds deceptively simple:

DORFMAN
There is no component problem. The port boom is undamaged and so, of course, are all the port-side components. If we remove the starboard wing and attach it to the port boom, and perform a similar operation on the tailplane, you'll see that we'll have the basis of, uh, an entirely new and aerodynamically sound structure...the center of gravity will allow us to distribute the payload — that means ourselves — on both wings.

Despite some eye-rolling, Towns has played along, but now he objects: "Now, wait a minute. Are you suggesting we string people along the top of that wing like sacks of potatoes?...We got an injured man in there. The doctor says he can't even be moved. Now, you're suggesting we tack him on to this thing and bounce him around like a wrangler in a rodeo?"

But Dorfman has an answer to that — cold-blooded, but practical: "That is not what I had in mind, Mr. Towns. With the material and personnel available, this project would require at least *twelve days*. How long did you say Mr. Scarnati might be expected to live? Six days? The problem does not even arise. Mr. Scarnati will remain here."

It is not an answer calculated to endear Dorfman to the rest, but it is practical and correct. For every objection Towns can raise, Dorfman has an answer. (From the book: "Towns knew he was having to speak to this kid down the length of a thousand runways, across whole skies where he had never been. How much of the message could he hope to get across, that far away?")

TOWNS

Now let me tell you something that makes nonsense out of this whole thing...and I'm not gonna give you the old veteran flyer routine. I just want you to know that I've been flying for quite some time now, and it hasn't always been for crummy outfits like this one...All right. You know a whole lot more than I do about aerodynamics and drag coefficients and stress factors. Okay. Your theory's fine, but you get this, mister. That engine's rated at 2,000 horsepower, and if I was ever fool enough to let it get started, it'd shake your patched-up pile of junk into a thousand pieces, and cut us up into mincemeat with the propeller!

DORFMAN

I told you there would be no difficulty building this aeroplane. I also told you it would require an outstanding pilot to fly it. The only thing outstanding about you, Mr. Towns, is your stupidity!

It is Doctor Renaud (Christian Marquand), who comes up with the deciding factor:

RENAUD

Perhaps there is one other thing. The way it is now, some of these men may not last as long as the water. But they need to believe that there is hope for them. I don't know, Mr. Towns, but maybe to build a thing like this could be a lot of help.

TOWNS

So we prove it can't fly and get killed in the process? What are you giving us? This is hard work. These men can't stand hard work.

> RENAUD
> *Watching each other die could be even harder.*

It takes them two nights to unship the starboard wing and haul it up onto the top of the fuselage. One other thing has happened, but only Watson has seen it, at the edge of the light: Captain Harris has crawled back to camp and collapsed. When work is suspended for the night, Watson takes to his makeshift bed, hoping Harris won't be seen — but Dorfman, who never seems to stop working, finds the man, who's brought inside and given water.

Another night's work and another tragedy: Gabriele, who had been flying home to a sick wife, comes to believe she has died, and commits suicide. Dorfman tries to prod his disheartened companions back to work, but Towns points up a new crisis:

> TOWNS
> *Before we start talking about who's gonna work and when, let me tell you somethin'. Somebody's been stealing water out of this tank...Now, I don't even want to know who it is. But I'm telling you this: If it happens again and I see who's doing it, I'll kill him.*

> DORFMAN
> *It was me...In any case, I didn't steal it. I took it...because whilst you people have been sleeping, or pursuing your own ridiculous little interests, I have been working. And since I was working harder than you were, I also needed more water than you did. However, it won't happen again, because from now on we shall all work equally hard. Is that clear now?*

> TOWNS
> *No, it isn't, but maybe I'm an idiot. Maybe you'll have to explain it to me. If you think being some kind of a boy wonder entitles you to other people's water, you've got another think coming. Why did you have to steal it? Why didn't you just come and ask me for it?*

> DORFMAN
> *Because you wouldn't have given me any!*

> TOWNS
> *You're damn right I wouldn't!*

Towns stalks off to the sand ridge about the wreck site, where Moran joins him to have it out:

> TOWNS
> *If you're coming to tell me I shouldn't be unkind to that miserable Kraut, you're wasting your breath…he isn't even concerned about getting out of here. All he wants to do is see that thing fly, and he doesn't care who gets killed in the process…I've done my share of killing. My score's five now. What does he want to do, improve on that?*

> MORAN
> *You know, I don't believe you're really all that concerned about those five men…What really gets you is the idea that maybe you're wrong. Or maybe that little, uh — little, uh, dried-up calculating machine down there really does know the answers. And maybe Frank Towns, who's flown every crate they've ever built and who could, oh, fly in and out of a tennis court if he had to — maybe that great hell-for-leather trailblazer's nothing more than a back number now! And maybe men like Dorfmann can build machines that can do Frank Towns' job for him, and do it better! All right. Let's suppose you have killed five men. And if it gives you any sort of satisfaction to sit up here feeling sorry for yourself, well, that's your — th-that's fine. But if you really mean that it is all your fault, then it's up to you to bloody well get us out of here, isn't it? And if you're not too proud to talk to Dorfmann, and you're half the pilot you think you are, well, maybe you will.*

> TOWNS
> *If! All right, if you hadn't made a career out of being a drunk, you might not have been a second-rate navigator in a fifth-rate outfit. And if you hadn't stayed in your bunk to kill that last bottle, you might have checked that engineer's report on the radio, and we might not be here! Awright?*

Turning away in anger, Towns turns back moments later with an abashed "Aw, Lew," but a shamed Moran has returned to the wreck. Towns follows him, and with a joke both apologizes and capitulates: "Come on, you drunken bum, let's get back to work."

Over the next several nights, with great difficulty, the starboard wing is dragged the rest of the way across the fuselage and mated with the port boom. The makeshift undercarriage begins to take shape, and, at least to some eyes, the project begins to resemble an airplane — enough for Standish to paint a name, *The Phoenix*, on both sides of the boom-turned-fuselage. At this point, voices are heard from the other side of the ridge — Arabic voices — a Razzia raiding party, on camels.

Opinions are divided: are they criminals, apt to kill the Westerners on sight — or harbingers of salvation? Harris determines that he and Watson will circle around and approach the Arabs on foot. But Watson has other ideas. This time, he cannot feign injury:

WATSON

I'm not going!

HARRIS

Sergeant, I don't think you quite understood. I'm giving you an order... If you refuse it, I shall have to assume that you're willfully disobeying a superior officer. Is that understood? Don't let yourself down, Watson. Report for duty and come with me.

Watson doesn't move. Nor will he surrender his revolver. Doctor Renaud steps forward to take his place, because "I do speak a little Arabic. Do you?" Harris' response is "Merci. Allons-y." Off they march, and the survivors' camp is kept dark and quiet, much to the disgust of Dorfmann.

The next morning, Watson willingly turns his gun over to Towns, who sets off with Moran to see what has happened. The Arabs are gone, but they have left behind a lame camel, along with the bodies of Harris and Renaud, their throats cut. Towns takes out his rage by emptying the revolver into the camel. Returning to camp, he's confronted by an evilly grinning Watson: "He's dead, isn't he?" (From the book: "Towns' fist smashed the man down.")

Work resumes, although Watson (from the book: "It was the end of all those years, but he wasn't free. He was lost.") experiences the vivid hallucination of an Arab dancing girl he knew in Benghazi. Even for this tiny role, the only female in the film, Aldrich's casting is meticulous: Barrie Chase, Fred Astaire's dance partner from his television specials.

It is Towns who interrupts the work with an unexpected question: "We testing this engine today?" Dorfman explains that "if we start this engine now, the vibration will put unnecessary strain on the whole structure." It is the very same argument the two had when Dorfman first presented his plans, when Towns claimed the engine would "shake your patched-up pile of junk into a thousand pieces," but now the two have unknowingly switched sides, leading Dorfman to remark: "Mr. Towns, you behave as if stupidity were a virtue. Why is that?"

Towns proceeds with plans to test-run the engine — until Dorfman heaves a heavy wrench in his direction, barely missing him.

Here, a strange thing happens. A scene from the book has been filmed *(see photo below)*, but has been deleted, presumably for reasons of time: Towns climbs up and tries to start the engine, only to find that Moran has removed the cartridges from the Coffman starter. Screaming, Towns leaps upon Moran, who fires Watson's gun at him.

(From the book: "Moran could still feel the recoil of the gun...with Towns flying at him it had been difficult to miss. The thing was, the shot had gone home, metaphorically: even in his crazed state Towns had realized that his best friend had fired a gun at him...it amounted to shock treatment. He was speaking quite normally and his eyes were quiet.")

The inclusion of a violent action scene might have provided a much needed spark in the midst of these "all-talk" confrontations. Its absence is almost palpable as the "normally speaking" Towns tells Moran:

TOWNS
Well, now I've really balled things up, haven't I?...I've been thinking about this thing. And I guess old Frank Towns just never could stand

being told what to do, that's all there is to it. And you know, funny thing: he was right about the engine, too. I guess I just wanted to make a point. That's what really gets you about him: he always has to be right!

If Towns has become reasonable, Dorfman has retreated within himself, where Moran cannot reach him: "Tomorrow's the last day. Then there'll only be what we get from the still, and that's n-not enough to keep us all going. Do you want them to fight over the water? Is that what you want? If we don't go back to work, we're gonna die — all of us… You told Towns he was behaving as if stupidity was a virtue. If he's making it into a virtue, you're making it into a bloody science!"

But the situation remains at a crossroads, until….

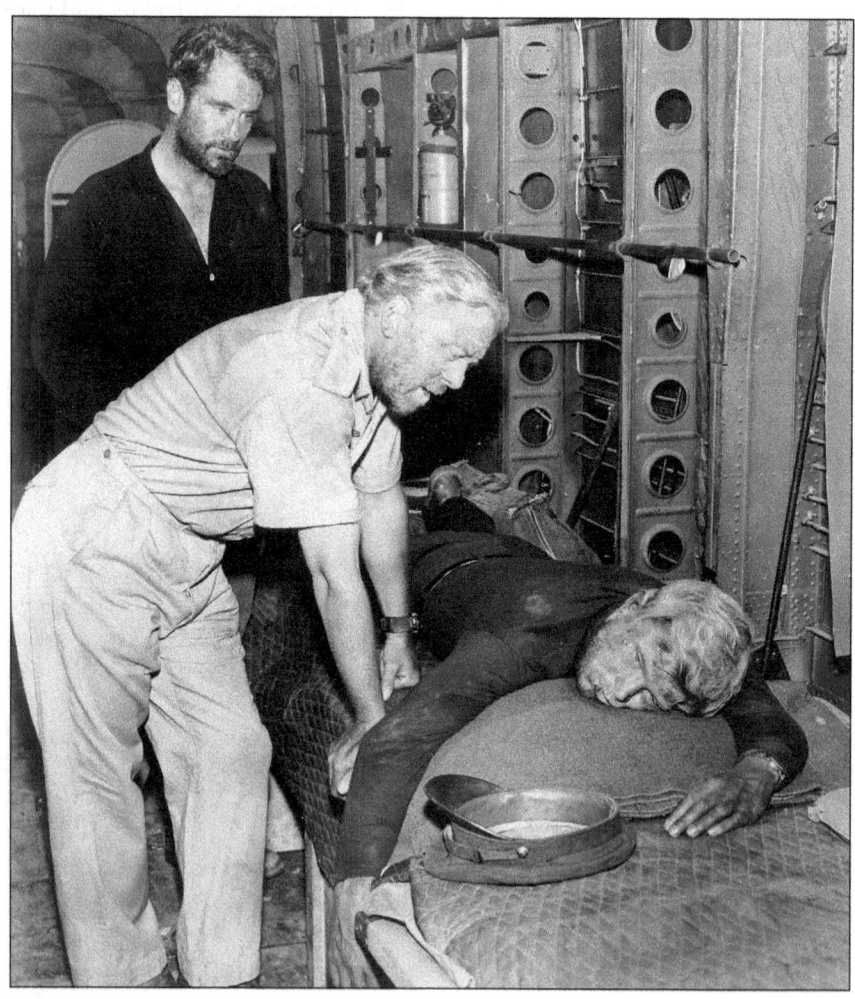

FRANK TOWNS MAKES HIS STAND

The next morning, Dorfman appears in the doorway of the fuselage, saying, "I want to talk to you. No, I — I want to talk to *all* of you."

Towns ("Of all people, Towns…." in the book) is the first to move, followed by the others. Dorfman's question is basic: "Mr. Towns, who is in authority here?"

Towns draws himself up to his full height, surveys the men around him — then he *visibly deflates*, as the words sigh out of him: "You are."

"Very well, then. Since I *am* in authority, I have decided to finish this plane — *and make it fly*. We shall now go back to work."

As work proceeds to the final phases, construction of the makeshift cockpit and control linkages, there is one more crisis to come. This is what Aldrich called "the twist that I don't think has even been done in film before." Towns and Moran spot Dorfman looking though the catalogue of the company he works for: a renowned builder of *model aircraft*. When they ask him "How much designing have you done on the, uh, *real* thing?" a proud Dorfman replies, "Oh, no, no, no. You misunderstand. We make nothing but model airplanes…but then, of course, the principles are the same."

"He…didn't even keep anything from us," Moran marvels when Dorfman has left. "He really doesn't think there *is* any difference." Now, Moran, the only one of the survivors who has maintained his equilibrium throughout, loses it: "We haven't enough water left to stay alive. We can die here — or we — or we can die in *that* thing. What's the matter? Haven't you any curiosity left? Wouldn't you like to know how it feels…to fly a toy airplane?" With that, he disintegrates into a long, vulgar, uncontrollable guffaw — which resolves into sobbing. (From the book: "Their chance of getting out of here hadn't gone: it had never existed. It had been a dream.")

The next morning, the two get the designer's attention when they suggest that he not "mention to the others about, uh, being a toy plane designer. Lew and I feel it might upset them."

DORFMAN

Mr. Towns, a toy plane is something you wind up, and it rolls along the floor. A model airplane is something totally different. Model airplanes have been flying successfully more than fifty years before the Wright brothers ever got off the ground. They were not toy planes…And there's something else you should remember, Mr. Towns: A model plane has to fly itself. There's no pilot to correct the trim. Therefore, if anything, a model plane has to be designed for greater stability than what you are pleased to call the real thing. In 1851, Henson and Stringfellow built a rubber-powered model that flew 600 meters before encountering an obstruction. Airfoil surfaces, lift and drag coefficients, weight/thrust equations, and the whole pattern of modern aviation originate from right there!

After another lecture from Dorfman about "unnecessary vibration," Towns climbs up into the cockpit, where the Coffman starter has only seven bullet-like cartridges to start the engine. Cartridges one, two, three and four spin the prop, but it fails to catch. To Dorfman's chagrin, Towns uses one of his three remaining cartridges "ignition off — clean out the cylinders." Despite Dorfman's cries of "I forbid you!" he does just that — then hits the next-to-last cartridge.

(From the book: "A spinner and she kicked, banging on the gears with the airframe shaking…the big prop spinning at a run and settling, putting out a roar from the pipe that drowned the sound of the sobbing in his throat as he eased the revs up and sat like a sack listening to the cylinders beating, hunting, one of them choked but picking up — then she was running with a will and in the long sweet sound he heard another, faintly, and turned his head and saw them standing there with their mouths open, cheering. His cracked lips hurt him and he knew he smiled.")

Dorfman and the other six climb into their makeshift harnesses and wearily pull the plane over into the nearby flat valley, then climb onto the wings. Towns revs up and the makeshift craft begins to move:

(From the book: "The wreck of the Skytruck was slipping past on the starboard wing-tip, the bones of a nightmare littering the ground, passing from sight as she made her run across smoother going…Towns got the stick back and held it against him, feeling the lift come into the wings…and all that was left of her on the sand was her shadow, falling away below…Soon she turned slowly, with the sun swinging across the port wing-tip, and headed west as they had planned.")

"What the hell is that?" is the cry of startled drillers at a small pumping station with its own oasis. "Hey, they aren't gonna try'n land that thing here, are they?"

"Well, it sure as hell looks that way!"

(From the book, last line: "Out of the desert there came seven men, and a monkey.")

PAUL MANTZ AND THE ACTUAL FIGHT OF THE *PHOENIX*

For the purist, the climax of the film is a bit of a disappointment: the *Phoenix* is never seen landing. It flies past a ridge, the sound of the engine dies, and the monkey comes climbing over to the oasis, the men trudging behind. Also, for eagle-eyed viewers (and those with pause buttons on their DVD players), it's obvious that the aircraft *changes shape*. There are good and tragic reasons for this.

The Associates and Aldrich (the company name) employed Tallmantz Aviation for the extraordinary flying requirements of this film. Tallmantz was the company formed by Paul Mantz, Hollywood's long-time purveyor of on-camera flying thrills in movies ranging from *Wings* to *Twelve*

O'Clock High, and his chief rival, Frank Tallman. By this time, the dapper, sixty-one-year-old Mantz had largely retired to the management side of the company, leaving the flying to the younger Tallman. It was after the *Phoenix* contract had been signed that Tallman, in a go-kart accident with his son, broke his leg, forcing Mantz to take over the flying duties. Mantz had no problem with this; he owed favors both to his old friend, Jimmy Stewart, and to the Fox studio.

What he did have a problem with was the airplane. While the craft the actors haul though the desert really is constructed from parts of a C-82, Tallmantz called on veteran aircraft designer Otto Timm to design something a bit more airworthy. The result was the one and only Tallmantz *Phoenix*, and whether it was more airworthy than a cannibalized Packet is debatable.

For greater controllability, the actual flying *Phoenix* was significantly different from the craft cobbled together in the film: the prop was two-bladed, rather than three, and the wings, rectangular on the original, were tapered. Also, the undercarriage, made up of "skis" in the script, actually camouflaged tires, since the skis would not stand up to repeated take-offs and landings. In testing, Mantz found many things wrong with the invented contraption, including the tires. These were replaced with larger ones, quite visible in the flying shots in the movie.

Despite weeks of tinkering, Mantz was never satisfied with the maneuverability of the ungainly aircraft; most alarmingly, he found the plane lost most of its lift when the dummies were in place behind fairings on the wing, simulating the passengers. These were eventually replaced by plywood cutouts, but even these dangerously impeded the plane's flying ability. (In the book, Trevor places his passengers not on the wing, but in makeshift "bunks" along both sides of the boom. It is interesting — if futile — to speculate whether Trevor's initial design would have proven more airworthy than that adopted for the film.)

In mid-July 1965, Mantz and stuntman Bobby Rose (simulating Stewart and Krüger) attempted the flying scenes for second unit director Oscar Rudolph, in a favorite locale for such shots, Arizona's Buttercup Valley. The first day yielded the exaggerated climb-out scenes visible in the film.

The second day, Thursday, July 8, Mantz and Rose tried the simulated landing approaches. The film is available for all to see on *www.youtube.com*.

The nose-heavy plane gets away from the veteran pilot and slams down hard on the desert floor. Mantz bounces it back into the air, but the craft has already begun to separate at the vulnerable joint behind the oversized wings. The front end cartwheels, and stuntman Rose "flipped my belt loose and dove out," while Mantz "just slid out, crushed."

With the small amount of aerial footage "in the can," the filmmakers had a few more shots they simply had to have, so they pulled a North American 0-47A observation plane out of the Air Museum for this work. Watch the movie carefully: this is the much-stubbier plane that is briefly seen before the off-screen "touchdown."

Ironically, the Civil Aeronautics Board labeled the cause of the real-life crash just as Towns had done in the film: *pilot error*. They concluded that Mantz had "misjudged his altitude" and was, surprisingly, "physically impaired by alcohol." The autopsy showed a blood-alcohol level of .013, which Mantz's friends scoffed at as a cause for the crash: they well knew he came from an era where drinking before flying was not frowned upon as it is now, and that he was accustomed to handling a certain amount. (Maybe not that much. As recently as 2007, a retired U.S. Air Force public relations officer researching the crash consulted several pathologists, who confirmed that rapid decomposition in the desert heat may well have compromised that blood-alcohol level.)

Whether the alcohol contributed to the crash or not, the accident was an unfortunate end for a man who had defined the concept of what he insisted was not "stunt flying," but *precision* flying. The film ends with this dedication: *It should be remembered that Paul Mantz, a fine man and a brilliant flyer, gave his life in the making of this film.*

THE BALANCE SHEET

Producer-director Robert Aldrich was embraced by European film critics as few American directors have been, since "his characters are adrift in a world both alienating and at times absurd, a world fraught with danger and conflict," according to *Whatever Happened to Robert Aldrich?*

His Life and Films. His biographers/filmographers, Alain Silver and James Ursini, contended, "His fables about bands of outsiders remain remarkably consistent across generic lines. *Attack!, Ten Seconds to Hell, The Flight of The Phoenix, The Dirty Dozen, Too Late the Hero, Ulzana's Raid, The Longest Yard* and *Twilight's Last Gleaming,* adventure films, war films and Westerns — all isolate a group of men in a specific, self-contained, and threatening...The truth is in the real world. The conflict or the dramatic dichotomy is in the characters working through their individual biases to discover that truth."

They then describe the standout characteristics of this particular film: "While in *Dirty Dozen* or *The Longest Yard*, the dramatic arc is a straightforward movement from disunity to unity. *The Flight of the Phoenix* is in many ways a more complete circle. The group starts out as sociable companions. Once the disaster occurs, their superficial camaraderie comes apart at the seams...like the characters in...[Jean Paul] Sartre's classic play, *No Exit (Huis Clos)*...this random assortment of individuals end *up battling each other* more than the hellish environment around them. For as one of the characters in *No Exit* states, 'Hell is other people.' Finally, the remainder of the film details how they put the pieces of this broken unit back together again."

Having made these salient points, the two writers overstep themselves: "The catalyst for this reactive behavior is not whom the viewer might expect. Rather than from the iconic James Stewart as Towns, who by billing and star-status would seem the anticipated hero or 'action-taker' of this drama, Aldrich plays against expectations. He makes the monomaniacal and egocentric Dorfman the one who leads this band out of the wilderness."

In a word, *no*. Aldrich has not "made" the designer anything; he has simply filmed Trevor's plot as written. Silver and Ursini are typical of those certain critics who credit, or blame, the director for all aspects of a film. Yet, in choosing to film a story of courage, Aldrich has demonstrated his own.

"I am against the idea of tragic destiny," Aldrich told fellow director Francois Truffaut. "Each man must fight even if he is broken. My characters have that suicidal attitude because the voluntary sacrifice of their lives is the height of their moral integrity. Suicide is a form of revolt."

Such an uncompromising Stand guaranteed that Aldrich's career would be a hit and miss affair. While *The Flight of the Phoenix* expired at the box office, it is refreshing to report that his very next film, *The Dirty Dozen*, caught the public fancy and recharged his career.

As for the actors, James Stewart had indeed endowed films with some of their best moments, in *The Flight of the Phoenix*, as he had elsewhere. Although there were a few more lead roles remaining for him, they were not mounted on the same scale as *Shenandoah* and *The Flight of the Phoenix*, and his career tapered off to choice cameos. His work as the doctor who tells John Wayne "You have a *cancer!* Advanced!" in *The Shootist* (1979) was especially moving. On television, he starred in the 1970s in a forgettable comedy, *The Jimmy Stewart Show*, and in a series of well-crafted mysteries as *Hawkins*, a crafty lawyer, who reminded viewers not a little of his role as Paul Biegler in *Anatomy of a Murder*. His happy marriage to Gloria, who had suggested he play the role of Frank Towns, continued up to her death in 1994. After that, an increasingly deaf and enfeebled Jimmy basically sat waiting to join her, which he did on Wednesday, July 2, 1997, to the sorrow of all.

The others all enjoyed future success, although Montoya and Duryea died before the decade was out. The producers had entertained high hopes for Oscars; the only actor so nominated was Ian Bannen (Crow). Always in demand as a supporting player, he enjoyed a late-career triumph as a lead in *Waking Ned Devine* (1998), only to die in a car crash near Loch Ness the next year. Two turned to directing: Christian Marquand helmed one of the most embarrassing excuses for a motion picture, *Candy* (1968), which managed to embarrass such stellar players as Marlon Brando, Richard Burton and Walter Matthau; Richard Attenborough was a bit more successful, directing the screen's all-time best anti-war war epic, *A Bridge Too Far* (1977), and one of its very best biographies, *Gandhi* (1982).

And Aldrich's son, Bill, who died on film in the crash of the Skytruck, lived until 2006, but finally expired from cancer. A couple of years before that, he sold the rights so that the film could be re-made.

THE RE-MAKE (2004)

20th Century Fox's 2004 remake starts out promisingly, with two and a half minutes of beautifully photographed opening credits and footage of a vintage C-119 Flying Boxcar flying over Mongolia. (The desert crash site has been transplanted from the Sahara to the Gobi.) From there, it becomes a six-point object lesson in how *not* to remake a classic film.

Change the characters — for the worse. The pilot is still Frank Towns, but as played by Dennis Quaid, he is a company "hatchet-man," who shows up at drilling sites to close them down, earning the nickname "Shut-It-Down-Towns." The other characters spring from the imagination of screenwriters Scott Frank and Edward Burns, but unlike those in the original film, these are all clichés. Two of them, Towns' crew chief (rather than navigator) and a driller, are now African-Americans, and played as standard bad-ass Blacks by two rappers, "Tyrese" (Tyrese Gibson) and "Sticky Fingaz" (Kirk Jones). Other stock characters include the overly concerned female (Miranda Otto), a self-absorbed company man (Hugh Laurie, rehearsing his upcoming role as television's *House, M.D.*), a mystical Middle Easterner (Kevork Malikyan) and a timid Mexican chef (Jacob Vargas). Even the "aircraft designer" (Giovanni Ribisi) is much more of a sanctimonious prick than Elleston Trevor's Stringer and Hardy Krüger's Dorfman put together. On the positive (?) side, he and Otto seem to be the only actors not chosen for how they'll look with their shirts off.

Minimize the danger. The remake characters are provided plenty of water and food, enough for at least a month. They never seem to undergo rationing; they drink what they wish and then bitch about the dwindling water supply. (When it's revealed the designer has been taking extra water, it begs the question: how could they *tell?*). They always have plenty of energy to dance to tunes on the Walkman, and nobody shows signs of exposure (it was consciously decided to avoid the blisters and peeling skin shown in the original because these would "distract" the audience!)

Goose up the special effects — past all reason. That's one area where one might reasonably expect major technical advances after four decades: instead, we're treated to a ludicrously exaggerated sandstorm straight out of a Hieronymous Bosch painting, a port engine that inexplicably disintegrates (so the propeller can ledge dramatically in the fuselage right behind Towns), and an extended crash sequence in which the C-119 is spun end-over-end, subjecting it to stresses that wouldn't leave pieces of a *real* Boxcar larger than a porthole, from which to build a *Phoenix!*

Escalate the violence whenever possible. Trevor's original story as adapted by Aldrich is surprisingly *non*-violent: two punches are thrown (by Towns and Cobb), while Harris and Renaud have their throats cut — *off-screen*. In the remake, these nasty-minded characters are ready to assault one another at the slightest provocation, when they're not engaging in gunfights with nomadic bandits (who "add excitement" by pursuing *The Phoenix* during its takeoff run).

"Modernize" the music. Frank De Vol's score from the original is sometimes criticized for its 1960s-style qualities of telegraphing the action, but it's far more timeless than the glut of "contemporary"–pop-rock tunes that are already beginning to date the remake!

Maintain a nasty attitude on everybody's part. Elleston Trevor's characters were tough men, oil drillers, and flyers, who treated each other with rough friendliness or, failing that, exaggerated politeness. These hip, updated, and "with-it" characters begin the remake as quarreling, self-centered egotists and end it precisely the same way; Towns especially, who has been humbled in the James Stewart version, is arrogantly shouting, in his Dennis Quaid incarnation, *"We make our own luck!"*

Director John Moore and his fellow filmmakers have not only missed the point of the original, they don't seem to realize there was anything there to miss. Check out the *Flight of the Phoenix* entries on the Internet Movie Database website for the verdict; when asked to choose, users are all but unanimous: in terms of quality, there is *only* the original.

When the hype over the remake has died down it is the original that endures, because it is the original that pays tribute to the essential heroism of the human spirit, in the face of both the petty distractions and the crushing realities that arise to daunt that courage. In their own, individual ways, the works of Jimmy Stewart, Robert Aldrich and those involved in the making of *Flight of the Phoenix* honor — and immortalize — that very same spirit that kept the men of the *Lady Be Good* walking into the desert when reason and hope had both been exhausted.

It is the function of films at their finest.

The late Burt Lancaster, a frequent Aldrich collaborator, recognized this about films. In his foreword to the Silver and Ursini Aldrich biography, he wrote this eloquent elegy:

"For all the fame those of us in this business may attain, we're all forgotten sooner or later. But not the films. I'd like to believe that in the future new generations will look at the work we did, look at all these pictures, and be moved by them. That's all the memorial we should need or hope for."

Attention to detail: William Windom bestrides the grand, operatic stage of Star Trek *as the haunted Commodore Matt Decker — with computer discs, in lieu of Captain Queeg's steel balls in* The Caine Mutiny.

STUDY III
Star Trek

To use Carl Sagan's signature phrase, "billions and billions" of words have been devoted to the vexing questions: what accounts for the lingering popularity of *Star Trek*? How did a low-rated, three-season network sci-fi show from the late 1960s come to spawn eleven feature films, four spin-off series, uncounted paperbacks, magazines, conventions, and a veritable galaxy of fan-generated product, in virtually all media?

Arguably, the answers can be boiled down to two: A, Gene Roddenberry's visionary, fictional future holds out the hope that mankind need not snuff itself out in nuclear holocaust nor drown itself in irrevocable pollution, but can instead move on to a universe of tolerance and cooperation, encompassing all sexes, all colors, all species, IDIC — Infinite Diversity in Infinite Combinations; and B, it's a hell of an entertaining stage for edge-of-the-seat drama involving the fundamental principles of good and evil, right and wrong, life and death: a Grand Opera of the Galaxy.

Every *Star Trek* fan (or "Trekker"), from the mildest to the most fanatic, could choose his or her favorites. The two spotlighted here violate the otherwise unbroken rule of this collection: that the selections be feature films. They're not; they're episodes of the original television series. But this is *Star Trek*, in which most of the best-conceived, best-written, best-directed, best-acted, even best-scored work has been produced not for the big screen, but the small. And these choices meet the fundamental test of this collection: the characters must make Stands that transcend their own inclinations and the expectations of those around them. The universe of *Star Trek* provides the ideal stage for just such fundamental and transcendent Stands.

STAND FIVE: *STAR TREK* "ARENA"

(1/19/1967: Desilu) Directed by Joseph Pevney; Written by Gene L. Coon, from Frederick Brown's story; Music by Alexander Courage; Photographed by Jerry Finnerman; Edited by Fabian D. Tjordmann.

KIRK
No, I won't kill him — do you hear? You'll have to get your entertainment someplace else!

Sometimes, heroes are defined by what they do not do — where they draw the line in terms of personal conduct. *Shenandoah*'s Charlie Anderson makes his Stand by refusing the temptation to strangle the soldier who has shot his son to death. Frank Towns makes his Stand by swallowing his pride and surrendering his authority so that the *Phoenix* can be completed. Likewise, that most iconic of iconic heroes, Captain James Tiberius Kirk (William Shatner), makes his Stand in this very early *Star Trek* offering by refusing to do the expected, although by that refusal, he is (theoretically) risking not only himself, but the ship and the crew that are his very reason for being.

Time to back up a bit: the legend that is *Star Trek* was still forming at the time of this, the eighteenth episode of its first season. Much of what is now regarded as sacred creed was still being arrived at: this was the very first episode that suggested the U.S.S. Enterprise represented something called "The Federation" (later the United Federation of Planets), and that established Warp Factor Six (six times the speed of light) as the maximum safe cruising speed for the Starship, with higher speeds attainable at considerable risk.

It is safe to say that, between this episode and that highlighted in our next chapter, "The Doomsday Machine," the series matured: the norms and practices of Starfleet in the twenty-third century were laid down and adhered to. The basic storyline of "Arena" contains, in fact, some plot holes "that could swallow a dozen Starships," to borrow a line from "The Doomsday Machine." And yet, so important is the conduct of Captain Kirk and his fellow explorers, so meaningful is the Stand shown here, that it is necessary to do what audiences have been doing since January 19th, 1967: take an uncritical pass at the story to appreciate it on its own terms. Later, we'll pick some interstellar nits.

Stardate 3045.6 (by our reckoning, the year is 2267): The U.S.S. *Enterprise* orbits the planet Cestus III, where Captain Kirk and his senior officers have been invited to dine by the commander of the remote Earth outpost, an officer known for his hospitality. One element of *Star Trek* that has already evolved is the bantering relationship between Lieutenant Commander Spock (Leonard Nimoy), the Vulcan First Officer known for his dispassionate logic, and Ship's Surgeon Leonard McCoy (DeForest Kelley):

McCOY

Spock, isn't it enough the commodore is famous for his hospitality? I, for one, could use a good non-reconstituted meal!

SPOCK

Doctor, you are a sensualist.

McCOY

You bet your pointed ears I am.

Materializing on the planet's surface, the six officers find the only hospitality is that of an ambush: the outpost lies in smoking ruins, and someone ("Not warm-blooded," Spock reads from his tricorder. "Living creatures, but not human"), too far away to be seen, is firing on them. While two *Enterprise* crewmen are killed, the encounter is otherwise inconclusive, as is a parallel encounter between the U.S.S. *Enterprise* in orbit and the enemy ship; weapons fire is deflected by "defensive screens." (Later in the series, these were formalized as "shields." This was the first episode to establish that the transporter could not be used through the screens/shields.) After the enemy ship retrieves its crew members and flees, Kirk and company return to their own ship with one survivor, a gravely wounded Lieutenant (Tom Troupe):

LIEUTENANT

Scanners reported a ship approaching...they came in at space normal speed using our regular approach run, but they knocked out our phaser batteries with their first salvo. From then on, we were helpless. We weren't expecting anything! Why should we? We didn't have anything anyone would want...they poured it on, like — like phasers, only worse, whatever they were using. I tried to signal them, we called up, tried to surrender. We had women and children; I told 'em that, I begged them! They wouldn't listen! They didn't let up for a moment...Why did they do it? Why? Why did they do it? There has to be a reason!

KIRK

The reason is crystal clear: the Enterprise *is the only protection in this section of the Federation. Destroy the* Enterprise *, and everything is wide open...I have all the proof I need on Cestus III...How can you explain a massacre like that?...The threat is clear, and immediate: invasion.*

SPOCK

Very well, then. If that's the case, you must make certain that the alien vessel never reaches its home base.

The rationale for doing so sounds very much like American foreign policy at the time, which is exactly the opportunity for commentary that Gene Roddenberry envisioned when he created the show:

KIRK

The colony of Cestus III has been obliterated, Mr. Spock...if the aliens go unpunished, they'll be back, attacking other Federation installations... It's a matter of policy. Out here we're the only policemen around, and a crime has been committed.

The *Enterprise* and its quarry are passing an uncharted solar system when, quite suddenly, the alien shudders to a halt, dead in space. "We've

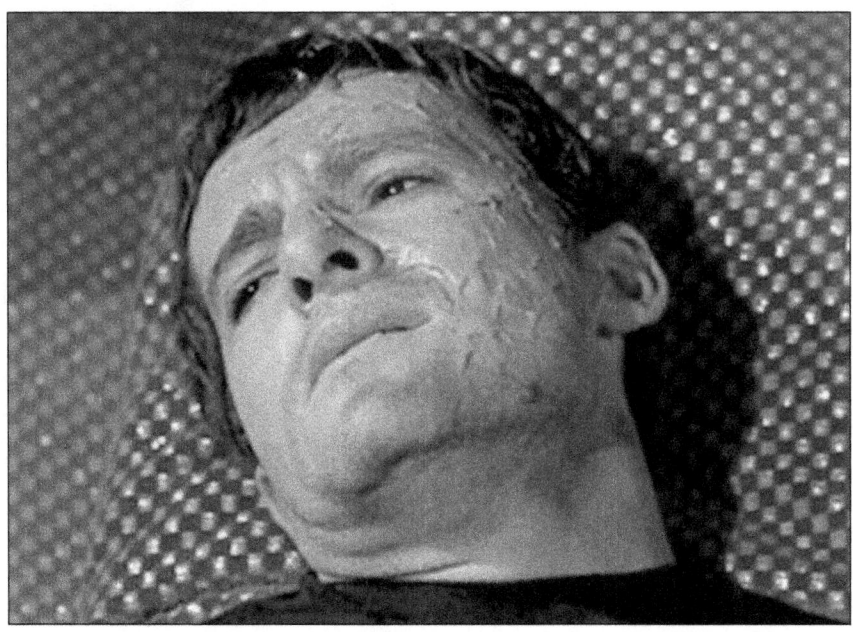

got him!" Kirk declares — until his ship, too, is stopped in its tracks, its weapons and propulsion systems locked up by an unknown technology:

SPOCK
We are being held in place, Captain, from that solar system.

KIRK
This far out? That's impossible.

SPOCK
We are being held.

The identity of their captors is soon heard over the communications system — although there is no corresponding picture on the bridge viewscreen, only pulsating lights.

METRON
We are the Metrons. You are one of two crafts which have come into our space on a mission of violence. This is not permissible. Yet we have analyzed you and learned that your violent tendencies are inherent. So be it. We will control them. We will resolve your conflict in the way most suited to your limited mentalities. We have prepared a planet with a suitable

atmosphere. You will be taken there, as will the captain of the Gorn ship which you have been pursuing. There you will settle your dispute. You will be provided with a recording/translating device, in hopes that a chronicle of this contest will serve to dissuade others of your kind from entering our system, but you will not be permitted to communicate with your ship. You will each be totally alone. The place we have prepared for you contains sufficient elements for either of you to construct weapons lethal enough to destroy the other, which seems to be your intention. The winner of the contest will be permitted to go his way unharmed. The loser, along with his ship, shall be destroyed in the interests of peace. The contest will be one of ingenuity against ingenuity, brute strength against brute strength. The results will be final.

Kirk immediately disappears from his bridge, and reappears face to face with a green, scaly, and formidable opponent. His attempts to defeat the Gorn through his own patented style of hand-to-hand combat — karate chops, flying drop-kicks — merely result in close encounters that are almost fatal for the Earthman. When it comes to throwing rocks at one another, the lumbering, lizard-like being can take anything Kirk can dish out, and return quite a bit more. Discovering a communications device on his belt as promised by the Metrons, Kirk records his situation:

KIRK

This is Captain James Kirk of the Starship Enterprise. *Whoever finds this, please get it to Starfleet Command. I'm engaged in personal combat with a creature apparently called a Gorn. He's immensely strong. Already, he has withstood attacks from me that would have killed a human being. Fortunately, though strong, he is not agile. The agility and, I hope, the cleverness, is mine. The Metrons, the creatures that sent us both here, said that the surface of the planet provides the raw material to construct weapons. There's very little here — scrub brush, rocks, an abundance of mineral deposits, but no weapons in the conventional sense. Still, I need to find one, bare-handed against the Gorn, I have no chance. A large deposit of diamonds on the surface — perhaps, the hardest substance known in the universe — beautifully crystallized and pointed, but too small to be useful as a weapon. An incredible fortune in stones, yet I would trade them all for a hand phaser or a good, solid club. Yet, the Metrons said there would be weapons — if I could find them. Where? What kind?*

Further encounters establish that, in terms of brute strength and endurance, the Gorn has the upper hand: Kirk is caught in a snare-triggered rockslide and escapes, limping, injured:

>KIRK
>
>*This may be my last entry. I am almost exhausted. Unless I find the weapon the Metron mentioned, I have very little time left. Native sulphur, diamonds... This place is a mineralogist's dream! Yet, there is something about sulphur, something very old. Something — if only I could remember.*

At this point, the aliens, who have overseen this mano-a-mano duel design to communicate with the *Enterprise* bridge crew:

>METRON
>
>*We are the Metrons. Your captain is losing his battle. We would suggest that you make whatever memorial arrangements are customary in your culture. We believe you have very little time left.*

>McCOY
>
>*We appeal to you in the name of civilization — put a stop to this!*

>METRON
>
>*Your violent intent and actions demonstrate that you are not civilized. However, we are not without compassion. It is possible you may have feelings toward your captain. So that you will be able to prepare yourselves, we will allow you to see and hear what is now transpiring.*

The human-Gorn duel fills the viewscreen — and the viewers of the episode are treated to a purely Shakespearean device: Spock, McCoy, Scotty (James Doohan) and Communications Officer Uhura (Nichelle Nichols) become a sort of Chorus, reacting in place of the viewer — and explaining what is going on.

>McCOY
>
>*If there were only some way we could contact him.*

>SPOCK
>
>*Yes, indeed, Doctor, if only there were. You'll notice the substance encrusting that rock? Yes, unless I'm mistaken, it's potassium nitrate.*

McCOY

So?

SPOCK

Perhaps nothing, Doctor. Perhaps — everything.

Meantime, a harsh, hissing voice issues from Kirk's communications device — which he seems to have forgotten was described as a translator:

GORN

Earthling! Captain! This is your opponent, earthling. I have heard every word you have said… I weary of the chase. Let us be reasonable. You have lost. Wait for me! I shall be merciful and quick!

KIRK

Like you were on Cestus III?

GORN

We destroyed intruders, as I shall destroy you!

Part of what defines the heroes of *Star Trek* is their willingness to question their own motives, their own actions. Thus, back on the Enterprise, McCoy is moved to ask:

McCOY

Could it be true? Was Cestus III really an intrusion on their space?

SPOCK

It may well be, Doctor. We know so little about that region of space.

McCOY

Then we could be in the wrong. The Gorns might have simply been trying to protect themselves.

SPOCK

Perhaps. That is something best decided by diplomats.

Spock continues to watch — "fascinated" — as Kirk acquires a bamboo tube and begins to collect various elements inside it:

SPOCK

Yes — yes, he knows, Doctor! He has reasoned it out.

McCOY

What is it, Spock?

SPOCK

Invention, Doctor. First, potassium nitrate. And now, if he can find some sulphur — and a charcoal deposit. Or ordinary coal...Diamonds: the hardest known substance. Impelled by sufficient force, they would make formidable projectiles.

McCOY

What force?

SPOCK

Recall your basic chemistry, Doctor: gunpowder.

And the obvious dawns: Kirk, limping, trying to stay one step ahead of his lumbering pursuer, is assembling a make-shift cannon.

McCOY

Can he do it?

SPOCK

If he has the time, doctor. If he has the time.

He does — barely. As the Gorn heaves into view, his hand-made knife poised for the kill, Kirk touches off his homemade weapon. The Gorn is knocked backwards, stunned, helpless. Kirk seizes the knife, brings it to his enemy's throat — and then —

CAPTAIN KIRK MAKES HIS STAND

All Kirk has to do is finish off his helpless enemy. He wins. Cestus III is avenged. His ship is saved.

But he can't. Or, more to the point: he won't.

"No," he tells the fallen Gorn, "I won't kill you. Maybe you thought you were protecting yourselves when you attacked the outpost." Then, he turns his attention above, to his unseen audience. "No, I won't kill him! Do you hear? You'll have to get your entertainment someplace else!"

His vanquished enemy vanishes into thin air, and Kirk finds himself confronting what appears to be a human teenager in a toga (Carole

Shelyne) — although the Metron tells Kirk that he is "approximately 1,500 of your Earth years old." The alien confesses to having been pleasantly surprised:

> METRON
>
> *By sparing your helpless enemy who surely would have destroyed you, you demonstrated the advanced trait of mercy, something we hardly expected. We feel that there may be hope for your kind. Therefore you will not be destroyed. It would not be — civilized.*

Having transported the Gorn back to his ship, the Metron offers to destroy both, but Kirk demurs:

> KIRK
>
> *No — that won't be necessary. We can talk, maybe reach an agreement.*

> METRON
>
> *Very good, Captain. There is hope for you. Perhaps, in several thousand years, your people and mine, shall meet to reach an agreement. You are still half savage — but there is hope.*

With that, a healed and restored Kirk finds himself back on the bridge of the Enterprise:

> KIRK
>
> *We're a most promising species, Mr. Spock, as predators go. Did you know that?*

> SPOCK
>
> *I have frequently had my doubts.*

> KIRK
>
> *I don't, not anymore. And, maybe, in a thousand years or so, we'll be able to prove it.*

THE BALANCE SHEET

Although this episode eventually cranks up to be one of *Star Trek*'s very best, capped by perhaps the purest and most provocative Stand in this entire collection, it almost doesn't make it out of the starting gate due to several staggeringly huge plot holes (and some embarrassing lapses, like the uncharacteristic use of the word "earthling.") The show opens with Kirk and his companions communicating with the Cestus III outpost commander, Commodore Travers, after which they beam down to find the outpost destroyed, and themselves in jeopardy. Problems:

Commodore Travers speaks to Kirk in the manner of an old friend, yet this is soon revealed to be a "faked" communication: faked by the Gorns, who we later learn have little or no knowledge of humanity, and cannot approximate our language, even through a translator, without lisping and hissing; the personalized impersonation of Travers seems far beyond their abilities. (It is possible — just possible — that there are language specialists on the Gorn ship, who have sufficient knowledge to fake the personal communications to Kirk. But this is a major stretch.)

The Enterprise transports its senior officers down to what is supposedly an active Federation outpost, without scanning it to see that it has been destroyed, or even noticing that the normal, subspace communications activity of such an outpost is totally missing.

When helmsman Sulu (George Takei) contacts Kirk to inform him that the Enterprise is under attack, no one has "taken the con," that is, occupied Kirk's command chair and function in his absence; though Sulu seems to be in authority (it should have been Chief Engineer Scott, as established in other episodes), he is still at the helm, and is ordered by Kirk to fire first his phasers, then his photon torpedoes, without bothering to aim either!

Other critics of the episode have wondered why, during their close-up struggles, the formidably-toothed Gorn doesn't simply take a bite out of Kirk (perhaps "Earthlings" are not kosher under Gorn dietary laws), why Kirk's standard-issue Starfleet boots are replaced with athletic shoes when he's transported to the planet/asteroid (very thoughtful, those Metrons), why the Gorn is seen plodding down a fairly well-defined dirt road on this planet/asteroid, and even why the Metrons say their own name with a short "o" (like "Klingon,") while Kirk and Spock pronounce it "Metrone." (Apparently, dialogue was recorded at different times.) All are quite valid criticisms, and most are errors the show did not make when it had matured a bit.

But, oh, that Stand!

Three of the world's great religions — Judaism, Christianity, and Islam — recognize the patriarch Abram, or Abraham. Familiar even to the non-religious is the story of Abraham, accompanied by his son Isaac, proceeding into the mountains to make a sacrifice unto the Lord — a sacrifice that God has told Abraham is to be Isaac.

"And Abraham stretched forth his hand and took the knife to slay his son," the Scriptures tell us in Genesis 22:10, whereupon "the angel of the Lord" stops him at the last minute and says, "Lay not thine hand upon the lad, neither do thou any thing unto him, for now I know that thou fearest God, seeing thou hast not withheld thy son, thine only son, from me."

And God richly blesses Abraham for his almost-act of unquestioning obedience.

A thoroughly heretical question presents itself: had the Lord not stayed his hand, what would have been Abraham's excuse for killing his son?

I was only following orders?

Spoken with a German accent, these words would be anathema to Jewish ears — and those of all men of decency — two thousand years later.

Yet, this is precisely what is being not only condoned, but praised and recommended in this Scriptural lesson: blind, unquestioning obedience.

Compare the two scenarios: ordered to "off" his own son, Abraham's reaction is "Well, okay, after all, you're God Almighty, Maker of Heaven and Earth, and me, I'm navel lint, I'm nothing, less than nothing, so Your Will be done!"

Whereas Captain Kirk is ordered to kill his reptilian enemy, a thoroughly hostile fellow, who has already caused the deaths of men, women, and children on Cestus III, and he says, "No, I won't kill him! Do you hear? You'll have to get your entertainment someplace else! "

What if Abraham had said, "No, I won't kill him! Do you hear? You'll have to get your entertainment someplace else!" What would have been the reaction of a just and righteous God?

What if Man's portion in this Scriptural lesson had not been blind, unquestioning obedience — but, rather, personal responsibility and accountability?

How might the history of mankind have been changed by this shift in focus?

How might it still be changed?

These are not easy questions. They are fundamental questions that penetrate to the deepest core of man's heart, mind, and soul.

These are the questions that make *Star Trek* unique.

These are the questions that spring from *Star Trek*'s Genes.

Most everyone knows of Gene Roddenberry, the "Great Bird of the Galaxy," from whose mind sprang the concept of the "Wagon Train to the Stars" that enabled him to make his creative comments about "what we are, where we should be going, and what we lack," and who went on fighting for his personal vision almost to his dying breath. Not so many know about Gene L. Coon, Roddenberry's initial successor as line producer and head writer, the man who, as Bill Shatner writes in *Star Trek Memories*, "...was directly responsible for the lion's share of the creative contributions that served toward making Roddenberry's good science fiction show into a frequently great one."

From Coon's fertile imagination sprang such *Star Trek* staples as the Klingons, the Organian Peace Treaty, and the Prime Directive, inventions with which, Shatner continues, "...Kirk, Spock, Bones, and the rest had specific goals, specific orders, rules to follow, and some terrific bad guys to fight." Most of these "specific contributions have generally been assumed to be Roddenberry's," which Shatner attributes to the fact that Coon died of cancer in 1973 — thus, almost alone among the initial architects of the *Star Trek* universe, he didn't live to give interviews or work the conventions. "Quite simply," Shatner concludes, "Roddenberry created *Star Trek*, and Coon made it fly."

Much of the dry *Star Trek* humor came from Coon, including the Spock-McCoy bantering, Kirk's pathetic attempt to drive a "flivver" in "A Piece of the Action," and his equally lame attempt to explain Spock's ears as the result of an encounter with "a mechanical rice-picker" in that perennial favorite of so many, "The City on the Edge of Forever." Even more important was Coon's deep-seated detestation of prejudice and preconceptions, evidenced in his very best stories, such as "The Devil in the Dark" (Shatner's all-time favorite), and "Arena."

Incidentally, the credits for "Arena" read "Teleplay by Gene L. Coon, from a story by Fredric Brown." Not so, according to *Star Trek* insiders, who say Coon worked out the story on his own, and then, when told how much it resembled Brown's "Arena" (first published in 1944 in the pages of *Astounding* magazine), telephoned Brown, who agreed to the use of his title in return for a screen credit.

Also, James Blish's novelizations of *Star Trek* episodes at the time they first aired had the unfortunate effects of robbing the stories of almost all depth, suspense, and poignancy, but his adaptation of "Arena" in *Star Trek 2* presented the information included in Coon's script, but omitted from the finished episode, that the Metrons admitted to Kirk that they had lied — that their intention had been to destroy the winner of the mano-a-mano duel, since the winner would pose the greater threat.

Layers upon layers, shadings upon shadings, complexities upon complexities, all of them contribute to this one unique episode, and *Star Trek* in all its variations, to the thoughtful considerations of human values and human conduct.

Many of these questions and conflicts were played out through *Star Trek*'s commanding officers, of whom James T. Kirk was the first and the perennial favorite of many.

But at least one Original Series episode took the character of the iconic starship commander where Kirk could not go — to a place where he has lost everything and everyone he loves.

In that episode, a surrogate Kirk had to be called in...

STAND SIX: *STAR TREK* "THE DOOMSDAY MACHINE"

(10/20/1967: Desilu) Directed by Marc Daniels; Written by Norman Spinrad; Music by Sol Kaplan; Photographed by Jerry Finnerman; Edited by Donald R. Rode.

>   DECKER
> *A commander is responsible for the lives of his crew, and for their deaths. Well — I should have died with mine.*

It really isn't Moby Dick in space, you know.

That's what author Norman Spinrad has consistently claimed as his inspiration for "The Doomsday Machine," explaining that Gene Roddenberry had asked him for a "bottle show," a story that could be shot entirely on the existing Enterprise sets, since the budget for "planetary" exteriors was being exhausted at this point in the series' second season. Spinrad says he went back to an unpublished novella he had written called "The Planet Eater," in which the title character/device compares to the white whale, and Captain Decker, the man obsessed with the machine's destruction, represents Captain Ahab.

All of which is okay, as far as it goes. But Matt Decker is not Ahab. Because Ahab is a loser, and Ahab is wrong.

Captain Ahab is a man who has surrendered himself to hate, and dies unrepentant: "…to the last I grapple with thee; from hell's heart I stab at thee; for hate's sake I spit my last breath at thee," wrote Herman Melville in *Moby Dick*. His obsessive quest has been motivated by nothing better than revenge, and he cares not that he has led his crew to death and destruction, excepting Ishmael, who is spared to tell the tale.

Matt Decker has also led his crew to death, but he feels it to the very depths of his soul, and the guilt threatens to unhinge him, his mistake threatens to undo him. But that doesn't happen. He perseveres, he hangs in there, and though it costs him his life, the ultimate victory is his.

Because Matt Decker is a winner, and Matt Decker is right.

The episode opens with the Enterprise proceeding through a series of solar systems in which the stars are intact but the planets are missing — along with her own sister ship. "Every solar system in this sector blasted to rubble," notes Captain Kirk, "and still no sign of the *Constellation*. Matt Decker's in command; what could've happened to him?"

As they approach a system in which the two inner planets are still extant, heavy subspace interference prevents Communications Officer Palmer from notifying Starfleet of the destruction, but she finally picks up a Starship's disaster beacon. (Elizabeth Rogers plays Palmer; this is one of the two episodes in which her character takes over from Nichelle Nichols' Uhura; ironically, the original *Star Trek* was first released on DVD in two-episode discs, and "The Doomsday Machine" is paired with "Wolf in the Fold," with the cover featuring Nichols as Uhura — despite the fact that these are two of the rare episodes in which she does not appear!)

Soon enough, the *Enterprise* encounters the drifting hulk of the U.S.S. *Constellation*, NCC-1017. (From the script: "She is canted at an odd angle and looks somehow grotesque in her helplessness.")

"She may have been wrecked," Spock suggests, "by whatever destroyed these solar systems."

Kirk sees it differently. "She was attacked," and orders his ship to red alert.

Sensors show all power plants dead on the wrecked ship, and reserve energy banks and life support systems still operating "at a low power level," so Kirk transports over with Chief Engineer Scott (Jimmy Doohan), Chief Medical Officer McCoy (DeForest Kelley) and a damage control party. They find the ship a shambles, phaser banks exhausted, warp drive "a hopeless pile of junk," impulse engines disabled but serviceable — but no casualties.

> **KIRK**
> *No clutter, no half-empty cups of coffee. Whatever happened, didn't happen without warning. The crew wasn't abducted, they just — left.*

With the bridge damaged, Kirk, Scott, and McCoy head for auxiliary control to play back the duplicate Captain's Log. There, slumped before the dead viewscreen, they find the one survivor of the *Constellation*: Commodore Matt Decker, haggard, unshaven, and semi-conscious. He is barely able to recognize his old friend Kirk — and when asked what happened, can only croak, "Ship — attack — that *thing* — !" While McCoy administers a stimulant, Scott plays back the last Captain's Log entry — in an authoritative voice reminiscent of Kirk's:

DECKER

Captain's Log: Stardate 4202.1. Exceptionally heavy subspace interference still prevents our contacting Starfleet command to inform them of the destroyed solar systems we have encountered. We are now entering system L-374, Science Officer Masada reports the third planet seems to be breaking up. We are going to investigate.

Reviving after McCoy's injection, Decker reveals more details:

DECKER

We tried to contact Starfleet…no one heard — no one! W-we couldn't run!

KIRK

Matt, what happened to your crew?

DECKER

Oh, well, I had to beam them down. I mean, we were dead — no power, our phasers useless. I stayed behind. The captain — last man aboard the ship; that's what you're supposed to do, isn't it? And then it hit again, and the transporter went out. They were down there, I'm up here…

KIRK

What hit? What attacked you?

DECKER

They say there's no Devil, Jim, but there is — *right out of* hell, *I* saw *it!*

KIRK

Matt, where's your crew?

DECKER

On the third planet.

KIRK

There is *no third planet.*

DECKER

Don't you think I know that? *There* was, *but not anymore! They called me, they begged me for help,* four hundred *of them! I couldn't…I-I couldn't…*

At this point, landing party member Washburn reports that something had apparently crashed through the deflector screens, knocking out the generators and deactivating the anti-matter in the warp drive pods. (Richard Compton, almost exactly twenty years later, directed a first-season episode of *Star Trek: The Next Generation*. His assistant director was Charlie Washburn, for whom his character had been named in "The Doomsday Machine!")

KIRK

Scotty, could some sort of general energy-dampening field do that — *and would the same thing account for the heavy subspace interference?*

SCOTT

Ay, it all adds up. But what sorta thing could do all that?

DECKER

If you'd seen it, you'd know; the whole thing's a weapon, it must be… it's miles long, with a maw that could swallow a dozen Starships…It destroys planets — *chops them into rubble!*

Spock radios from the *Enterprise* with an analysis of the *Constellation's* computer tapes that confirms what Decker has said: the planet killer is "…essentially a robot. Its apparent function is to smash planets, and then to digest the remains for fuel. It is therefore self-sustaining as long as there are planetary bodies for it to feed on." What's worse, helmsman Sulu has computed the course of the machine: it has come "…from outside, from another galaxy…" and is headed "…for the most densely populated section of our galaxy."

Kirk theorizes that the machine is the product of a long-dead alien technology — and he has a good idea just what it is:

> KIRK
> *Bones…did you ever hear of the doomsday machine?*
>
> McCOY
> *No; I'm a doctor, not a mechanic.*
>
> KIRK
> *It's a weapon, built primarily as a bluff; it was never meant to be used. So strong it could destroy both sides in a war — something like the old H-bombs were supposed to be. That's what I think this is: a doomsday machine that someone used in a war uncounted centuries ago. They don't exist anymore, but the machine is still destroying.*
>
> DECKER
> *Aw, forget about your theories, that thing's on its way to the heart of our galaxy! What're you gonna do about it?*

Kirk's response is to send Decker over to the *Enterprise* for treatment. Decker's reluctant to leave his ship, but Kirk is blunt: "There's no ship to leave! She's a dead hulk!" Only after Kirk offers to stay aboard the *Constellation* and ready her to be towed does Decker consent to beam to the other ship with Doctor McCoy. As soon as they materialize, however, they discover the *Enterprise* on red alert and rush to the bridge. There, a funnel-shape maw full of crackling energy fills the viewscreen. Spock is updating Kirk over on the blinded *Constellation:* "It looks very much like Commodore Decker's Planet Killer. And it is pursuing — us."

Gone is the thought of a tow. "Lower your deflector shields long enough to beam us aboard," Kirk orders. As though sensing the momentary vulnerability, the Planet Killer fires its deadly anti-proton beam, knocking the *Enterprise* off-kilter — and disabling both the transporter and ship-to-ship communications. Significantly, it is Decker, rapidly recovering his wits, who is first to reach Sulu's console and stabilize the ship.

On the *Constellation*, Kirk has just heard that his ship was under attack before his communicator fails. Now, he's stuck aboard a blind, deaf, and paralyzed ship, but he has one formidable weapon — his "miracle-working" Chief Engineer:

> KIRK
> *We can't just stand here while that thing attacks our ship. You've got to get me some maneuvering power —*

> SCOTT
> *Ah can't repair warp drive without a space dock —*

> KIRK
> *Then get me half-speed, quarter-speed, anything. If we can get this hulk moving, maybe we can do something!*

> SCOTT
> *Aye, the impulse's engines aren't too badly off; I might coax 'em —*

Scotty heads for engineering, while Kirk and Washburn address the matter of the dead viewscreen: "I've got to see what's happening out there!"

On his ship, however, things are taking an unexpected turn, as the Planet Killer breaks off its attack — the *Enterprise* is evidently outside of its programmed defensive sphere — and resumes course for the next solar system, which Sulu advises is the Rigel colony. A rapidly reviving Decker quizzes Spock on his future plans:

> SPOCK
> *We'll maintain a discrete distance and circle back to pick up the Captain.*

> DECKER
> *You can't let that thing reach Rigel! Why, millions of innocent people would die.*

> SPOCK
> *I am aware of the Rigel system's population, Commodore, but we are only one ship. Our deflector shields are strained; our subspace transmitter*

is useless; logically, our primary duty is to survive in order to warn Starfleet command.

DECKER

Our primary duty is to maintain life, and the safety of Federation planets! Do you deny that?

SPOCK

Mr. Sulu, you will lay in an evasive course back to the Constellation.

DECKER

Belay that last order, helmsman. 180° turn, hard about. We're going to attack…Mr. Spock, I am officially notifying you that I am exercising my option under regulations as a Starfleet Commodore, and that I am assuming command of the Enterprise.

SPOCK

You have the right to do so, but I would advise against it.

DECKER

That thing must be destroyed!

SPOCK

You tried to destroy it once before, Commodore. The result was a wrecked ship…and a dead crew.

Decker's quick look downward indicates that Spock has scored — but it's not enough.

DECKER

I made a mistake then; we were too far away. This time, I'm going to hit it with full phasers at point-blank range.

SPOCK

Sensors show the object's hull is solid neutronium; a single ship cannot combat it.

DECKER

Mr. Spock, that will be all. You have been relieved of command. Don't force me to relieve you of duty, as well.

This is followed by a very typical Spock-McCoy exchange:

> McCOY
> *You can't let him do this!*
>
> DECKER
> *Doctor, you are out of line.*
>
> McCOY
> *So are you — sir! Well, Spock?*
>
> SPOCK
> *Unfortunately, Starfleet General Order 104, Section B, leaves me no choice; Paragraph 1A clearly states —*
>
> McCOY
> *To blazes with regulations! You can't let him take command when you know he's wrong!*
>
> SPOCK
> *If you can certify Commodore Decker as unfit for command, I can relieve him under Section C.*
>
> McCOY
> *I'll certify that right now!*
>
> SPOCK
> *You will also be asked to provide your medical records to prove it.*
>
> McCOY
> *Now, you know I haven't had time to perform an examination on him.*
>
> SPOCK
> *Then your statement would not be considered valid.*

Matt Decker is no Jim Kirk; he wants no medical man on the bridge second-guessing him:

> DECKER
> *Doctor, you may leave the bridge.*

McCOY

Spock? Do something!

DECKER

Mr. Spock knows his duty under regulations, Doctor — do you?

Back on the *Constellation*, Kirk has finally gotten the viewscreen working, only to be greeted by a stomach-sinking sight: Decker has taken the *Enterprise* into combat with the Planet Killer. The results are distressingly similar to those achieved with his last command: the phasers simply "bounce off" the enemy's neutronium hull, the shields are quickly knocked out, and the ship is seized in a tractor beam, which begins to pull it inside the machine. This is where Decker comes close to losing either the command — or the ship itself:

SPOCK

We are being pulled inside, Commodore. You must veer off. We have lost warp power. If we do not break the tractor beam within sixty seconds, we never will.

> DECKER
>
> *But don't you understand? We've got to* destroy *it!*

Spock sees his chance:

> SPOCK
>
> *That, sir, is illogical. It is suicide. Attempted suicide would be proof that you are psychologically unfit to command. If you don't veer off, I shall relieve you on that basis.*

Disgustedly, Decker orders Sulu to veer off — but it's too late, they haven't enough power to break free. The Planet Killer is sucking them relentlessly inside.

Scotty, however, is no less a miracle worker in the engine room of the *Constellation* than that of the *Enterprise;* in short order, he delivers the power Kirk wants — "Just enough to move 'er, ah can't do better" — and the wrecked ship lurches and groans, throwing the few men aboard it about; then, as Kirk masters his cross-connected controls, the dead hulk begins to move, slowly but steadily.

> SCOTT
>
> *Captain, ah still don't know what we're doin.'*

> KIRK
>
> *We're moving, and the* Enterprise *isn't. Maybe that thing will see us, and let the* Enterprise *go. If I only had some phasers —.*

> SCOTT
>
> *Phasers? Ya got 'em: Ah have one bank recharged.*

That's enough. One phaser beam strikes the alien machine — which immediately releases the *Enterprise,* turning to face the new threat. "Mr. Scott, it worked! Great!" Kirk enthuses — then changes his tone. "I think it's great; Scotty, get us outta here!"

"Kirk pulled us outta there by distracting it," observes Decker. "Now it's our turn: fire phasers!" Sulu does, after which Decker orders a strategic retreat: "Hard about! Get me some distance!" With no immediate Starships attracting it, the machine returns to feeding off planetary debris. The impasse between Decker's obsession and Spock's logic remains:

SPOCK

We can maintain this speed for only seven hours before our fuel is exhausted, but it can refuel itself indefinitely.

DECKER

Then we'll have to fight it now, before it gets any stronger.

SPOCK

Illogical. We cannot destroy it, therefore we cannot save Rigel. We must transport the Captain and the others from the Constellation *and escape this thing's subspace interference to warn Starfleet Command.*

At this point, the equation changes: the subspace interference is pierced locally, Kirk can communicate with his ship — and its self-styled commander.

DECKER

Enterprise *to Kirk, Commodore Decker speaking.*

KIRK

Matt? What's going on? Give me Spock.

DECKER

I'm in command here, Jim. I assumed command according to regulations, since our first officer was reluctant to take aggressive action against the —

KIRK

You mean you're the lunatic who's responsible for almost destroying my ship?

DECKER

I told you, I am in command and I will give the orders, Captain; we are going to turn and attack.

KIRK

Not with my ship, you don't! Mr. Spock, relieve Commodore Decker immediately — that's a direct order!

DECKER

You can't relieve me, and you know it! According to regulations —

KIRK

Blast *regulations!* *Mr. Spock, I order you to take command on my personal authority as Captain of the* Enterprise.

At this point, Spock motions over the two guards posted by the turbolift (who are not posted there in most episodes).

SPOCK

Commodore Decker, you are relieved of command.

DECKER

I don't recognize your authority to relieve me.

SPOCK

You may file a formal protest with Starfleet, assuming we survive to reach a Starbase; but you are relieved…Commodore, I do not wish to place you under arrest.

DECKER

You wouldn't dare. You're bluffing.

SPOCK

Vulcans never bluff.

DECKER

No — no, I don't suppose that they do. Very well, Mr. Spock; the bridge is yours.

Spock orders one of the guards, Montgomery (Jerry Catron) to escort Decker to sick bay. Then, he and Kirk began planning a rendezvous, but Matt Decker's not going to give up now…

COMMODORE DECKER MAKES HIS STAND

Emerging into an isolated corridor, Decker fakes a cough and disarms the younger guard. In the hand-to-hand combat that follows, Decker overcomes Montgomery (in what writer Peter David notes is the only scene in all of *Star Trek* to show a "vaguely futuristic style" of hand-to-hand fighting) and escapes to the hangar deck. Next thing anyone knows — including Kirk on the approaching *Constellation* — a shuttlecraft is exiting the *Enterprise*. Lieutenant Palmer hails the smaller vessel; a weary Decker replies. Spock insists that he return to the ship.

DECKER

You said it yourself, Spock; there is no way to blast through the hull'a that machine, so — I'm gonna take this thing right down its throat.

KIRK

This is Kirk — Matt, you'll be killed!

DECKER

I've been prepared for death ever since I — ever since I killed my crew.

Neither Spock's logical appeals nor Kirk's impassioned pleas can move Decker; simultaneously terrified, fascinated, and perhaps relieved, he pilots the shuttlecraft directly into the fiery heart of the infernal device — where it is disintegrated. Kirk laments that "It's regrettable that he died for nothing," but Sulu's instruments show a minute, but measurable, drop in the machine's power emanations. Spock judges the decrease negligible, but Kirk has other ideas:

KIRK

Spock, listen, maybe Matt Decker didn't die for nothing: he had the right idea but not enough power to do it. Am I correct in assuming that a fusion explosion of ninety-seven megatons will result if a Starship Impulse engine is overloaded?

SPOCK

No, sir; ninety-seven point-eight-three-five megatons.

KIRK

Ninety-seven point — eight-three-five. Will it be powerful enough to destroy that thing out there?

Spock maintains that nothing can penetrate neutronium; his stubborn logic has not caught up with Kirk's intuition: "Not *through* it, Spock — from *inside* it!"

Now Spock understands, but his sensors cannot give a conclusive answer. Nevertheless, Kirk orders Scotty and the damage control party back to the *Enterprise* via the just-restored transporter: he has directed Scotty to rig up a thirty-second delay detonation device to ignite the damaged engine. "The shape that thing's in," Scott confirms, "it's hard to keep 'er from blowin'!"

The *Enterprise* transporter is in much the same condition: "Bridge, it's shorted out again!" shouts Transporter Chief Kyle (John Winston) as Scotty rematerializes. In perhaps *Star Trek*'s most vivid "countdown" sequence (spoken in appropriately sepulchral tones by Sulu), Scott races to jerry-rig the transporter in time — and barely succeeds; even as the *Constellation* explodes, effectively "killing" the Planet Killer, agonizing seconds tick by before Kyle can confirm, "Bridge, we got him through!"

Back on the Bridge, Kirk and Spock agree that Decker shall be shown in the log as having "died in the line of duty" — and so that the allusion to the present is not missed, Kirk compares the Planet Killer once again to the twentieth century H-Bomb: "Probably the first time such a weapon has been used for constructive purposes."

THE BALANCE SHEET

It is a hallmark — and wonderment — that *Star Trek* in its multiple incarnations exhibits the uncanny ability to be both entertaining and meaningful, in the face of gaping plot holes that gravely threaten the viewer's "suspension of disbelief." This is true of our previous Stand, "Arena," but refreshingly, not the case with "The Doomsday Machine," which holds up as solid storytelling on all levels: writing, performance, timing, suspense; even the magnificently evocative score by Sol Kaplan compares favorably with a great many motion pictures. (The episode was nominated for a 1968 Hugo Award as "Best Dramatic Presentation.")

The only glaring weakness in "The Doomsday Machine" — at least, some perceive it that way — is the 1960s-era special effects. Critics noted that the *Constellation* lacked the detail of most of the show's miniatures, even then. The AMT company had just begun producing *Enterprise* model kits, and it was one of these, attacked with a soldering iron, that became the derelict *Constellation*. That's why the ship's registration number is "1017": so the decals of the *Enterprise* number, "1701," could be rearranged. In addition to a plastic *Constellation*, the episode's villainous robot greatly disappointed writer Norman Spinrad: he had envisioned a sophisticated machine bristling with weaponry (something like the Death Star eventually produced for *Star Wars*) and he complained to Gene Roddenberry that the actual Planet Killer looked like "a windsock dipped in cement." Roddenberry concurred, but explained that they'd simply run out of money to do it better.

Doing it better has been the entire rationale behind the remastered or "enhanced" versions of the Original Series episodes produced for *Star Trek's* 40th Anniversary. "The Doomsday Machine" is the prize exhibit: the extensive exteriors present themselves as prime targets for digital enhancement. (Not that everyone was enchanted. Spinrad thinks the new Planet Killer looks like a slightly more sophisticated windsock.) The digital upgrade helps, but the storyline is not essentially altered in any way: it's a very human story, propelled by very human performances.

One of these performances apparently doesn't sit well with writer Spinrad, either: to this day, he seems to resent the fact that he wrote the character of Decker, as instructed, to be played by the hard-edged Robert Ryan, in a defiant and vengeful manner, only to find, upon shooting, that the part had been reassigned to the "softer," and much more nuanced, William Windom.

Windom admits in a recent interview in *Star Trek Magazine*, "I was known in those days as "Willie the Weeper…They would give me these terrible parts that never went anywhere, including, God help me, that one on *Star Trek*…It would always lead up to me falling apart on camera." Many would argue that Windom's wide range of emotional expression gave the episode a quality of identification missing elsewhere. Andy Lane writes in the same issue: "Interestingly, other episodes of *Star Trek* and its various offspring, including the movies, have shown us planets being laid waste, but nowhere else have we felt that sheer gut-wrenching terror of what it actually *means*."

One of Windom's strongest proponents was episode director Marc Daniels, who said in *Star Trek Magazine:* "William Windom is a terrific actor, and…when you get an actor like that *you* don't get a performance out of him. Maybe you need to steer him in some direction if he's going wrong, but the chances are that he does it himself."

From the "right-back-atcha" department, all the original *Star Trek* stars, excepting the gentlemanly De Kelley, published their memoirs, in which their opinions were often at odds with one another — and often uncomplimentary to Bill Shatner. One thing everyone agreed on was that the finest directors of the original series episodes were Joe Pevney and Marc Daniels, who are represented in our collection by "Arena" and "The Doomsday Machine," respectively.

In Stand Five, "Arena," we pointed out that James Blish's paperback adaptation of the original *Star Trek* episodes tended to rob them of almost all depth, suspense, and poignancy. Never was this more true than in his version of "The Doomsday Machine," where Commodore *Brand* Decker steals no shuttlecraft, but stands by and watches as Kirk conceives the idea out of thin air to explode the derelict *Constellation* inside The Planet Killer, after which Decker retires with the comparatively undramatic statement, "I cannot forget that my first attempt to attack that thing cost four hundred lives — men and women who trusted me — and that I had the bad judgment to try it again with your men's lives. When a man stops learning, he's no longer fit to command."

Several sources, including *Star Trek Magazine,* claim this comes from earlier drafts of the story supplied to Blish, but writer Spinrad demurs: "I never wrote anything like that and I don't remember anyone else bringing up such a thing because it wouldn't make any sense. There is no story. He doesn't die, and then what happens? How do they kill the thing?…I never wrote a thing where Decker didn't die…That is the whole end of the thing, that is *Moby Dick!* Dialogue got changed here and there but the fundamentals of the story were never changed."

The human story was filmed with some very human limitations: shortly after the *Enterprise* encounters the wrecked *Constellation*, Spock scans the derelict and announces, "The bridge is damaged and uninhabitable; the rest of the ship seems able to sustain life." Yet the exterior shots of the *Constellation* show many areas of the saucer section damaged, while the bridge area is absolutely pristine! Oddly enough, this error from the original episode was actually repeated and extended when the exterior shots were redone in 2006: the new footage shows huge sections of the saucer blown open and certainly not "able to sustain life," while the bridge, again, looks relatively undamaged. (Of course, the original idea of declaring the bridge "uninhabitable" stemmed from the fact that

there was not enough time to shoot the *Enterprise* scenes on a pristine bridge set, and the *Constellation* scenes using the same set "distressed.")

This relatively minor inconsistency hasn't measurably damaged the episode's legacy: the episode, along with its recent remastering, was the cover story of *Star Trek Magazine's* July/August 2007 issue. Most "Top 10" polls among *Star Trek* fans rank "The Doomsday Machine" in the Top 5, Jimmy Doohan (Scotty) called it his favorite episode, and it has become a part of the larger legend: In *Star Trek: The Motion Picture* (1979), Admiral Kirk regains command of the *Enterprise* from its new captain, Willard Decker. (Oddly, the film never mentions that Will is Matt Decker's son, but "The Great Bird of the Galaxy," Gene Roddenberry, confirms it in his paperback novelization of the film: "It hasn't been easy for him to live down the old man's legacy. Apparently, losing a Federation starship is still frowned on, whether it is the captain's fault or not.") In *Star Trek IV: The Voyage Home*, the probe that devastates the earth when it can't find humpback whales vaguely resembles a giant mailing tube set in concrete, with a ball protrusion at one end; one could be forgiven for wondering if the effects department was intentionally trying to bring to mind "The Doomsday Machine."

The Letters pages of *Star Trek Magazine* have hosted a debate over what some perceive to be a plot hole: after being relieved of the *Enterprise* command by Spock, Commodore Decker is able to overcome his guard, Montgomery, and steal a shuttlecraft. The question is asked: how could an emotionally drained and physically exhausted older man overcome a young, alert security guard? The answer is simple: Montgomery is on an *assignment*, but Decker is on a *mission* — so committed and totally invested is he to destroying the Planet Killer that one guy with a phaser doesn't really stand a chance.

As noted before, Decker is very much a surrogate Kirk. This is borne out by parallels with the film *Star Trek III: The Search for Spock*. Decker, to fulfill his mission, steals and ultimately destroys a shuttlecraft; Admiral Kirk, to save his friends Spock and McCoy, steals and ultimately destroys the *Enterprise*. He survives because, as McCoy so eloquently puts it, he does "…what you had to do, what you always do: turn death into a fighting chance to live."

And speaking of turning death into life, people who read or watch tragedies over and over again often do so with an unexpressed, perhaps unrealized and totally unrealistic hope that, this time, it'll turn out differently: Hamlet will overcome his indecision and live; Arthur, Guinevere, and Lancelot will solve the romantic triangle; Scarlett will persuade Rhett to stay; Commodore Decker will figure out how to defeat the Planet Killer and survive.

In *Tales of The Zombie* #6, writer Tony Isabella called such ideas "Walt Disney concepts in a Sam Peckinpah world."

But in a Gene Roddenberry universe…?

Even as Paramount's franchise graduated to new and bigger *Enterprises*, fancier uniforms, and more sophisticated bells and whistles, hard core fans continued to yearn for the sets and settings of the original five-year mission. This was largely expressed in written fiction until an Elvis impersonator named James Cawley amassed enough money — along with an impressive array of duplicate Original Series sets — to produce his own series of films, *Star Trek: New Voyages*, for distribution on the web.

The first such, "Come What May," released in January 2004, was uneven but enthusiastic, and tapped into a fan hunger for traditional *Star Trek* that Paramount has largely ignored in recent years. The second episode, "In Harm's Way," was a far more ambitious undertaking, no less than a sequel to two classic *Star Trek* episodes: "The Doomsday Machine" and "The City on the Edge of Forever." (By this time, their work was well thought-of to the point that Rod Roddenberry, The Great Bird's son, signed on as an Associate Producer.)

The plot involves a timeline that has been radically altered by multiple Doomsday Machines traveling back in time. Kirk, Spock, and McCoy use the time-traveling device established in "The City on the Edge of Forever," the Guardian of Forever, to try and undo the damage. Their quest leads them to a suburban American neighborhood in the early years of the twenty-first century, where a stunning older woman named Veronica (BarBara Luna, who played Captain Kirk's "woman" in "Mirror, Mirror") astonishes the Starfleet time-travelers by *recognizing* them. She then invites them into her living room and plays them a homemade videotape.

The man on the video is *an elderly Matt Decker* — who then explains how the explosion did not destroy his shuttlecraft, but sent it back in time to the late twentieth century, where he returned to Earth and lived out another forty years of life.

For aficionados of original *Star Trek,* the casting of new actors in the classic roles is a bit hard to take (and this is long before J. J. Abrams' colossal 2009 reboot), no reflection on the actors, but the parts are so closely identified with Shatner, Nimoy, and Kelley that Cawley and his companions cannot help but suffer in comparison (Jeff Quinn, in particular, comes off as sort of an "I was a teenage Spock" — even in later scenes, where he plays an elderly Spock!), and thereby, the episode lacks credibility. This one scene goes a long way toward remedying that — because, just as the "new" heroes gasp in recognition of Matt Decker, the audience gasps in recognition of William Windom.

Star Trek abounds in moments that bring a lump to the throat. In the original "The Doomsday Machine," when the shell-shocked Decker recognizes Kirk, there is a slight chuckle to Windom's voice, as he speaks the line, "Why, it's Jim Kirk." His first line as an elderly man on the videotape is, "If you're watching this tape, it means that someone from Starfleet has come looking for me. I'm betting it's Jim Kirk," — and it's said with that very same almost-chuckle.

A fan of the original episode cannot help but react as though encountering an old, dear friend — which, of course, is what the *Star Trek* characters have become.

Since the events of "In Harm's Way" conveniently occur in an "alternate timeline" — similar to the much later Abrams reboot — a fan of the original show may choose to believe either scenario: that Decker died in the shuttlecraft explosion, or that he was hurled backward in time to become "the only man to see three centuries." And like the remastering of the original episode, it detracts in no way from the magnificent Stand of Matt Decker. That Stand is all the more remarkable in that Decker was driven not by his error in judgment, but by his passion — not necessarily to revenge his crew, but to give their deaths meaning, which he did. And First Officer Spock, for all his vaunted Vulcan logic, was wrong — he had adamantly maintained that "we cannot save Rigel, our only logical alternative is to escape to warn Starfleet Command." Had it been left to Spock, the millions in the Rigel colonies would have died, because his logic dictated that they could not be saved — whereas Decker's intuition (and Kirk's) said they could be, and indeed they were.

Decker's Stand has, in the words of Bertrand Russell's *A Free Man's Worship*, "…become eternal by the immortality of the past," just as the Stands taken by the wonderful characters in Roddenberry's universe — in its many incarnations — continue to dazzle, to delight, and to inspire.

Still questing: Errol Flynn near the end of his life, in Cuba.

STUDY IV
Errol Flynn

Like Rock Hudson, Errol Flynn built his career on his looks — and the camera's affinity for those looks — only to be eclipsed by his off-camera reputation. Hudson's frustration with this state of affairs was confined to private conversations and an even more private journal. Flynn's journal entries, by contrast, were reprinted in his posthumously published autobiography:

> "I had by now made about forty-five pictures, but what had I become? I knew all too well: a phallic symbol. All over the world I was, as a name and personality, equated with sex. Playboy of the Western World. That was me. But what had I set out to become a long time before, when I was young and the world opened to me? How far afield had I gone from my early ambitions? Does any man ever set out to become a phallic symbol universally, or does this not happen to a man in spite of himself? The old bromide came back to me, how some were born to greatness, some achieved it, and others had it thrust upon them. I had no greatness, only a deadly fear of mediocrity. But time had set upon me this stamp of lady-killer *par excellence*."

Time didn't do it alone, of course. Flynn was an eager and enthusiastic participant. But the image expanded to grotesque proportions with Flynn's trial on charges of statutory rape in 1943. The verdict was "Not guilty," but —

> "I had become something other than what I set out to be. Now my name was simply associated with sex. I was a male Mae West, as it were. Me, Errol Leslie Thomson Flynn, son of the respectable biologist, student of Darwin, lover of culture — and nothing that I had wanted had happened. Instead I was in a swamp of Flynn jokes, dirty stories, snide innuendoes…What was I doing with a sword in one hand and a garter in the other?"

By the mid-1950s, Flynn was living in Europe , mostly on board his yacht, *Zaca*. After the last — and loudest — of his many rows with Jack Warner, the contract was canceled by mutual consent, and he was off to Italy to "…make my own pictures. I will make a mint and show them I don't need them or their studio."

He didn't make a mint; he lost one, when the principal Italian investor reneged on his commitment to finance one-half of a Cinemascope production of *William Tell*. The other half had come from Flynn, all the cash he had, followed swiftly by the death of his less-than-honest business manager, and the news that he owed the IRS a million in back taxes. Added to the crippling alimony payments to his first wife — a ruinous settlement that went up when his salary did, but not down when the money dried up — this spelled financial failure, on top of what Flynn perceived to be failures as a writer (he'd published two books, but lacked the discipline to go further), failure as a husband (he was married by then to wife number three), failure as a father to his four children, and finally, failure as an actor. The last, though, he refused to take full blame for:

> "I wonder if you can imagine what it might mean to be one who believes that, given the chance at good and great roles, he might be able to act, say, like a Barrymore — but never to be given that chance. Only to be given those sure-fire box-office attractions — entertainment pictures that often didn't entertain — action, action, action…If a stereotype makes money, keep the stereotype alive. Don't make a switch. Don't experiment, don't pander to an actor's whim that he might like to do something special, different. Keep the sword shiny, shoe the horse and turn Flynn loose on a new one."

By this time, he was being offered little more than third-rate films and occasional television work, yet he had his chance in the eleventh hour to "act like a Barrymore."

> "The first break came when Darryl F. Zanuck, whom I hardly knew then, for some obscure reason he has never explained to me, thought of me for a juicy part in his *The Sun Also Rises* and all the critics were unanimously very kind, for once. Then, of all people, Jack Warner (remember I was going to teach him how to make pictures?), my old friend and antagonist, thought I was right for the role of John Barrymore in *Too Much, Too Soon* and again the critics leaped into the breach for me, saying I made a good Barrymore and

I was welcomed home. Then came *Roots of Heaven*, another one for Darryl. In all of these I played a drunk and a bum. What people believed I was and had become. Maybe these roles were right for me. I was a natural, I guess. A bum, a rake, a character. Yet, apparently, all the world loves a comeback."

Unfortunately, in the words of film writer George Morris, "The years of narcotics, excessive drinking, and sensual indulgence had begun to consume Errol Flynn," and the comeback was limited to those three films, none of which was a hit — though Flynn's performance in the Hemingway film earned the ultimate in left-handed compliments from Papa himself in *Papa Hemingway* by A. E. Hotchner: "Any film in which Errol Flynn is the best actor is its own worst enemy." The part of Mike Campbell, the man who'd gone bankrupt "two ways — gradually and suddenly," offered Flynn the opportunity to show such varied emotions as loss, embarrassment, and desolation, covered by a transparent façade of false jocularity. Actually, he'd demonstrated this talent many times over the years: as the flamboyant ace turned haunted commander in *The Dawn Patrol* (1938), the jewel thief turned reluctant patriot in *Uncertain Glory* (1944), and the heartless husband of Greer Garson, *That Forsyte Woman* (1949), but the blinding dazzle of his costumed, period roles tended to obscure these subtler performances. Now, nearing fifty and prematurely aged by dissipation, he experienced a new-found satisfaction from merely doing his best in these three movies.

The latter two are on display here: *Too Much, Too Soon* adapts the sordid, depressing life story of Diana Barrymore, but it's even more the story of her father and Flynn's mentor, John Barrymore. Flynn's portrayal, walking a paper-thin tightrope between affectionate tribute and savage indictment, says perhaps as much about himself as it does about his subject, though it's open to question whether a man who ultimately self-destructs can be said to "triumph over himself," the guiding principle of this collection. No such dilemma arises in *The Roots of Heaven*, where circumstance gives Flynn top billing but a secondary role: one of the followers of Morel (Trevor Howard), the eccentric ex-P.O.W. dedicated to preserving the African elephant. Ultimately, that quest saves precious few pachyderms, but yields a measure of personal resurrection to those very followers, none more so than Flynn's character.

So here are the Flynn characterizations in this collection of Stands: the real-life John Barrymore and the fictitious Major Forsythe, portraits of extraordinary depth and poignancy from the swashbuckling star who could, after all, act.

STAND SEVEN: *TOO MUCH, TOO SOON*

(4/17/1958: Warner Bros.) Directed by Art Napoleon; Written by Art & Jo Napoleon, from the autobiography by Diana Barrymore with Gerold Frank; Music by Ernest Gold; Photographed by Nick Musuraca & Carl Guthrie; Edited by Owen Marks.

From *S.O.B.* (1982), screenplay by Blake Edwards:

> **FELIX FARMER**
> *You think I'm crazy... What if I'm right? If my vision is valid, Culley, not so crazy, a more acceptable insanity...sane and miserable? Or insane, and bursting with creative joy, and happiness...and in the final analysis, who says "He's sane, therefore he should?" or "He's insane, therefore he shouldn't?" Culley, c'mon. Even if I'm wrong — and I'm not — I'm full of fire, Culley! I'm a blazing comet!*
>
> **TIM CULLEY**
> *Comets burn out, pal.*
>
> **FELIX FARMER**
> *But, ah, my foes and oh, my friends, it gives a lovely light!*

Okay, so the opening quote isn't even from this movie, but it accurately describes why Warner Bros. made a movie about the sordid slide into self-destruction of Diana Barrymore, and why audiences, then as well as now, are drawn to such stories as surely as they are drawn to crash sites: *Comets burn out...but they give a lovely light.* Or, if not lovely, at least fascinating and absorbing.

Too Much, Too Soon is Warner Bros. adaptation of Diana Barrymore's confessional autobiography, detailing her unsuccessful attempt to follow in her family's celebrated acting footsteps and her somewhat more successful (if you can call it that) journey down her father's path of career and personal and professional degeneration. Both were the kind of "comets" the Messrs. Farmer and Culley discuss in the scene from *S.O.B.*, the primary difference being that while Diana mainly lit up the sky with her own self-immolation (in more ways than one), John first set it afire with his own blazing talent. When the man who had dared to take an American version of *Hamlet* to London — and in the process, to inspire

two star-struck youngsters named Laurence Olivier and John Gielgud — died broken and wasted in 1941, many pious tongues wagged in haughty tones of self-righteous condemnation. An anonymous editorial writer in the *Herald Tribune* struck a more realistic balance:

> "The moralists said it was 'sad' that in his latter years he became a 'caricature' of a once magnificent figure. But none of this was news to Barrymore, nor did he allow it to disturb him unduly…Here was an actor. Was ever there a better in America?…No matter what he touched, he gave it a manner and a dash. He was born to be an actor, and when he conscientiously set himself to a task he could blend his genius with a thoroughly sound and intelligent craftsmanship… *He was a mortal whose head at times reached very close to the stars.*"

Beneath a cheap and tawdry veneer, *Too Much, Too Soon* examines how John Barrymore and his daughter, Diana, met that ordeal, and indirectly, how Errol Flynn did the same.

In a sense, all three felt the dull anger of the congenital non-conformist, born into a world that demands conformity. Flynn expressed it in his autobiography:

"It seems absurd, ridiculous and laughable that somebody should tell me how to behave during my brief span on this earth. I feel like rebelling every time I think of it. A rough, bemused, rugged individualist, I was born this way and that is the way I will die. I have no clear-cut system of philosophy. I want none. I want no design for living. I want no one to tell me how to live. I will take it from day to day. I follow no leaders, no set of rules, and don't anyone lay down rules for me."

Although its details are vague, whitewashed, or outright made up, *Too Much, Too Soon* captures this spirit of doomed rebellion.

MICHAEL STRANGE
Really, Diana, you're old enough to know men don't have yachts to entertain their adolescent daughters — certainly not Jack Barrymore!

Played with glacial frostiness by Neva Patterson (Mrs. Kramer in our Stand Two, *The Spiral Road*), poet-playwright Michael Strange (pen name for Blanche Oelrichs) is rearing her teenage daughter Diana in loveless splendor in a magnificent New York mansion. (Conveniently missing from the story is Diana's stepfather, Harrison Tweed, and her two step-brothers.) Diana is shown as pining for the father she hasn't seen since infancy, the legendary stage and screen star John Barrymore, who represents, along with siblings Ethel and Lionel, the Royal Family of Broadway — but by this time, John's crown has been thoroughly tarnished by his drinking and outrageous behavior.

Learning that her father is cruising off Miami on his magnificent yacht *Infanta*, Diana writes asking to join him. Both mother and daughter are surprised when he agrees, but the aging actor and the gushing teenager end up talking past one another:

DIANA
You're world-famous, didja know that, Daddy? Really! They couldn't believe I was your daughter, you look so young — on the screen, that is. Isn't that funny, Daddy?

JACK
Hilarious…

The father-daughter reunion, such as it is, is rudely interrupted when the *Infanta* is hailed by another yacht, captained by "Bill Heming," who has been "writing a book on the war in Spain" — a none-too subtle knockoff of Ernest Hemingway. "Heming" is accompanied by "all your old friends," shown only in silhouette (one of them, "Lynn," sounds alarmingly like Lauren Bacall). These cronies shine the spotlight on the old

Shakespearean and inspire him to a recital from Henry V (Flynn's only spoken Shakespeare on film — for which the crew gave him a standing ovation) — after which the Great Profile falls over the railing into the ocean. Instead of returning to the Infanta, Jack accepts the invitation of his cronies to join them on their way to Rio de Janeiro, leaving Diana in charge of his hired captain, Crowley (John Doucette):

CROWLEY
Won't do any good. Whatever he's looking for, he won't find it in Rio, either...don't feel bad, Miss. He was just lonely for his kind of people again. He didn't mean to hurt your feelings.

DIANA
My feelings aren't hurt. I'm just jealous. I'm jealous of every one of them!

In reality, Diana's first adolescent meeting with her father occurred when he took her to dinner from boarding school outside Baltimore, along with a classmate — an outing that ended with Barrymore hitting on the other girl, then passing out drunk in the taxi. He did later invite Diana on the yacht, but there was no "swimming away" incident.

In the film, Diana is next seen at her "coming out" party, announcing her ambitions to her childhood companion, Lincoln Forrester (a composite character played by young Martin Milner, prior to his television fame on *Route 66* and *Adam-12*):

DIANA
What I want you can't buy with money...It's a world, a whole special world of exciting people who write, and paint, and act, and don't care about anything else.

LINC
Well, at least you've learned that much...that they don't care about anything else.

This, of course, doesn't stop Diana from wangling a Broadway debut as an ingénue in a show called *Alexander Hamilton* (in reality, *The Romantic Mister Dickens*). Her mother needs no crystal ball to predict the future:

MICHAEL
You've watched her stumble through rehearsals. You know as well as I how good she's ever going to be.

LINC
So, she'll get it out of her system. Maybe then she'll marry me, forget about acting.

MICHAEL

They'll never let her. The name of Barrymore is a commodity in this business. There isn't a producer in the country who won't jump at the chance to cash in on it. By tomorrow morning she'll have a dozen offers — a dozen chances to make an even bigger fool of herself.

Diana soon has in hand a contract from "Imperial Pictures" (in reality, Universal), which her mother must co-sign since Diana's still a minor. Michael, in return, exacts a promise that Diana will not live with her father in Hollywood. Diana misinterprets the motive as hatred of the man:

MICHAEL

No, I don't hate him at all — I only hate what he's done to himself. If you'd known him as I once did — with a face like a Renaissance prince, a body bursting with talent and vitality, you'd hate what he's become — but you could never hate him.

Diana's train is met by her father and his "keeper," the male nurse Gerhardt (played by John Dennis, and based on the real-life Karl Steuvers), who take her to visit his legendary mansion, "the Castle" on Tower Road. Diana is stunned to discover that, although this "Grand Central Station" is largely devoid of furniture (claimed by his creditors), one room has been lavishly outfitted for her use.

JACK
I suppose your mother's been briefing you about past history. She told you how I was drunk and disorderly and disgraced her over two continents. It's all true, y'know, every word of it. But she was telling you about her husband, and we're talking about your father — a man who's given up the search for the fountain of youth, and only wants, and loves, his daughter.

Charmed, Diana moves in, only to learn that her father's continental charm can easily turn to earthy obscenity whenever he is able to sneak liquor past the male nurse, who must then physically subdue the obstreperous drunk.

At her urging, he agrees to, "…for as long as I can…give you a whole and sober father." This is followed by a month of magical sobriety (totally fictitious), at the end of which the dissolute actor has recovered enough to charm reporters at a press party for Diana's debut film:

JACK
In those old days, Hollywood was the most exciting place in the world. Overnight, telephone operators, cowpokes, glove salesmen became millionaires — the idols of the country. Every one of us was like — well, like a kid in a candy store. We built palaces on hilltops, bought custom-made cars. Every man got his mother that chauffeur he'd promised her when he was a kid, y'know?

Diana's producer, Charlie Snow (Murray Hamilton, see page 169) is moved by Barrymore's "reformed" behavior to offer him a screen test for the role of Sheridan Whiteside in *The Man Who Came to Dinner* — a possible return to screen greatness. (This actually occurred, prompted by Bette Davis, but Barrymore miserably failed the test, and Monty Woolley was called back to play the part he had originated on Broadway in 1939.)

However, when father and daughter return to Tower Road, he is moved to telephone Michael and beg for reconciliation ("Actors make comebacks; why not marriages?"). To bolster his courage, he sneaks a drink, after which she hangs up on him — and Diana berates him for taking his "whole new life" and "throwing it all away!" Barrymore is astonished at the strength of his daughter's possessiveness:

JACK
What do you think you'd do to me? Stick me in that — in that cage over there, with pipe and slippers, so that Daddy wouldn't get away from you again?

DIANA
You've no right to talk to me like that! A little while ago you said you owed a whole new life to me!

JACK
Yes, most women I've known waited a little longer before they tried to collect!

He has hit a raw nerve, as her slap proves. His attempt to recover touches on the truth of the situation:

JACK
I'm your father — and no matter what I said to you, I love you. Your mother and I gave you such a dirty deal when you were small, I know that. We gave you so little love and affection — but now you seem to feel you want to hoard it, like a miser with his gold. But, darling, love doesn't work that way. The moment you try to force it, it — it dries up and blows away as if it never existed.

But Diana is unmoved, and stalks out of the house. The final shot of her father is a pitiless portrayal of dejection and despondency:

JACK

Baby, I am fifty-nine years old, and I'm not as drunk as you think. Won't you take what little I have to offer and not make me jump through hoops?

Once again, it's instructive to sort fact from fiction. The final parting of Jack (who was sixty-one, not fifty-nine — a sop to Flynn's ego, possibly, though at forty-nine, he looked twenty years older), and Diana was far more prosaic: Her ailing father asked her to phone a *call girl* for him — which, outraged, she did, then stalked off in righteous indignation. It haunted her for the rest of her life, as she wrote in the autobiography:

> "I shouldn't have been that way about my father. I shouldn't have been such a Goddamned boarding school-bitch! When I let that girl into the house that night I should've said to her, 'All right, honey, be kind to him. I'll be here when you come down....' I should have realized that my father was sick and broken and lonely and old and unhappy. I thought, oh, if he were alive, I'd know how to be a daughter to him now, no matter what he did, no matter what he asked, no matter how shocking a life he led. But I'd been brought up too bloody much "society" and too strictly and too everything else! And I could not take it. I could not take it that my own father should ask me to get him a whore! *Oh, Daddy,* I prayed, *forgive me.*"

In the movie, the fictionalizing continues. In reality, Universal had cast Diana as Robert Stack's love interest in *Eagle Squadron*, a performance which was received as neither a resounding hit nor an unmitigated flop. *Too Much, Too Soon* positions her as the star of *Forever In My Heart*, which bombs at its preview.

Leaving the theatre, Diana learns that her father has collapsed after a month's solitary drinking and been hospitalized. On her way to his room, she takes no notice of the body wheeled past her, or its name tag: "John Barrymore." Very Hollywood and complete nonsense: In reality, John Barrymore lingered for ten days after his final collapse, impressing all with his courage and gallantry.

Flynn biographer George Morris hits the nail on the head at this point:

> "Depressing as it is, Flynn's appearance in this tawdry little tale is the brightest spot in the movie. When he dies midway through the film, *Too Much, Too Soon* degenerates even further into a sordid parade of paramours, sadists and occasional husbands mistreating and abusing a perpetually sneering Dorothy Malone."

Morris has said almost everything that need be said about the rest of the film. To sum up briefly: Diana marries actor Vince Bryant (a fictionalized version of Bramwell Fletcher, and played by Efrem Zimbalist, Junior), but her possessiveness ruins the marriage; on the rebound, she marries the sadistic tennis player John Howard (ruthlessly portrayed by Ray Danton), a real-life creep about whom Diana says lamely in her book "At least the record shows that I left him long before he was jailed for white slavery;" her third and final husband is another actor, Robert Wilcox (Edward Kemmer), a recovering alcoholic whose shaky recovery is abruptly derailed by their relationship.

As for Diana's career, *Too Much, Too Soon* paints it in much harsher terms than it warrants: she is shown as giving up after the initial, disastrous preview. In reality, Diana made several more films, and gave what was generally regarded as a standout performance in the film noir classic, *Nightmare* (1942) co-starring Oscar-nominated Brian Donlevy. But the studio's insistence on pushing her into leading roles she wasn't ready for resulted in low box-office returns, and the quality of the vehicles offered her dropped sharply: she accepted a six-month suspension rather than appear in an Abbott and Costello comedy, and offers dried up after that to the point that she left Hollywood, tail between her legs, in 1943.

Nevertheless, Diana was far from the abjectly awful actress shown in the movie, nor was her personal and professional decline as steep and straight as portrayed. Her story, like that of most alcoholics and abusers, is one of fits and starts, stumbles and falls, and rising to promise to do better; second, third, and fourth chances that are honored for a while and then broken, and golden opportunities muffed. One of the most poignant stories in her book involves her shot at a television hosting gig on CBS in 1950: beset by the usual insecurities, she showed up loaded, and was replaced by Faye Emerson — who went on to become a celebrated success in that role.

Having sunk to the depths of depression, the film is somewhat salvaged by a charming ending involving Martin Milner (see page 173): after descending to the point of hospitalization in a sanitarium, Diana is approached by writer Gerold Frank with the offer of collaborating on her life story. Clutching at this last straw, she leaves the clinic for Frank's house, but it is sixty-seven blocks away in Washington Square, and she hasn't even the money for bus fare. She stops a well-dressed man to ask for change, and is horrified to find he's her childhood friend, Linc (Milner). She is too embarrassed to face him, claiming she's "old and ugly and changed" — until he removes his fedora to show that he's changed, too: he's gone bald in the intervening years!

Cheered up, Diana boards the bus for Frank's house and the book that will hopefully straighten her out — with Milner, looking very much like Joe Garagiola, waving from the sidewalk.

Two years after the film's release, Diana Barrymore was dead of third-degree burns suffered in a kitchen fire, her death ruled a suicide. If she had not achieved redemption with her book, she had at least achieved a measure of honesty:

> "Damn them for giving me nothing and taking it away before I had it! Damn mother for her grandness and her indifference and her disdain of me, and damn daddy for the crazy, mixed-up life he led and the daughter he never gave a damn for, and damn uncle Lionel for treating me like the boarding-school bitch I am, and damn aunt Ethel who doesn't even know I'm alive, and damn me for being a silly, arrogant, affected schoolgirl! God damn us all! We deserve everything we get!"

The film press book shows that, in some respects, Warner Bros. had gone to great lengths to produce a memorable film. To recreate John Barrymore's *Infanta*, they borrowed the *Caronia*, "...the largest pleasure craft in Southern California waters." When John Barrymore's Tower Road "Castle" proved inaccessible, they borrowed a similarly striking mansion "...built by silent screen star Madge Bellamy in 1920."

Yet, one press book item ironically symbolizes the final fate of this largely forgotten film. John's macabre "pet" in The Castle, a huge hunting hawk, is portrayed by "Goldie, the only motion-picture trained eagle ever given screen credit in Hollywood...a character in many pictures, Goldie was awarded screen credit for its role with John Wayne in *The Conqueror.*"

Ah, yes, *The Conqueror*, the celebrated screen turkey in which the Duke played Genghis Khan, inspiring one wag, Harry Medved, to crack, "Perhaps Mr. Wayne fails to understand the distinction between a Mongolian and a Mongoloid." That's fitting company for this film, whose dim screenplay runs the gamut from sophomoric to soap-opera. Director Art Napoleon, who shared screenwriting credit with his wife, Jo, had very little on his resume before this picture, and less afterward. He seems to have been of little assistance to Dorothy Malone, who had just won an Academy Award for her work in *Written on the Wind* (1956, with our Stand One and Stand Two star, Rock Hudson), yet could not create any earthly reason for the audience to sympathize — or even identify with — Diana Barrymore as written.

For our purposes, it is not Diana Barrymore who makes a Stand in this film, nor is it her father. If there *is* a Stand made here — a triumph of a man over himself, a shining moment that surprises him and those around him — it is made by Errol Flynn, and eloquently described in his own words.

ERROL FLYNN MAKES HIS STAND

"In making *Too Much, Too Soon*, it would have been easy for me to simulate Jack Barrymore's physical characteristics, for I can do, with the lifted eyebrow, an imitation about as good as anyone else's. In fact I have often, at gatherings, told stories of him and mimicked his motions, such a fabulous human figure the man was.

"Jack turned himself into a burlesque of himself at the end, and many who had known him and his work were distressed to see this, because he typified to them the greatest actor they knew or heard of in their lifetime; the public remembered this final phase of his and they may have come to look upon Jack as a clown, and perhaps they expected to see that in my portrayal.

"When I started to try to get Jack into focus, I wanted to delve into his inner self, not to imitate him — that was too easy. I wanted to show a man with a heart, a man eaten up inside — as I knew him to be in those final days when I was close to him — a man full of regrets and all ready to die, but with one last thing to live for, the love of his daughter, Diana, his desire to get back her love.

"I determined that I would stay away from the least suggestion or imitation of manners. That would have been deadly wrong. The only concession I made to that was to try to look like him. To facilitate that, the studio put a tip on the end of my nose which aided in conveying his profile.

"There was much controversy about my playing him. Some said I was the only one who could do it, others said I'd foul it up. It was a challenge, because it was almost impossible to be right, no matter what you did.

"I determined I would show the inner Barrymore as I knew him: right or wrong. I would win, lose or get a draw. For once in my long career I worked hard at the characterization that I thought should be presented. I tried hard to underemphasize, and in this way to get nearest to the recesses of the mind and heart of a great human being."

THE BALANCE SHEET

The film, as shown, is a hodgepodge of misrepresentation and gross inaccuracies, among them, the idea that Barrymore spent his last days unemployed: he could always get film parts as a faded caricature of himself — as opposite, in *Playmates* (1941), with bandleader Kay Kyser — and he took them, not wanting to owe anyone anything. He was doing the same on radio, rehearsing NBC'S *Rudy Vallee Show* at the time of his final collapse. Equally false is the suggestion that he was without friends and companions. As far gone as he was, John was actually surrounded by a cast of equally colorful characters: his brother Lionel, the cynical, and equally wasted comedian W.C. Fields, artist John Decker, gadfly extraordinaire Sadakichi Hartmann, and writer Gene Fowler, who penned Barrymore's biography, *Good Night, Sweet Prince*. In a later and lesser-known work, *Minutes of the Last Meeting*, Fowler had enough professional detachment to appreciate these men for just what they were:

> "They were extraordinary men, vital and forthright, with extraordinary staying powers. Clocks run down. Men run down. You can rewind a clock. What hand is there so cunning as to wind up a man?"

It's often fashionable to look down the nose at those who visibly and publicly disintegrate. Being the wordsmith of the group, Fowler rises to an eloquent defense:

> "Fields and his companions actually did not belong to this century, for all had been born before its coming. In effect they were misfits, whatever their fame, and unable to conform to an age of regimentation that, for good or ill, marked the rise of science and the decline of art. Each member of this group had known tragedy and pain, but elected to wear the mask of comedy for the world to see, if not to applaud...If I were to apologize for W.C. Fields, or for any other member of our group for that matter, their shades would cry out with indignation. False praise is the province of the epitaph-maker and is best done with a chisel on a stone seldom visited. I needed no pretext to like these men, nor they me. They were not hypocrites; they never changed character; and at bottom, they were men, every one of them, to the end. And as I looked on — or rather, participated — it became quite clear to me, if not to the men themselves, that they were severally enacting the final

scenes of a tragedy — no matter the comic masks they wore. Each in his own fashion had lived too much in conflict with his God-given talents, as well as against the world of thou-shalt-not; and so they now must walk in the long shadow; but never for outsiders to see them except in their caps and bells. They were their own executioners...Decker had said: 'We are too big for our bodies. We spring the seams, then blow to pieces.'...Notwithstanding their shortcomings — their lack of self-discipline among other things — the members of this group acted valiantly in times of adversity. They blamed no one but themselves for the outcome of their follies; self-pity was a stranger to them. They paid all penalties without welshing and lived their last hours without cringing."

Depending on the biases of the individual reader, that's an acceptable defense — or not.

Fifteen years after leaving in triumph as *Hamlet* and two years before his death, John Barrymore, a man given to doing bizarre things, outdid himself by returning to the stage. The vehicle was an unfunny spoof called *My Dear Children*, and the ailing Barrymore resorted to much mugging and clowning to make it work. Many saw it as merely a further act of self-debasement. Others, more perceptive, saw what Fowler had seen: a mortally sick man masquerading as a well one, and overcoming the depths of depravity with the craftsmanship of a master, celebrating talent and decline in tandem: no one can go downhill as fast, or as thoroughly, as a thoroughbred.

After filming *Too Much, Too Soon*, Errol Flynn unconsciously embarked on yet another parallel with his mentor: he accepted a stage role, his first since leaving England for Hollywood in 1934. *The Master of Thornfield* was playboy/playwright Huntington Hartford's adaptation of *Jane Eyre*, and he considered Flynn perfect for the part of Mr. Rochester.

Flynn should have known better. Harrowing experiences on the sets of *The Sun Also Rises* and *Too Much, Too Soon* had demonstrated that he suffered memory impairment not unlike Barrymore's own, and was by this time barely able to retain the few lines of dialogue necessary to shoot a single scene — memorizing a full-length text was long since beyond him, and he was grateful when Darryl Zanuck came again to his rescue, giving him an excuse to leave the show and fly off to Africa to make *The Roots of Heaven*.

One experience while struggling with the play in Cincinnati offers a unique perspective on not only Flynn, but also Barrymore and perhaps the others cited by Fowler:

"One cold night, after the performance, I left the theatre disgruntled. I disliked the play, wondered what I was doing out here, in this town, in this unconvincing drama. I felt like a dog who has had his day — that is, was late in the afternoon professionally. Dejection had really set in.

"As I walked out of the theatre a crippled old lady in a wheelchair blocked the stage entrance. I excused myself and tried to get by. She took me by the arm. Gently she said, 'Thank you. Thank you so much.'

"What had I done? Maybe I had given her a couple of tickets to the show and didn't remember, or what?

"She said, 'Thank you for all the wonderful hours of happiness. If you knew what my life has been you would know what I am saying.'

"I was embarrassed. She kissed my hand and said, 'Go home to bed now.'

"I walked off, thinking maybe I haven't been such a loss after all. Anybody who can bring a few moments of happiness to another human life certainly can't be wasting his time in an otherwise fear-ridden and very often drab world. Maybe it hasn't been so futile. Maybe it wasn't all a waste.

"Maybe all that I am in this world and all that I have been comes down to nothing more than being as touch of color in a prosaic world. Even that is something."

In the twilight of his own career, Flynn had taken a Stand — to tell the world that John Barrymore was more than just a "touch of color"—that, as Gene Fowler said, "Here was a champion, a man to be remembered."

Flynn had one more big-screen appearance in him, in a movie as bedeviled in its own way as *Too Much, Too Soon*, but a film full of important and challenging ideas…

STAND EIGHT: *THE ROOTS OF HEAVEN*

(8/15/1958: 20th Century-Fox) Directed by John Huston; Written by Romain Gary & Patrick Leigh-Fermor, from Gary's novel; Music by Malcolm Arnold; Photographed by Oswald Morris; Edited by Russell Lloyd.

MOREL
They're the strongest creatures on Earth, yet no animal fears them. They're friends with the birds, the gazelles roam among them. Man, only Man, is their enemy. He has to pursue, kill and maim them, turning their gentleness into hatred, then he calls them "rogues." The greatest elephant slaughter in history took place here thirty years ago, during a drought like this. Ivory poachers seized the opportunity and killed over five hundred in a day. After it was over, the lake ran red with blood — blood of animals who feed on tender green branches that grow on the top of forest trees, and wild young water lilies.

Noble sentiments, nobly expressed, but oddly enough, they're not what *The Roots of Heaven,* made back in 1958, is actually about. "The quality of the novel that attracted me to the subject matter in the first place was never realized," director John Huston freely admitted in *The Cinema of John Huston.* "The depths of the novel — a good, a very interesting book indeed — were not touched, became in our hands a kind of adventure story, a shoot-up." Posters for the film luridly proclaimed, "A New Mold of Dramatic Adventure Has Been Shaped In the Cradle of Civilization. Where The Elephants Make Their Death Pilgrimages!" and "The Towering Adventure That Crashes Against Heaven Itself!"

Flynn biographer George Morris is absolutely withering — but closer to the point:

"Director John Huston and Romain Gary…have done little more than film a tract — one that does not even have the courage of its convictions. Its concerns are verbalized too often. Each character spouts self-aware philosophy every five minutes…it's the kind of film in which a bald German aristocrat with a monocle speaks fourteen languages but remains mute, communicating only though guttural grunts, because of the injustice and inequity of the world."

Ah, but therein lies all the charm of the film — if the viewer is prepared to accept it on its own terms: not those of breast-beating jungle adventure, but a deft duel of ideas and irony.

Actually, the book, by the wry writer-soldier-diplomat, Romain Gary, is a sharp satire of dry, tongue-in-cheek delights, gentle but telling jabs at both the increasingly impotent colonial masters and the wild-eyed, stout-hearted African revolutionaries who have learned all the wrong lessons from their European overlords. It is also a simmering brew of truly revolutionary ideas, the most controversial of them being an outright condemnation of the entire idea of nationalism. These ideas — just as inflammatory today as the were then, if not more so — are given lip service in the film, but, as Huston points out, largely lost in the emphasis on adventure.

The Roots of Heaven has yet to be officially released to the general public, on VHS, DVD, or anything else (though a DVD is generally available on eBay). It *could* be marketed to a present-day audience, though. One effective way would be to advertise the spectacle of Orson Welles playing a character virtually identical to the real-life Rush Limbaugh forty years later!

True, "El Rushbo" was only seven in 1958, and his fame (or infamy) was decades away, but Welles, now well into the cameo character portion of his own checkered career, nailed him: an overweight, pompous blowhard of a broadcaster, much given to exhorting his audience of "decent and right-thinking Americans" to follow his will. Cy Sedgwick is broadcasting from French Equatorial Africa, on safari to shoot "the big ones — and that's what we've got here, friends, the *big ones*," he solemnly intones, his massive buttocks filling the screen, just as they are torn apart by buckshot.

Even back in Welles' glory days of the all-Black *Voodoo Macbeth* in Harlem, the *War of the Worlds* radio broadcast, and finally, the glorious but all-too-brief triumph of *Citizen Kane*, he approached each role, in the words of his producer-partner John Houseman, "…with a curious mixture of narcissism and self-loathing." This is certainly true of Sedgwick, narcissistic enough to become a broadcast celebrity, while still possessed

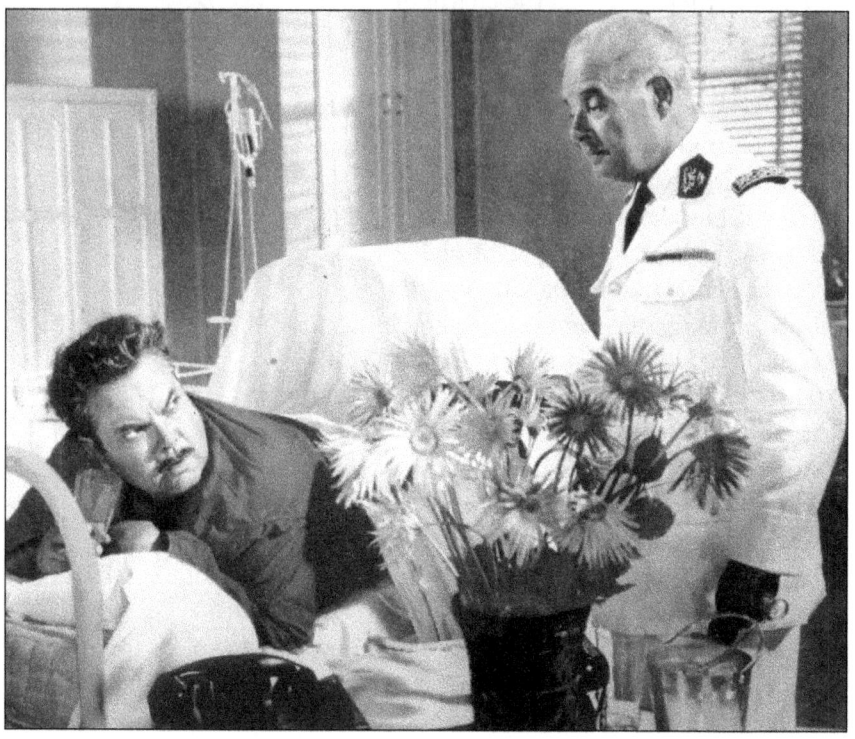

of a fundamental self-hatred.

When the colony's Governor (Andre Luguet) apologizes for Sedgwick's wounding at the hands of Morel, the man fighting to save the African elephant, and the broadcaster, prone on his hospital bed, is truculent. "I like him [Morel]. He spits on us, on all of us, and he's right. I been waiting all my life for somebody to spit on me — now, finally, someone's had the guts to do it and you know what? Suddenly it gets to be almost bearable — to be a man."

Welles' appearance in *The Roots of Heaven* lasts all of four minutes and forty-five seconds, and yet the story turns on it: prior to this point, Morel is called by Waitari, the African nationalist, "little more than a crank," almost unknown outside his own area; it is the publicity from

Sedgwick's broadcast that makes Morel a celebrity. Actually, the film could have done with more of the Welles touch: *Citizen Kane* presents the story of a legend as told in scattered flashback as his various associates are encountered. Romain Gary's dryly witty and gently barbed book tells the story of the elephant activist Morel in much the same way. Yet, the screenplay produced by Gary in partnership with Patrick Leigh-

Cavorting among the natives: stars Errol Flynn and Juliette Greco, producer Darryl F. Zanuck, and director John Huston.

Fermor presents the story in a straight, linear timeline — and strangely enough, the same incidents don't play out as interestingly this way as they do when revealed as successive elements of a mystery. (Imagine *Citizen Kane* presented in linear fashion, not that *Roots of Heaven* is any *Citizen Kane*.)

Much has been made of the fact that the film came out a good decade ahead of its time. It failed to find the audience that turned out in droves for *Born Free* (1966), the story of two gamekeepers (played by the real-life married couple Virginia McKenna and Bill Travers), who first adopt the orphaned lioness, Elsa, and then face the heartbreaking, and nearly impossible, task of returning her to the wild. The accepted wisdom is that the environmentally-conscious audience that took *Born Free* to its heart simply didn't exist when *Roots of Heaven* came out.

Well, maybe, but the fact is that the makers of *Born Free* went to great lengths to present Elsa the Lioness as cute, loveable, naïve, noble — in other words, endlessly appealing to the audience. In contrast, Gary, Leigh-Fermor, Zanuck and director John Huston filled *Roots of Heaven* with

Trevor Howard, cast at the last minute as Morel, joins Errol Flynn (Forsythe) and Maurice Cannon (Jacob Haas) en route to French Equatorial Africa for an adventure that was far more exciting than the resulting film.

reels and reels of noble *talk* about the endangered pachyderm — yet there is only one scene early on, where a mother elephant rescues her baby from the fenced enclosure of zoo supplier Jacob Haas (Maurice Cannon), that even remotely excites the empathy of the viewer. (Even then, Huston resists a zoom shot that would emphasize and personalize the event!) Much of the time, the great gray behemoths are seen in monotonous long shots, and come off to the audience as at best distant, at worst vaguely frightening. The result is that the passion of the film is far too often intellectual, rather than emotional.

All right, then, take it as a passion of the intellect. You'll arrive at the emotions soon enough.

Certainly Darryl F. Zanuck did. One of the last and most flamboyant of the moguls, Zanuck, according to the pressbook, "…personally led a safari of 120 actors and technicians into danger-infested regions of the Dark Continent" for one basic reason: to find a good starring vehicle for his then-girlfriend, French singer-actress Juliette Greco. He had featured her in his mammoth production of *The Sun Also Rises* in a cameo as a Parisian prostitute, who propositions the impotent Jake Barnes. Now, he brought her back, along with two of that film's standouts, Eddie Albert and Errol Flynn, but the original idea had not been to star Flynn, as Flynn explained in his autobiography:

> "I had top billing. That was very funny, because William Holden was supposed to do this, and I was going to co-star with him, but Holden got into some kind of beef with Paramount, to whom he is under contract — and Zanuck switched to another just as brilliant actor, Trevor Howard. However, when Holden bowed out, I had to take star billing. This was strange, because the main burden had to be carried by Howard."

In retrospect, it's difficult to imagine William Holden playing what the original book described as the "tough, bad-tempered" and yet dryly humorous Morel. The film opens with Morel having beaten an ivory hunter (Marc Doelnitz) within an inch of his life: "You can tell Habib the next time I find this piece of filth round an elephant herd, I'll make such an unholy mess of him, the elephants themselves won't be able to do better!"

Despite this surface show of ferocity, Morel is largely pursuing his goals at this point through peaceful means: circulating a petition to stop the killing of elephants, and other animals, for sport:

MOREL

Anyone who's seen the great herds on the march across the last free spaces of the earth knows there's something the world can't afford to lose! But no, they have to capture, kill, destroy everything; all that's beautiful has to go, all that's free. Soon we'll be alone on this earth with nothing else left to destroy but ourselves... We've reached a point on this earth where we need all the friendship we can get. We need all the African herds! All the elephants! All the birds! We need friendship.

Seeking signatures, he is quickly turned down by the French Governor. ("My dear fellow, our first duty is towards mankind.") The local missionary, Father Fargue (Francis de Wolff) also turns him down. ("I have an idea that you want me to sign not for the animals, but against men — you're fed up with men, so you've gone over to the animals.") He is also turned down by everyone else.

Eventually, Morel secures only two rather dubious signatures: those of Minna (Juliette Greco), a hostess (and prostitute, though the film plays this down) at the local watering hole, Le Tchadien, and a disgraced English military man called Major Forsythe (Flynn). Incidentally, Flynn biographers have generally assumed that his character is based on the book's Johnny Forsythe, the American who broadcast for the Communists during the Korean War. Actually, it's a composite of that character and Colonel Babcock, which the book describes as an "essentially decent"

retired English soldier whose only companion is a Mexican jumping bean named Toto — an eccentricity carried over to Flynn's role.

Finally, Morel is pushed to another stage of his own particular Stand:

MOREL
You can't wipe out an entire race to keep the world supplied with billiard balls — and paper knives!

Morel quickly graduates to shooting elephant hunters and ivory traders, as the governor's aide-de-camp (Alain Saury) cheerfully reminds everyone, "…in the rear, sir?" Still, he remains in obscurity until he trains his sights on the American broadcaster, Sedgwick — and Sedgwick, bemused by the man who has had the courage to spit on him, informs "the vast TV public," and Morel's crusade is world news.

Now, Le Tchadien is beset by what Minna calls a "plague of journalists" from all over the world (two of whom, in a quick cameo, are John Huston, dressed in white suit and fedora as in *Treasure of the Sierra Madre,* and Darryl Zanuck). Those sympathetic to Morel's cause can earn a drink on the house from Minna, or a proclamation from the inebriated Forsythe:

FORSYTHE
This man Morel isn't really defending elephants, he's defending us! We're all threatened with extinction! One more of those hydrogen bombs,

couple'a those Sputniks whizzing around up here — and we'll all go up in smoke like the poor ruddy old elephants!

The besieged Governor calls in one of his veteran administrators, Saint Denis (Paul Lukas), who has been around long enough to go native ("When I die, one of the local witch doctors is having me reincarnated as a tree.") He seeks out the fugitive Morel and finds him in the company of several followers and compatriots, including the famous Danish naturalist, Peer Qvist (Friedrich Ledebur), who makes no bones about the Stand he is taking:

PEER QVIST
My duty is to protect all the species, all the living roots that Heaven planted into the earth. I've been fighting all my life for their preservation. Man is destroying the forests, poisoning the ocean, poisoning the very air we breathe with radiations. The oceans, the forests, the race of animals, mankind are the Roots of Heaven. Poison Heaven at its roots and the tree will wither and die, the stars will go out, and Heaven will be destroyed.

More tellingly, Morel is also traveling with Habib (Grégoire Aslan), the owner of Le Tchadien and a local ne'er-do-well, and Waitari, a would-be "African Napoleon" (Edric Connor):

WAITARI
Monsieur Morel pointed out, quite rightly, that the elephants are the symbol of African freedom. They will be the symbols we put on our banners, and when the power is firmly in our hands, we will protect them.

Saint Denis warns Morel that he is being used by Waitari, which is fine with Morel: "Let's say we're useful to each other." Advised that if he surrenders now, he'll be let off with a slap on the wrist, Morel counters, "They sent you to tell me that? It wasn't worth tiring your horse."

Returning to Fort Lamy, Saint Denis tarries at the bar of Le Tchadien, unwilling to report to the Governor. To Minna, he confides that Morel had the audacity to ask him for arms and supplies, "…as if he really thought I was going to get them for him. As a matter of fact, I almost did. He has something about him that makes you want to help him."

That's what Minna wants, too. First, she persuades Saint Denis to part with an amulet that will guarantee her safe passage through the native tribes to Morel's hideout. Then, she persuades Forsythe to procure the supplies — and a car.

Earlier, Minna had told Morel the reason she had come to Africa: to escape the memory of bone-chilling cold and implied forced prostitution in wartime Berlin. Now, we learn why Forsythe is running away from himself: he had been dropped into the Balkans in command of a squadron of paratroopers — and captured.

FORSYTHE
The other fourteen got shot. They got shot because they wouldn't talk, the damn fools. These ruddy fools wouldn't talk! And so, there they all are, now (thumbs down)—and here am I! On top of the ruddy world!

Delivering their supplies, Minna and Forsythe join Morel's rag-tag band: Peer Qvist, the "mute" Baron mentioned earlier (Olivier Hussenot), the petty thief Korotoro (Habib Benglia), and several of Waitari's soldiers, one of whom, Yussef (Bachir Touré), has "special" orders. Morel then performs his most audacious raid so far, on the Sionville home of the oily newspaper magnate Orsini (Herbert Lom). The purpose is twofold: to publicly chastise Madame Orsini, known as the woman champion of big game hunting in Equatorial Africa (she is spanked before her dinner party guests by Professor Qvist), and to print up Morel's "Communiqué

of the World Committee for the Protection of Nature"—on Orsini's own printing presses!

> MOREL
>
> *The committee recalls that it has no political character, and that considerations of ideology, doctrine, party, race, class and nationality are completely foreign to it. It appeals solely to the feelings and dignity in every human being, without discrimination, and with no other thought than to call for a new international agreement on the protection of nature, beginning with the elephants, the biggest of man's company on Earth.*

The Sionville raid is everything Morel could have hoped for, but Waitari's soldiers are miffed that the Communiqué deliberately avoided mention of their pan-African movement; they steal Morel's transportation, killing Korotoro in the process. Morel and company then set off on foot for Lake Kuru, where a massive herd of elephants has gathered to escape the drought. Watching the pachyderms, Minna begins to understand the concept of what Morel called the "gigantic freedom" that motivates Morel.

The idyll doesn't last long: first, a crashing plane deposits in their midst the world-famous (and crassly commercial) photographer Abe Fields (Eddie Albert). Then, poachers arrive on the scene, led by Habib and Waitari.

As the sun rises, Morel and company attempt to scatter, and thereby save, the huge herd. For Forsythe, this is his moment of personal redemption, as he moves among the trees with his machine pistol, obviously relishing the adventure. He pays for it with his life (in a moment of Hustonian exaggeration, perhaps honoring the screen hero of a quarter-century of costume epics, it takes ten bullets to bring Flynn down). The Baron is also killed. Thoroughly demoralized, Morel is ready to pack it in. Minna makes her Stand trying to dissuade him:

MINNA
And what about the people who follow you, and love you? What about us? There are lots of us, thousands and thousands who would like to do what you are doing. But they haven't the courage — they are too tired, too done for. But they understand, they know what you are trying to

Headed for the final showdown with ivory poachers: the Baron, Yussef, Abe Fields, Forsythe, Morel, and Qvist. Two will not return.

say. Even the stupidest — like me! They think of you, and they think of the elephants — and suddenly, they find themselves smiling. They can't help it — we can't help it! You must go on!*

He *is* going on, Morel retorts; he's going on to the Army post at Biondi, where the injured Fields and the feverish Minna can receive medical attention and Morel can turn himself in. Before this can happen, though, Morel, under the pretext of fetching water from a well, contrives to be alone with Yussef, who aims a fatal shot at him, but cannot fire.

MOREL

Go on, what're you waiting for?...Your orders were not to let me be captured alive, weren't they?

YUSSEF

Waitari's orders. But I couldn't do it!

Once again, Morel has, almost in spite of himself, compelled loyalty — and Yussef has made his own Stand.

There is one more Stand of note to be made in this film — by Cerisot.

CERISOT MAKES HIS STAND

Cerisot? Who the hell is Cerisot?

Cerisot (Jacques Marin) is called in the book the "plump, energetic" commandant of the Biondi army outpost. As Morel and his survivors struggle toward their fateful rendezvous, and the world press watches, Cerisot is reading a magazine article entitled *Nuclear Scientists Predict "End Of Mankind" Unless Atomic Race Halted...Where Do We Go From Here?* and makes his own decision: *"I'll show them..."*

From the book: "Cerisot wasn't caught unprepared; he didn't miss the opportunity so dear to the heart of each Frenchman to speak his own mind..."

Dramatically, Morel staggers into the outpost, with Minna begging him to flee: "I know soldiers! They will kill you!" Undaunted, Morel strides boldly up to Cerisot and his men, rendering a proper military salute. Cerisot returns the salute, and gives the order to his men:

"Present — arms! Corporal, let them pass."

One more Stand, in a long series of them — and Morel and his followers are free to continue their adventurous quest.

THE BALANCE SHEET

"The ending, where Howard just walks out of the gate, was as it was in the novel too," lamented director John Huston in *The Cinema of John Huston*, "but it had a much greater significance in the novel. Everything was significant in the novel, whereas very little was of significance in the picture." He added, "I think the whole practice of re-making successful pictures is absurd. I would gladly remake *The Roots of Heaven*, however."

Of course, that opportunity never presented itself in Huston's lifetime. But it's debatable whether the more significant issues presented in the book — and the film — would be any more palatable today than they were in the 1950s.

Roots of Heaven was one of the very first films to touch on the idea of man's loyalty to his humanity and to his planet, possibly overriding the importance of loyalty to one's class, creed, or even country. Consider again the wording of Morel's Communiqué: "The committee recalls that it has no political character, and that considerations of ideology, doctrine, party, race, class and nationality are completely foreign to it. It appeals solely to the feelings and dignity in every human being, without discrimination."

The book is, on an elemental level, a plea for *decent treatment* — of nature by man, and of men by men, and it dares to whisper the heretical thought that *such conduct is only possible outside the constraints of ideologies and nationalism*. It was, and is, a touchy subject, and the movie version of Morel struck but a glancing blow in this direction:

MOREL
Personally, I've no patience with nationalists, any of them. But no one paid the slightest bit of attention to my petition. Now, when they find out its being used politically, they'll get frightened. They'll have to do something about it.

The Morel of Gary's book is somewhat more direct:

"Nations — I don't give a damn about them. The old ones, the new ones, mine, yours, the lot of them. I don't play marbles, I've outgrown that...As for ideologies, I distrust them on principle: they usually take up all the room. As for nationalism, limited to just that — the sort you can see all over the place at present, and a hell of a lot it cares about the protection of national splendours — that sort of nationalism's just one more foulness invented by man in this world, and he's invented a fair number. As for nationalism, it has no right to exist except in football matches."

In the words of Thomas Lethbridge: "I may not believe it, you may not believe it, it is an idea worthy of our consideration."

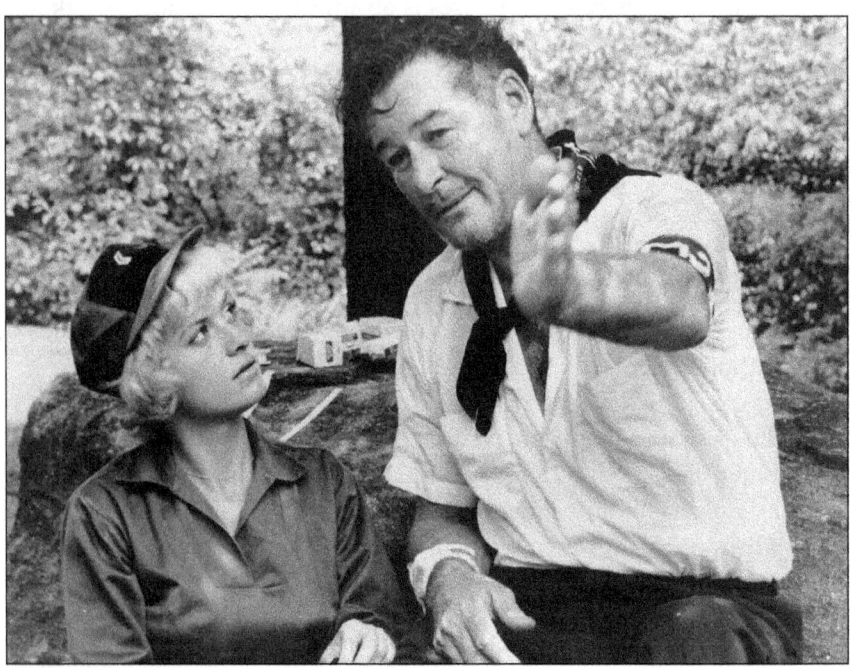

AFTERMATH

Lead roles largely eluded Trevor Howard, but his idiosyncratic presence added delight to many more films. Eddie Albert had more movies ahead, but he found lasting fame as businessman-turned-farmer Oliver Douglas on television's *Green Acres*. Orson Welles continued a nomadic existence, which he described as "20% filmmaker and 80% huckster," yet he maintained a childlike enthusiasm up to his death. Juliette Greco went back to singing in France, while Darryl Zanuck sought smaller roles for his girlfriends in future films (such as Irina Deming, who plays a bicyclist distracting German soldiers in *The Longest Day*). John Huston continued to direct modest hits and misfires, then confounded his critics by making one of his biggest successes, *The Man Who Would Be King* (1975).

Errol Flynn's much-ballyhooed "comeback" was largely played out after *The Roots of Heaven*. He proceeded to Cuba as what he considered a "special correspondent" to participate in the revolution of a man he (and many others) admired at the time, Fidel Castro. This led to his writing, narrating, and playing himself in the one of the lamest excuses for a movie ever made.

Cuban Rebel Girls (page 194) was directed by Flynn's old friend and sometime agent, Barry Mahon, said to have been the inspiration for the Steve McQueen character in *The Great Escape,* and evidently a much better pilot than filmmaker. Cheaply staged, badly photographed, and scored apparently by playing record albums onto the soundtrack, the movie was a attempt to enable Flynn's fifteen-year-old (!) girlfriend, Beverly Aadland, to break into films. (Didn't work. She never made another.)

Flynn's fans have lamented the fact that one of Hollywood's legendary leading men finished his career with a film that was not only utterly dreadful, but showed him noticeably drunk on screen. (He had played

drunks in his last three roles, but there's a big difference between an actor playing a drunk and an actor who is drunk.)

But there was one more personal redemption for Flynn. In the summer of 1959, he appeared in an episode of *The Alcoa-Goodyear Theatre* called

"The Golden Shanty," based on an Australian short story, but transplanted to the American West. The central character is Cedric "Doc" Boatwright, a con man and purveyor of "Doc Boatwright's Celebrated Stomach Bitters," who learns that the saloon he'd snookered a young couple (Peter Hansen and Patricia Barry) into buying has flakes of gold embedded in its brickwork — hence the title.

As with *The Roots of Heaven*, most Flynn biographies and filmographies recount in great detail the rigors of the three-day shooting schedule: how Flynn's memory was so completely gone that he had to read his lines from giant TelePrompTers, or have them spoken to him off-camera by sympathetic director Arthur Hiller (shown on page 195 with Flynn and his teenage daughters, Rory and Deirdre). Yet, the strain doesn't show. Flynn is old and tired, but these qualities are absolutely right for the part — and he's also charming and mischievous. The role of "Doc Boatwright" offers Flynn fans a tantalizing glimpse of how he might have fared as an older, character actor had he lived. It is a gift sometimes afforded to the really good actors: even while ailing, they are able to summon their talents and experience for one more golden performance, one last chance to hit it out of the park. Rock Hudson did it in a television movie called *The Vegas Strip Wars* (1984), Edward G. Robinson in *Soylent Green* (1973), Henry Fonda in *On Golden Pond* (1981), and perhaps the most famous example, John Wayne in *The Shootist* (1976). Flynn managed it in *The Golden Shanty*: a last, small triumph and a vindication of his acting ability.

Shanty was Flynn's next-to-last work as an actor. In the first week of October 1959, he appeared as a gentleman hobo on *The Red Skelton Show*. In the on-set shot opposite, he and Beverly are oddly pensive — in John Huston's words, "…looking into his future, of which there wasn't much left." A week later, she watched him die of a heart attack on the floor of a Vancouver, B.C. apartment.

And among his many screen legacies, costume extravaganzas such as *Captain Blood, They Died With Their Boots On, The Sea Hawk,* and *The Adventures of Robin Hood*, there lurks the subtly subversive *Roots of Heaven*, a film — and book — which dare to suggest that man's duty to humanity — and simple decency — might just trump his duty to flag and country.

It's an idea just as revolutionary now — and just as urgently needed — as then.

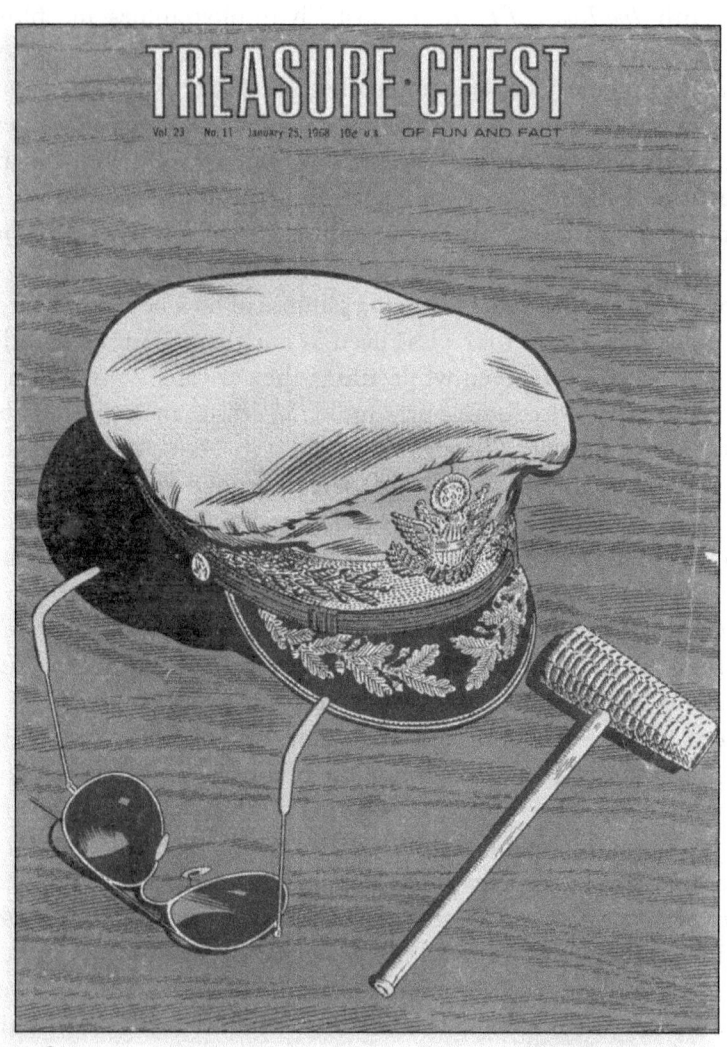

Cover of *Treasure Chest of Fun and Fact*, January 25, 1968, by Joe Sinnott. USED BY PERMISSION.

STUDY V
Real-Life Heroes

Up to this point, this collection has spotlighted fictional characters making fictional Stands — with the possible exception of the Barrymore film, which was itself highly fictionalized.

These two are very *real*. And so are their stories.

It is easy to deify heroes, but that is the ultimate cop-out. It's basically an excuse, a convenient way to let the admirer off the hook: *He wasn't a regular human being like me, with aches and pains and burdens and obligations and wants and needs. He was Different. He was Special. He was a Saint. I can't be expected to do what he did, so I needn't even try.*

Nonsense!

It is not only possible for "regular human beings" to make such Stands — to overcome and transcend their very natures — it is absolutely essential to the survival of the species.

Otherwise, men and women will continue to fight one another over politics, over color, over custom, over religion, over slogans and dogmas and doctrines until, finally, there *is* no future — or the future there *is*, is not worth living.

The warrior — who won the *peace*. The playboy profiteer who wanted to do well — and ended up doing *good*.

Their stories point the way for all of us. They should be required studies, for everyone, everywhere.

The film biographies are as good a place as any to start.

STAND NINE: *MACARTHUR*

(6/30/1977: Universal) Directed by Joseph Sargent; Written by Hal Barwood & Matthew Robbins; Music by Jerry Goldsmith; Photographed by Mario Tosi; Edited by George Jay Nicholson.

> MacARTHUR
> *I pray that an omnipotent providence will summon all persons of goodwill to the realization of the utter futility of war... The destructiveness of the war potential, through progressive advances in scientific discovery, has in fact reached a point which revises the traditional concept of war.* War, the most malignant scourge and greatest sin of mankind, can no longer be controlled — only abolished. *We are in a new era. If we do not devise some greater and more equitable means of settling disputes between nations, Armageddon will be at our door.*

If you're still reading this book after the first eight Chapters/Stands, chances are you're sympathetic to the sentiments just expressed, their quality of noble resolution, and at the same time, painfully aware that the very grandeur of their heroic aspiration is all but doomed by the baser tendency of humanity to continue settling its differences through war and bloodshed.

These are not the words of a fictional character spoken in an invented setting. Though the words are spoken by the actor Gregory Peck in 1976, the scene represents the actual acceptance of the surrender of the Empire of Japan thirty-one years earlier — and indeed, the scene is photographed where it happened, on the deck of the battleship U.S.S. *Missouri* (then, in Tokyo Bay; at the time of the filming, in Bremerton Navy Yard).

Entire forests have been felled to print the praises of General of the Army Douglas MacArthur as the predominant soldier/statesman of his time — and an equal number dedicated to the proposition that he was a conceited, narcissistic, self-promoting poseur of no real merit. A somewhat smaller number of pages pursue neither his deification nor his demonization, but some approximation of the truth.

This chapter will uncover no blazing, unprecedented revelations about Douglas MacArthur. He appears in these pages because he made a Stand like none other, and because a movie was made about it. Unfortunately, while the man was, love him or loathe him, absolutely unique, the film is decidedly ordinary: a perfectly serviceable World War II movie. "From the producers of *Patton*," it was billed and marketed; the idea seemed to be, if one movie about one WW II general scored a hit, another one will do equally well.

And therein lay the fallacy: MacArthur was not another Patton. MacArthur was not *another* anything. Patton was a brilliant and audacious commander of a field army, and that was as far as it went: he never served as Superintendent of West Point, he never succeeded to the highest Army post of Chief of Staff, and he never rebuilt an entire shattered nation, body, soul, and spirit, from the ground up. Yet the film *Patton* captured both the man and the imagination of the audience in a way that *MacArthur* never did.

Oddly enough, the potential was there. Before becoming a film producer, Frank McCarthy, as a Brigadier General, had served as an aide to wartime Chief of Staff George C. Marshall. He used his own knowledge, together with his unique access to the Marshall papers, to inform both *Patton* and *MacArthur*, yet screenwriters Hal Barwood and Matthew Robbins seem to have rendered the MacArthur story as a series of vignettes, seldom managing to probe beneath the surface.

The director was a good choice for telling the story of a complex individual, whose flamboyance and bravado may have masked more subtle qualities. From the very early *Star Trek* episode "The Corbomite Maneuver" (1966) to the recent HBO films *Something the Lord Made* (2004) and *Warm Springs* (2005), Joseph Sargent has emerged as one of the most expressively human directors in film, a man capable of subtly shaping the emotional shadings of his actors' performances, and carrying the audience exactly where he wants them to go. How much of this he was able to achieve in *MacArthur* is debatable.

The same composer who scored *Patton* scored *MacArthur:* the legendary Jerry Goldsmith, whose long list of films includes *The Spiral Road*

(Stand Two in this collection) and *Star Trek: The Motion Picture* (its stirring theme was lifted for the *Star Trek: The Next Generation* television series). A comparison of the *Patton* and *MacArthur* themes may illustrate how the latter fell short: Goldsmith's "Patton March" is filled with brass and bravado, breaking at one point into 1940s-style swing, yet also featuring haunting undercurrents and disturbing countermelodies that

Gregory Peck as MacArthur: he disliked the General, until his research revealed the man's complexities.

amplify and augment the complexities and contradictions of the man's character. Just such a multi-layered melody is called for, if not more so, by *MacArthur*, but the theme is a fairly light-hearted, perfectly serviceable parade-ground march, and not much more. To be blunt, it's just another march, and *MacArthur* suffers for want of the emotional resonance and depth of feeling that Goldsmith's theme brought to the earlier film.

And finally, there's Gregory Peck in the title role, a somewhat daunting assignment, since extensive newsreel footage exists of the actual man, and it's easy for a student of acting to compare MacArthur's actual speeches — his 1951 speech to Congress, or his 1962 farewell at West Point — to Peck's recreation. Also, while MacArthur was known as a sharp and incisive speaker in a one-on-one environment, his public utterances tended to be stagy and filled with theatrical pauses — difficult for an actor to reproduce with any degree of sincerity. Most critics praised Peck's impersonation, though his cerebral interpretation was inevitably compared with George C. Scott's bravura performance as Patton — and Scott, being (at the time) less well-known and more heavily made up, was better able to disappear into the role.

This movie begins promisingly enough in May, 1962, on the occasion of MacArthur's last visit to his beloved West Point. His address to the Corps of Cadets is both folksy and flamboyant:

MacARTHUR
As I was leaving my hotel this morning, the doorman asked me, "Where are you bound for, sir?" When I replied "West Point," he remarked, "It's a beautiful place. Have you ever been there before?" Duty — honor — country. Those three hallowed words reverently dictate what you ought to be, what you can be, and what you will be. They are your rallying points. They give you a temper of the will, a quality of the imagination, a vigor of the emotions, a freshness of the deep springs of life, a temperamental predominance of courage over timidity, an appetite for adventure over love of ease. In this way, they will teach you to be an officer and a gentleman. From your ranks come the great captains who will hold the nation's destiny in their hands the moment the war tocsin sounds. The Long Gray Line has never failed us. Were you to do so, a million ghosts in olive drab and brown khaki, in blue and gray, would rise from their white crosses thundering those magic words, Duty — honor — country! *This does not mean that you are warmongers; on the contrary, the soldier, above all other people, prays for peace, for he must suffer and bear the deepest wounds and scars of war. But always in our minds ring the ominous words of Plato: Only the dead have seen the end of war.*

Here is where the film goes astray: as one might expect, this is where it goes into flashback — but it flashes back only as far March, 1942, three months after what President Franklin Delano Roosevelt labeled "a date that will live in infamy," which was the sneak attack not only on Pearl Harbor, but other key points throughout the Pacific, including MacArthur's beloved Philippines. Forced back into the island fortress of Corregidor, he's promising the "battling bastards of Bataan" that help is on the way from Washington. In the White House, however, Roosevelt (brilliantly impersonated by Dan O'Herlihy) is conferring with General Marshall (Ward Costello) and Admiral Ernest J. King (Russell Johnson, the Professor from *Gilligan's Island,* in a rare triumph over typecasting). Roosevelt's speech sets the tone for a movie in which much of the story will be told in set speeches:

>ROOSEVELT
>
>*Like everything else, Douglas is going to take our strategy personally. He thinks the blockade is a figment of my imagination, and that I'm somehow, deliberately robbing him of glory. I wish you people would send Douglas a globe of the world to remind him we have obligations all around it. We have to support Stalin while he fights the bulk of the Nazi army, we have to assist Churchill to keep England functioning, we have to protect our flanks, the Panama Canal, and General Douglas MacArthur. I need him, the country needs him, we can't leave him to the Japanese.*

So, from Roosevelt's words, we know that "General Mac" is a legend, a man with whom Roosevelt is on a first-name basis, but not *why*. Armchair quarterbacking is just as painless, and pointless, a pastime for the film viewer as for the sports enthusiast; still, there is a huge amount of back story that the film omits by beginning its story in the sixty-third year of its subject's life:

MacArthur's birth in a frontier barracks in Arkansas still subject to attack by Native American tribesmen, thus establishing that his remarkable life spanned the distance from bows-and-arrows to thermonuclear war.

His graduation from West Point, first in a class of 95.

How he joined his famous father, General Arthur MacArthur (who had earned the Medal of Honor at Missionary Ridge in the Civil War) on assignments in Japan, China, and most importantly, in the Philippines.

His heroic exploits in the 1914 excursion into Vera Cruz.

How he fought in the trenches of World War I, often wounded, earning seven silver stars, and promoted with blinding speed to Brigadier General.

His postwar service as West Point's youngest and most progressive commandant.

His participation in the court-martial of air-warfare pioneer Billy Mitchell in 1924 (though Mitchell's family thanked him for his efforts, many airmen bore a lingering resentment).

His routing of the Bonus Marchers in 1932 (these were the World War I veterans who camped out in Washington demanding early payment of postwar benefits to combat the effects of the Depression; wearing medals and riding on horseback, his flamboyant breakup of the demonstrators garnered harsh criticism).

His efforts to sustain a woefully under funded Army as Chief of Staff in the early 1930s which brought him into frequent conflict not only with Congress but with Roosevelt. After one such memorable face-off, the general vomited on the steps of the White House.

His retirement from the U.S. Army to become Field Marshal (!) of the Army of the Philippines (not his shining hour, perhaps because his self-designed uniform looked like that of a Banana Republic dictator).

The reactivation of his commission by Roosevelt shortly before the outbreak of World War II.

All this has been omitted from the film, and although time constraints can be cited, they don't appear to be all that critical. After MacArthur is ordered to leave the Philippines by Roosevelt, we are treated to prolonged footage of the General trying to fight off seasickness while he, his wife (Marj Dusay), and young son (Johnny Brogna) are evacuated to Australia by PT boat; thus, we appreciate neither the reasons for his celebrity, nor why the opinions of cowardice held by some of his men were so wounding to "Dugout Doug," the utterly unjustified name they had saddled him with.

MacArthur has left the Philippines on the understanding that men and materiel will be waiting for him in Australia, ready for an immediate return to the islands. He is dismayed by the realization that troops and supplies are not only insufficient for an offensive operation, but perhaps not even up to the defense of Australia. There is good news to balance this, sort of: Roosevelt has awarded him the Medal of Honor. "My father was awarded the same decoration when he was only nineteen. I had to wait just a little bit longer. But at this moment, I would swap it for just one trained division." He then addresses the press and crowds gathered to greet him, in apparent off-the-cuff wording that will echo dramatically:

MacARTHUR
The President of the United States ordered me to break through the Japanese lines and proceed from Corregidor to Australia for the purpose of organizing the American offensive against Japan, a primary object of which is the retaking of the Philippines. I came through, and I shall return.

There's more bad news to follow: MacArthur's leave-taking of the Philippines had been punctuated by a solemn farewell to his successor,

Major General Jonathan M. Wainwright (Sandy Kenyon). Now, word comes over the radio that Wainwright has surrendered, which leaves MacArthur in a state of total denial:

> **MacARTHUR**
> *He struck Old Glory and ran up a bedsheet! The only possible explanation is that he's temporarily deranged! For that reason alone, his orders have no validity. I place no credence in this alleged "broadcast."*

> **GENERAL SUTHERLAND**
> *He had no supplies, no food left! The malaria was totally out of hand. If he had tried to hold out one more day, we would have had a dreadful massacre...There's some talk in Washington of a Medal of Honor for Wainwright. They want you to recommend it.*

> **MacARTHUR**
> *Medal of Honor? If Wainwright received it, it'd constitute an injustice to others who've done far more.*

As MacArthur exhorts his troops-in-training, his remarks are typically unfortunate regarding his fellow officers:

> **MacARTHUR**
> *If I don't get going, the Navy's gonna win this war. Look what Nimitz did up at Coral Sea and Midway...I know you don't have everything you need. That's because our friends in Washington are sending it all to George Patton in North Africa, so he can run around in the desert, fighting a see-saw tank battle.*

MacArthur finds little more to praise in the status report of his chief Australian subordinate, General Sir Thomas Blamey (Gerald Peters):

> **GENERAL BLAMEY**
> *The recent bombings of our northern airfields give us every reason to believe that the Nips' next move will be a massive invasion of the Australian continent. The garrison at Darwin, up here, doesn't have enough troops to hold for more than forty-eight hours. So our best plan, therefore, is to show token resistance and fall back rapidly to this, the Brisbane line. To the north, the enemy will find only burnt offerings. Meanwhile, in the southeast, we will throw everything into the fight for the cities and*

the farmlands around them. This is the living heart of Australia, and we shall defend it with our lives.

MacARTHUR
Gentlemen, I've been deeply moved and deeply stirred by the Allied efforts, and by the courage and determination of the Australians as expressed by General Blamey. But, as supreme commander of the southwest Pacific area, I will not be the leader of another lost cause. We are attacking, gentlemen! I am going to make the fight for Australia up here, in New Guinea.

The attack begins in New Guinea, but progress is minimal. This leads MacArthur to call in the man who would become one of his most able combat commanders, Major General Robert L. Eichelberger (G.D. Spradlin):

MacARTHUR
Bob, I sent for you because I don't think you like a stalemate any better than I do, and that's what we've got here in New Guinea. They tell me that American boys are actually throwing away their rifles and turning tail. That hasn't happened since the first Battle of Bull Run...I'm sending you in, Bob. I want you to remove all officers who won't fight. If necessary, put sergeants in charge of battalions and corporals in charge of companies, anyone who will fight! I want you to take Buna or don't come back alive, and that goes for your Chief of Staff, too...Bob, if you come through this all right, I'll give you the Distinguished Service Cross, I'll recommend you for a high British decoration, and I'll release your name for newspaper publication.

Buna is finally taken, but MacArthur shakes his head sadly as he peruses a battlefield filled with dead bodies:

MacARTHUR
I'm thinking about Hansa Bay still up ahead.

GENERAL EICHELBERGER
Yes, and Hansa Bay is not some little outpost that we can overrun with galoshes and determination. We need men, supplies, plenty of both.

GENERAL KENNEY
Well, bombing Hansa Bay is one thing, taking it is another.

> MACARTHUR
> *Well, let's just say we won't take Hansa Bay. That's it. We don't want it! We don't want Wewak, either! We'll bypass their strong points, cut their supply lines, and leave 'em to wither and die on the vine Starve Hansa Bay! Starve Wewak! Starvation is my ally!*

Here, the film skips ahead: Colonel Courtney Whitney (Dick O'Neill), who will eventually become one of MacArthur's closest aides, arrives on the scene just as Colonel Diller (Allan Miller) is assembling a propaganda film for new recruits, which helpfully covers several months of the war:

> NARRATOR
> *Okay, soldier, welcome to the fight. So the cut of the cards has dealt you a tour of the Pacific. What's it going to be like fighting the Nips, and who is this man, Douglas MacArthur, your new commander? Let's take a look at the general who, in a few short months, has turned the tide toward victory. Just remember, America's greatest combat general will be leading you into battle. "Hit 'em where they ain't." That's his motto. This is the MacArthur touch, combining sea and air power as never before, he's leapfrogging right over the enemy's strongholds to cut their chow line, all the way to the Philippines. Now you get your chance to fulfill the immortal pledge, "I came through, and I shall return."*

Now, Whitney joins Diller and Colonel Sid Huff (Nicholas Coster) as MacArthur's closest advisors. Here they are reading the General his fan mail, which has been uniformly adulatory, until Huff reads: "Uh-oh. Here's a little boy in Moline, Illinois wants to know, 'Why do you carry a cane? Are you feeble?'" MacArthur, who has carried the cane as a prop, abruptly drops it in the nearest trash can. There is another matter concerning his image:

> COLONEL HUFF
> *General, what we wanna do is to print "I shall return" on candy bars, matchbooks, chewing gum, sewing kits and pencils, and drop them on the Philippines to boost morale.*

> COLONEL WHITNEY
> *But back in Washington, the Office of War Information wants to know if, before things get going, you'd be amenable to a small revision of the wording...they feel that "We shall return" is more to the point.*

MacARTHUR
We shall return? I fail to see what purpose that would serve.

Another skip ahead to 1944: MacArthur is called to Pearl Harbor for a conference with Admiral Chester W. Nimitz (Addison Powell), the Navy Commander-in-Chief Pacific (CINCPAC) and President

Generals MacArthur, Eichelberger (G. D. Spradlin), and Kenney (Walter O. Miles), working out the concept of "Hit 'em where they ain't."

Roosevelt. Ensconced on the deck of a Navy ship, Roosevelt and Nimitz await MacArthur's arrival:

> NIMITZ
>
> *That's our general. And you should see the fire-engine red car he just drove up in.*

> ROOSEVELT
>
> Douglas MacArthur, *starring Douglas MacArthur! He keeps me waiting half an hour, and then he gets a bigger reception than I did. Now I see what Eisenhower meant. He said he spent nine long years with MacArthur — studying dramatics!*

The Joint Chiefs of Staff are mulling over a final plan for the conquest of Japan, and Roosevelt has come to hear the plans of his two Theatre Commanders. Nimitz presents the Navy plan: to proceed straight west across the Pacific, seize the island of Formosa and use it as a jumping-off point for the invasion of Japan. This calls for completely bypassing the Philippines, an idea which horrifies MacArthur. He outlines his own ideas for continuing his northward island-hopping efforts, culminating in an invasion of the main Philippine island of Luzon. Both Nimitz and Roosevelt object on the basis of casualties, and MacArthur escalates his attack:

> MacARTHUR
>
> *In my two years of fighting in the Southwest Pacific area, and they have been long, hard years, fewer Americans have been killed than in the single battle of Anzio. The days of the frontal attack are over. Only your mediocre commanders use it. Your good commanders do not turn in heavy losses…Franklin, all the years we've known each other, I don't believe I told you how my father won his Medal of Honor…It was during the battle of Missionary Ridge. At the height of the fighting, he saw the flag go down. As others around him faltered, he seized up the colors and rallied the troops to victory. Admiral Nimitz is one of our greatest admirals. But just now, as I listened to the plan, I thought I saw our flag going down.*

> ROOSEVELT
>
> *Oh,* did *you?*

MacARTHUR
Mr. President, had we the will to do so, we could have saved Bataan and Corregidor in the first place! To sacrifice Luzon a second time cannot be condoned or forgiven…bypassing Luzon has implications which stain American honor. Do you realize what the Japanese propagandists are telling the Filipino people? That Americans will never shed their blood to save the colored peoples of the earth!

He then unfolds and reads to Roosevelt a quote:

MacARTHUR
"I give to the Philippines my solemn pledge that their freedom will be redeemed. Entire resources of men and materiel of the United States stand behind that pledge." Your words, sir.

Roosevelt informs him that both plans will be presented to the Joint Chiefs — and gets in one last jab:

MacARTHUR
I'd like to return to my command as soon as possible. For forty years, I've held a firm conviction that a commander's place is at the scene of the battle.

ROOSEVELT
I agree entirely, Douglas. That is why I am here.

For whatever reason, MacArthur's plan is eventually approved, and on October 16, 1944, he wades ashore with his troops onto Philippine soil (and is famously photographed doing so). A light rain begins to fall as he addresses the people by radio:

MacARTHUR
People of the Philippines, I have returned. By the grace of Almighty God, our forces stand again on Philippine soil. The hour of your redemption is here. Rally to me! Let the indomitable spirit of Bataan and Corregidor lead on. As the lines of battle roll forward, rise and strike, for your homes and hearts! Strike for future generations of your sons and daughters! Strike in the name of your sacred dead! Strike! Let no heart be faint. Let every arm be steel! The divine guidance of God points the way. Follow in His name to the Holy Grail of righteous victory!

(In reality, some in the U.S. criticized this as one of MacArthur's more baroque and imperial utterances, some branding it "sacrilegious;" Court Whitney pointed out that the words were not intended for the "folks back home," but the largely Catholic — and still captive — Filipinos, with whom they resonated dramatically.)

Though MacArthur's troops suffer serious setbacks (glossed over in the film), he has indeed Returned.

The film skips ahead to April, as a new and somewhat bewildered Chief Executive enters the Oval Office:

TRUMAN
Ladies and gentlemen, if you've ever had a load of hay fall on ya, then you know how I feel right now. I don't know if any of ya pray, but if y'do, you could pray God to help me...I never felt so outta place in all m'life.

As played with brittle feistiness by Ed Flanders (best known for television's *St. Elsewhere*), Harry S Truman enters into office as a man of humility — though that won't last. He is soon handed a document by Chief of Staff Marshall that shakes him to the core: "Well, the President — Mister Roosevelt — never told me."

MacArthur's reaction to news of the atomic bomb is decidedly negative:

MacARTHUR
They never told me. We spent months of staff time, tens of millions of dollars in preparation for the greatest invasion in history, and when we're primed and ready, they send an air force officer to tell me they've constructed this — this — apparatus!

COLONEL WHITNEY
General, what happens if it doesn't work?

MacARTHUR
What happens if it does?

As history records, it did, although two nuclear explosions were required before the pro-peace factions in the Japanese government, backed by the prestige of the Emperor, overcame the diehard militarists and instructed the people to accept the unthinkable: surrender. Allies converged on the Japanese capitol, including an old friend of MacArthur, just released from the prison camp where he had languished for more than three years: the emaciated General Wainwright.

WAINWRIGHT
I'm sorry…I've disgraced you and the army…We were starving…I had to shoot my horse. I realize they'll never restore me to active duty —

MacARTHUR
That's not true, Jim. You can have whatever you want.

WAINWRIGHT
Command of a corps? That's all I want.

MacARTHUR
Your old corps is yours whenever you're ready, General.

Although the friendship of the two men was restored, MacArthur still refused to recommend the Medal of Honor for the ex-P.O.W., but others pushed it through. Wainwright is shown at MacArthur's side, as the General accepts the surrender of the Empire of Japan on board the U.S.S. *Missouri*, after which he begins the most important assignment of his life, as Supreme Commander Allied Powers (SCAP) in the vanquished Japan.

GENERAL MacARTHUR MAKES HIS STAND

MacARTHUR
Court, I want you to tell Washington that I'm transferring food and medical supplies to the Japanese. The next priority is to get those men home, get them to work rebuilding this country. A new Japan with new ideas, but preserving the best of the old. All of our troops will be judged by me for their conduct as men and as soldiers. I want them to understand that the Japanese must be treated with courtesy and respect. Alexander, Caesar, Napoleon all failed as occupiers of conquered countries because of the harshness of their policies. I do not intend to fail.

COLONEL WHITNEY
We're coming up on the palace now. I wonder whether it wouldn't be a good idea to summon the Emperor to explain your policies — show of authority to the Japanese people.

MacARTHUR
After a lifetime of studying the Oriental mind, I can tell you that I must not directly challenge the authority of the Emperor. He lives there in that palace, across that moat, half God, half King. His decrees limit the degree of each man's freedom, his word is absolute. The time will come

when Hirohito, of his own volition, will cross that moat and come to me, and that will mark the beginning of the end of his absolute power over the Japanese people.

This was MacArthur's true Stand. What he proposed to do, what he proceeded to do, was to institute a series of reforms that would remake that part of the world, reforms both simple and sweeping: destroy the military power. Build the structure of representative government. Modernize the constitution. Hold free elections. Enfranchise the women. Release the political prisoners. Liberate the farmers. Establish a free labor movement. Encourage a free economy. Abolish police oppression. Develop a free and responsible press. Liberalize education. Decentralize the political power. Separate church from state.

Many considered these to be impossible goals, including the officers of MacArthur's own staff. But such dreams began to assume concrete form, when MacArthur was approached by the newly elected Japanese Prime Minister (Yuki Shimoda):

PRIME MINISTER SHIDEHARA
General, our new constitution must forbid any military establishment in Japan whatsoever. There must not be an army, a navy or an air force. We must renounce now and forever the use of force as an instrument of national power. In this way, and only this way, can we eliminate forever the power of the militarists. Only in this way can we reassure the world that Japan no longer has warlike design against any people. We are a poor country, with seventy million persons to feed and clothe. We cannot afford armaments. We cannot afford the trapping of power. And never, never again can we suffer Nagasaki and Hiroshima. Let us renounce war, sir. Please. Let us renounce war in the new constitution, and forever.

MACARTHUR
Mr. Shidehara, no man detests war more than this soldier. My abhorrence for it reached its height with the development of the atom bomb. No man, sir, could be more moved by your offer, or more determined to accept it.

However, both historically and in the film, the very success of MacArthur's administration of Japan, and his lack of reluctance to capitalize upon it, was already beginning to deteriorate his relationship with the new President:

TRUMAN

Well, it's damned embarrassing. I been tellin' Congress for months we need four hundred thousand men in Japan, and MacArthur holds a press conference, says he can make do with half that number...I invited MacArthur to come home. I wanted to discuss occupation policy with him, and I expected him to back up our position before the Congressional committees. So I held out the big carrot to him. I told him we'd set up a series of welcome-home demonstrations and a joint session of Congress. Well, you know what he replied? He said he thought the situation here was just too dangerous for him to come home right now, he said he was just too busy. That's what he said to the President of the United States, dammit!

This disagreement aside, the years of MacArthur's tenure as SCAP proceed with a surprising smoothness, marred only by the efforts of certain Republican leaders to enter his name in the Presidential ring, an attempt which fizzles before it can get underway. Otherwise, the ongoing shift in Japanese society is shown in newsreels, spotlighting the Japanese embrace of such American icons as baseball and swing music. This continues until the night of June 25, 1950, when General and Mrs. MacArthur are watching *Winchester '73* with Jimmy Stewart (good trick, since that film was not released until July 12), when the phone rings:

JEAN MacARTHUR

Why, General, what's happened?

MacARTHUR

One last gift to an old warrior.

North Korea has invaded South Korea, steaming southward across the thirty-eighth parallel. A recitation of the factual timeline of the Korean War, not to mention the hot debate it still engenders, exceeds both the space limitations and the inclinations — of this chapter, and the movie as well. Here it is primarily a stage for the struggle between MacArthur and President Truman. The General seemed to have enjoyed, with Roosevelt, a relationship of exasperation tempered by genuine respect. The respect is utterly lacking in Truman's response to MacArthur's conference with Chiang Kai-shek, the Nationalist Chinese leader, now relegated to the island of Formosa, and things go downhill from there:

TRUMAN
Dammit, didn't we send MacArthur to Formosa to do just the opposite? Call off Chiang and tell him he couldn't send his troops to mainland China or anywhere else? We didn't send him over there to forge his own personal alliances — hell, that sounds like we're concludin' some kind of mutual defense treaty. Mister Secretary, I want you to radio a message to His Majesty MacArthur.

MacARTHUR
What's the matter with them back there? Have they lost their nerve? I know all about Chiang. If he had two horns and a tail, we should use him as long as he's anti-Communist; we can reform him later. It's my destiny to defeat Communism, and only God or those Washington politicians will keep me from doing it!

TRUMAN
You didn't read this one, didja? It's a letter to the Veterans of Foreign Wars. "Nothing could be more fallacious than the threadbare argument by those who advocate appeasement and defeatism in the Pacific that if we defend Formosa, we alienate continental Asia. Signed, Douglas MacArthur." Ya hear that? Appeasement — defeatism — now that's me he's talkin' about. Did any of ya know in advance this letter was gonna be printed? Well, I want it withdrawn right now!

Nothing soothes hurt feelings like success, though, and this is where MacArthur executes a military maneuver that not even his harshest critics could gainsay. With his forces driven far down the peninsula to the painfully small Pusan perimeter, MacArthur stages a brilliant and audacious amphibious landing far behind the enemy lines, at the port of Inchon — an operation dismissed as impossible by the North Koreans, and many American officials as well. With the war temporarily going the United Nations' way, Truman resolves to fly to Wake Island in the Pacific for a face-to-face confrontation with the general he's never met. Forced to wait for the other man, as Roosevelt had been before him, Truman's reaction is far less charitable:

TRUMAN
They probably had a little trouble gettin' him down off his cross. Wait a minute, there he is. That son of a bitch isn't in uniform, he's in costume. I dunno why it is, an old man like that, and a five-star general to boot,

has to run around dressed up like a nineteen-year-old second lieutenant. I'll tell ya one thing, if he was an officer in my outfit, I'd bust him so fast he wouldn't know what happened. And makin' me wait — he can do that to Harry Truman, but not to his Commander-In-Chief.

Nevertheless, when they finally meet, the tone is conciliatory:

MacARTHUR
Mister President, you know that I'm not involved in politics in any way. I did let the politicians make a chump out of me in the '48 elections. If a general is going to be running against you, his name will be Eisenhower, not MacArthur.

TRUMAN
Eisenhower? That man doesn't know as much about politics as a pig does about Sunday.

In the official briefing, MacArthur tells Truman that the situation is well in hand, and that he hopes to have the troops home by

MacArthur and Truman: they met but once. How might history have been altered if they'd truly known one another?

Christmas — enabling the President to put on a smiling face upon his return to Washington:

> TRUMAN
> *Well, I've, uh, I've never had a more satisfactory conference since I've been President. Now General MacArthur is a member of the government of the United States, and he's loyal to that government, and to the United Nations, and he's loyal to the President and his foreign policy, and he's confident that the fighting in Korea will soon be over.*

Then disaster strikes: the Red Chinese invade South Korea in full force, completely changing the complexion of the battle, and reigniting the war of words between the Commander-in-Chief and his Far East Commander:

> MacARTHUR
> *The defeat of the North Koreans was decisive. In the face of this victory, the Chinese Communists have committed the most offensive act of international lawlessness in history! We are now facing a new, fresh, highly trained army! What does Truman mean by calling this a "police action?" Isn't it a fact that the casualties are mounting daily? This "police action" has almost destroyed the Korean nation — for what? I've seen as much blood and disaster as any man now living. Every time I come out of here, I could just — just — be sick! It curdles my stomach...I requested permission to bomb the Chinese airfields in Manchuria. The request was denied. I requested permission for hot pursuit of enemy aircraft into their privileged sanctuary above the Yalu. That request was denied. I requested permission to bomb the Yalu bridges to keep the Chinese out of Korea. They said, you might bomb the southern half of the bridges only. In my fifty years of military service, I have never learned how to bomb half a bridge! It's the most imbecilic order ever given to a commander in the field. For the first time in military history, a commander has been denied the use of his military power to safeguard the lives of his soldiers and the safety of his army. It leaves me with a sense of inexpressible — shock.*

The next to last incident is not long in coming:

> COLONEL WHITNEY
> *Excuse me, General. We just got word that Washington wants you to stop all offensive operations immediately. They want to effect a political rather*

than a military solution. They're planning to draft a cease-fire proposal. Well, sir, in view of Mr. Truman's feeling you want to substitute your policy for his —

MacARTHUR

I couldn't substitute my policy for Mr. Truman's, because Mr. Truman doesn't have a policy!...I have a better idea. We'll send a message to the Chinese commander. Put it on all the wire services, I want maximum exposure!

COLONEL WHITNEY

Sir, you have been specifically prohibited from issuing any statements. Sir, that is a direct order from the President!

MacARTHUR

And that is part of a dangerous concept: that men of the armed forces owe their primary allegiance to these temporary occupants of the White House instead of to the country and the Constitution we're sworn to defend!

Here, the film oversimplifies, as film often must: MacArthur's personal, very belligerent message to the Chinese is shown as the straw that breaks the President's back (though, in fact, the dismissal did not take place until a Congressman took a supposedly confidential letter filled with MacArthur's anti-Administration opinions, and read it into the Congressional Record):

TRUMAN

I oughtta kick his insubordinate ass right in the Sea of Japan. The lousiest trick he's pulled: I travel fourteen thousand miles to reach an understanding face-to-face, and he still thinks he can do what he damn well pleases!...Y'know, there's a story where Abe Lincoln was tryin' to mount a horse that was skittish, and the horse kicked a hind hoof into the stirrup. So Lincoln says to him, "If you're gonna get on, I'll get off." Well, I'm not gettin' off! I think Roosevelt should'a pulled Wainwright outta Corregidor, and left that five-star brass hat MacArthur there to be the martyr. That man's tryin' to start World War III, an' I'm tryin' to prevent it. I'm gonna fire that brass hat prima donna right now. Who the hell's he think he is, God?

The MacArthurs are entertaining dinner guests when word of the general's dismissal reaches Tokyo by radio. The news is whispered by Sid Huff to Jean; she relays it to her husband, whose reaction is simply, "Well, Jeannie, we're going home at last."

Truman is in hot water with the press and the political opposition. For the television cameras, he stubbornly defends his action:

TRUMAN
Well, people who think they're God are bound to get in trouble sooner or later. Y'see, whatcha have to understand is that the people of this country are men and women'a common sense, and whenever anybody gets too far outta line, the people are gonna take charge an' put him outta business.

MacArthur receives a tumultuous welcome home, culminating in an invitation to address a joint session of Congress. To them, he defends his own actions, and his lifelong tenets: "War's very object is victory, not prolonged indecision. In war, there can be no substitute for victory." He then segues into a remarkably poignant farewell:

MACARTHUR
I am closing my fifty-two years of military service. When I joined the army, even before the turn of the century, it was the fulfillment of all my

boyish hopes and dreams. The world has turned over many times since I took the oath on the plain at West Point, and the hopes and dreams have long since vanished. But I still remember the refrain of one of the most popular barrack ballads of that day which pronounced, most proudly, the old soldiers never die, they just fade away. And, like the old soldier of that ballad, I now close my military career and just fade away, an old soldier who tried to do his duty as God gave him the light to see that duty. Good-bye.

Although Truman angrily responds, "Good-bye, hell! He's runnin' for President!" that's not to be, a fact the movie teases by showing television convention coverage of "the greatest war hero our country has ever known…the next President of the United States, five-star General — Dwight David Eisenhower!" MacArthur is allowed to fire off the quip, "I think he'll make a fine President. He was the best clerk who ever served under me."

Skipping MacArthur's years of retirement as President of Remington Rand, and his sentimental visit to the Philippines in 1961, the film cycles back to where it began: his farewell address to the Corps of Cadets in 1962, which was, if anything, even more poignant than the "old soldier" speech to Congress:

MacARTHUR

The shadows are lengthening for me. The twilight is here. My days of old have vanished — tone and tint. They have gone glimmering through the dreams of things that were. Their memory is one of wondrous beauty, watered by tears and coaxed and caressed by the smiles of yesterday. I listen vainly, but with thirsty ear, for the witching melody of faint bugles blowing reveille, of far drums beating the long roll. In my dreams I hear the crash of guns, the rattle of musketry, the strange, mournful mutter of the battlefield. But, in the evening of my memory, always I return to West Point. Always there echoes and re-echoes: duty — honor — country. Today marks my final roll call with you. But I want you to know that when I cross the river, my last conscious thoughts will be of the Corps, and the Corps, and the Corps. I bid you farewell.

In this scene, Jean MacArthur is depicted as being on hand to applaud her husband. In filming the scene, actress Marj Dusay became only the third woman in history to sit in the West Point Cadet Mess "Poop Deck" while the Corps of Cadets was assembled. The second had been the real Mrs. MacArthur during the actual speech; the first, Queen Elizabeth II.

Many who have tried to tell the MacArthur story have seen this as the perfect place for the "fade-out." The list includes the makers of this film — and MacArthur himself, who ended his remarkable autobiography, *Reminiscences*, the same way. (One year before his death, the old soldier, in his West Point bathrobe, sat down in a comfortable chair with legal pads and sharpened pencils and wrote out *Reminiscences*. With practically no revisions and precious little editing, it represents a nearly direct communication between the General and the reader. Those who rush to sit in judgment on the man are obliged to read his book first.)

THE BALANCE SHEET

There exists a little-known, "expanded" version of *MacArthur*, designed for television viewing. It includes an entire Japanese subplot built around the real-life General Yamashita (played with grave solemnity by James Shigeta), executed for atrocities including the Bataan Death March, (which some people, in reality, believed was unfair), and his son-in-law (Evan Kim), who, in the film, tries to prevent his father-in-law's execution by shooting MacArthur, but cannot go through with it.

While this detour from the main storyline is not particularly effective, there is much in the expanded version that greatly improved the version now available on DVD: more explanatory footage with Roosevelt, King, and Marshall; extra footage of the arrival of the MacArthur family in Japan; MacArthur's first meeting with Emperor Hirohito (surreptitiously observed by Jean and little Arthur); contemporary television coverage of the Korean years (featuring archive footage of Richard Nixon, Joe McCarthy, and other senators), and — most importantly — a black-and-white prologue that begins with still photos of the real MacArthur as a youngster, proceeding on to newsreel footage from the World War I period, and morphing Peck into the footage seamlessly at the time of the Bonus March. Early in this chapter, we lamented the lack of back story in the DVD version; inclusion of this prologue in future releases of the DVD would alleviate many of these objections.

What it wouldn't do, unhappily, is change *MacArthur* from an ordinary film to one worthy of its subject. The fact that *MacArthur* is another "General movie" in the wake of *Patton* continues to burden the film: similarity breeds tedium, and familiarity breeds contempt.

In this sterile and almost textbook production of *MacArthur*, director Sargent and the producers seem to painfully distance themselves from adorning historical record with their own approval or disapproval: If MacArthur's actions appear noble, let them be presented as such; if they appear egotistical or bombastic, let those conceptions register sans comment. This refusal to offer opinion may be commendable in a purely

historical sense, but it nearly defeats the efforts of the viewer to place this extraordinary man in any kind of rational perspective.

There was inarguable vanity and pettiness in that man, but there was also greatness. Love him or loathe him, one must acknowledge the fact that, in reality, MacArthur did what no military commander before him had done: *he won the peace.*

Peace was very much on the mind of that old soldier. One statement from *Reminiscences* says it all, on the occasion when his troops liberated the Japanese prisoner-of-war camp at Santo Tomas: "It was a wonderful and never-to-be-forgotten moment — to be a life-saver, not a life-taker." And again, at the long-awaited liberation of Manila, MacArthur — a man never at a loss for words — was too choked up to speak. He later wrote, "It had killed something inside me to see my men die." Five years before his death, he considered the verdict of history: "Could I have but a line a century hence crediting a contribution to the advance of peace, I would gladly yield every honor which has been accorded by war."

This side of the man is lost on a great many people. For that, he, himself, must shoulder a large share of the blame. He was, and is, known as a vain, egotistical braggart who strutted across the stage of world history. Yet is it not possible that it was these very qualities of ego and vanity that enabled this creature of military indoctrination and military orientation to *maintain the qualities of a free-thinking, autonomous individual?* Only such a man could have written of the Japanese people he ruled so absolutely — and so well: "As they increasingly sensed my insistence upon just treatment for them, even at times against the great nations I represented, they came to regard me not as a conqueror, but as a protector."

"Even at times against the great nations I represented?" But that flies in the face of the three words by which the old soldier actually lived. Or does it?

Duty — Honor — Country. These are the words MacArthur kept returning to, in the West Point address that bookmarks the film. In fact, he proclaimed these words to be the lodestone of his existence: *Duty — Honor — Country.* He might be surprised to hear us say that his actions demonstrated otherwise.

Duty? By all means. Honor? Absolutely. Country? Well....

In a life absolutely unique among military commanders, MacArthur showed that his country was not just the United States of America. It was the world. It was *humanity at large.*

The prologue deleted from the final release print stated that MacArthur's "greatest battles were not always with the enemy." Sadly, that is a fact of life for those who place the welfare of humanity over an assumed allegiance to those who look like them, who worship from the same book, who salute the same flag.

That sense of he's one of *us* — his loyalty should be to *us,* affected not only MacArthur, but the man whose story follows...

STAND TEN: *SCHINDLER'S LIST*

(11/30/1993: Universal) Directed by Steven Spielberg; Written by Steven Zaillan, from Thomas Keneally's book; Music by John Williams; Photographed by Janusz Kaminsky; Edited by Michael Kahn.

> STERN
> *The list is an absolute good. The list — is life. All around its margins lies the gulf.*

What is a Rusesabagina?

He's a man — a man, thankfully, still very much with us, and a man who has honored the people chronicled in this book, especially Douglas MacArthur and Oskar Schindler, by applying their methods, and achieving similar results. Rusesabagina puts it very simply in his autobiography: "I am a hotel manager. In April 1994, when a wave of mass murder broke out in my country, I was able to hide 1,268 people inside the hotel where I worked." To add a bit more detail: For seventy-six days, Rusesabagina wined, dined, bribed, and cajoled the leaders of the warring factions, and kept his charges safe — men and women of both sides. Like Schindler, his story has been made into a movie, *Hotel Rwanda,* with Don Cheadle quite effective as Rusesabagina. (Also like Schindler, his film often sits on the shelves of the video rental stores, while those who would most benefit from his example check out the latest teen sex comedy or shootout-and-car-chases-epic.)

Paul Rusesabagina expressed his own philosophy of dealing with one's "enemies" in words that could have been written by Oskar Schindler — and words that would be anathema to the political leaders of most countries, not the least of which is our own beloved United States:

"People are never completely good or completely evil. And in order to fight evil you sometimes have to keep evil people in your orbit. Even the worst among them have their soft side, and if you can find and play with that part of them, you can accomplish a great deal of good. In an era of extremism you can never afford to be an extremist yourself."

That's the philosophy that Rusesabagina shared with Schindler: "It is very hard to hate someone with whom you have shared a beer. There is too much laughter and good feeling between you. Even people who might be predisposed to be enemies will come together over a beer."

For Oskar Schindler, it wasn't only beer — schnapps, cognac, champagne, caviar, chocolate, or cash — whatever did the trick. The goal, for

this German Catholic businessman, was initially to make himself rich beyond the dreams of avarice where the pickings were most lush: in Nazi-occupied Poland. In the end, the goal was to keep alive over a thousand people who otherwise would have been swept up in the sea of faceless victims of that incomprehensible expression of man's inhumanity to man called the Holocaust.

In this way, a man who came to do well — wound up doing good.

Another man who had done well made this film to do good, and many doubted his ability to do so. Steven Spielberg had become, in name and face, the most recognizable director in the world, synonymous with gigantic menaces — and even more gigantic optimism. At the time, he had directed four of the highest grossing films of all time, and others evidencing a rare and innate understanding of the potential of film storytelling — and nearly every moviegoer had their favorites. Mine are *Duel* (1971), with Dennis Weaver chased by a malevolent eighteen-wheeler,

Jaws (1975), where Roy Scheider, Robert Shaw, and Richard Dreyfus trade bon mots as they hunt a rapacious Great White Shark, and *E.T.* (1982) in which Henry Thomas befriends the cuddliest alien in the universe. Few believed that this master purveyor of cinematic warmth and charm could do justice to a story set inside what very well may be the ultimate genocide in human history. They feared he would reduce the story to the level of a Holocaust Theme Park.

They needn't have worried. Drawing on his own Jewishness (which was heretofore largely unnoticed by the public and unpublicized by himself), his growth as a husband and father, and his innate professionalism, Spielberg was able to discard the gimmicks of a lifetime and retain the craftsmanship. *Schindler's List* is a magnificent motion picture on every level — technically, artistically, financially — and, most important, emotionally.

Yet, it has its critics, most of whom base their objections on their own individual biases, rather than any shortcomings in the movie. Claude Lanzmann, whose nine-hour *Shoah* stands as the definitive documentary treatment of the Holocaust, questions the propriety of anyone recreating these events with stage-sets, actors, and scripted dialogue. David Thomson, in *Film Comment,* objects to the appearance on-screen of the name of Spielberg's company, Amblin Entertainment: "Whatever its faults and virtues, *Schindler's List* is *not* an ambling entertainment." (That's called a cheap shot.) Others find Elie Wiesel's pronouncement "How is one to tell a tale that *cannot* be — but *must* be — told?" to be a prohibition rather than a challenge.

But these critics miss the point. In the more than half-century since World War II ended, outright denial of the Holocaust has grown by leaps and bounds. Movies are in a unique position to do something about that. But while nine-hour chronicles such as *Shoah* have their place, a great many people who would never subject themselves to Lanzmann's grueling marathon, will sit through and learn from three hours of edge-of-the-seat storytelling by one of cinema's master storytellers. Spielberg's film makes the whole Holocaust setting accessible to a viewing audience that might never otherwise come anywhere near experiencing it, and that's not a sin, though some would have us believe it is. By handling the subject with rarefied kid gloves, they honor neither the dead nor the survivors. The survivors want the story told, and *Schindler's List* does that and will continue to do so. The experience of making the film prompted Spielberg to found the Survivors of the Shoah Visual History Foundation, preserving and cross-cataloguing the verbal recollections not only of Schindler's Jews, but any and all who were willing and able to add their voices to the record.

Also, if the cinematic retelling of this most important true story happens to occur in the form of an absolute masterpiece, that's all to the good, too.

The three central roles in *Schindler's List* are inhabited by actors whose performances are so vivid, so visceral, that the viewer can see himself/herself in them — when it is pleasant to do so, and when it is not. It is certainly pleasant to see oneself in the role of hero, albeit one who backs into it at first: with his myriad flaws — greed, lechery, hedonism — Liam Neeson's Oskar Schindler is one of the most *human* heroes in film.

If it is not quite as exhilarating to see oneself as the victim, it's certainly a role many of us are inclined towards, and some would say that society in recent years has encouraged this identification far too much. In his carefully controlled portrayal of Itzhak Stern, which was based on a real person, but whose part in the story is combined with that of Abraham Bankier and several other Emalia executives, Ben Kingsley, with an outward poker face and eyes that tell all, compels identification with the victim, albeit a victim who is morphing into the role of action-taker, the whole reason for the creation of the State of Israel shortly after the war.

It is the third actor in this trilogy of razor-sharp performances who holds up the mirror we *don't* want to look into, allowing us to see ourselves in the role of the *villain*. Ralph Fiennes (pronounced Rafe Fines) as the Plaszow camp commandant Amon Goeth (pronounced Gert) is so incredibly effective, that he lingers in the viewer's memory much as the real Goeth haunted the dreams of his charges (and may still). But Spielberg will not allow us to dismiss Goeth as an inhuman aberration — that's too easy.

Some viewers will wonder why Spielberg shows us a shirtless, pot-bellied Goeth shooting prisoners at random from the balcony of his villa, and follows that with a scene of him walking to the toilet and urinating. Why are we compelled to watch the man taking a whiz? The keyword in that question is "man." Spielberg is graphically demonstrating that the Nazi commandant is *not* some demon from the depths, *not* some alien creature from another world, but a man who has a pot belly, as so many of us do, pees, as we all do, and kills without qualm, as we are all quite capable of doing.

That is the whole point of these three incredible performances: to show us *ourselves*. We have it within us to be a hero like Schindler. We have it within us to be victims like Stern, and like it or not, we have it within us to be a beast like Goeth. This may explain why so many to this day deny that the Holocaust ever occurred: they don't want to admit, they *cannot* admit, that they themselves are capable of such evil, so they desperately deny the truth they find so unacceptable.

That's the true glory of Fiennes' performance: he reveals the beast that dwells in all of us, and must always be guarded against. Because the beast denied is not the beast vanquished. It merely waits, watches, and observes the opportunity. It is always ready to emerge again, in any government, nation, or people. Constant vigilance is required to empower the cry of the Holocaust survivors: *never again*.

The film begins with the lighting of a Shabbat candle, in a glorious burst of color which will not be seen again for some time. The vast majority of the film is shot in black and white, giving a documentary feel to the proceedings. The smoke from the guttering candle resolves into the steam exhaust of a train entering Krakow, and a title card gives us the setting:

> "September, 1939, the German forces defeated the Polish army in two weeks. Jews were ordered to register all family members and relocate to major cities. More than 10,000 Jews from the countryside arrive in Krakow daily."

This will be a film about *lists* — lists of those selected to die, and of those selected to live — and we see folding tables set up, paper, pens, and ink pots laid out, as the arriving Jews are dutifully recorded. The Nazis are nothing if not punctilious in the keeping of lists by which some of them will be convicted of their hideous crimes in years to come.

We then focus on a man of a different sort, dressing for a dinner party, choosing from between various suits, ties, cufflinks, and what appears to be a limited supply of folding money. He has at least one thing in common with the listmakers, though: he affixes a prominent *Hakenkreuz* (swastika) pin to his lapel.

In a Krakow nightclub, he surveys the scene with cold, calculating eyes, he signals the maitre d' (Branko Lustig, co-producer of the film and a Holocaust survivor) and puts the currency to work. Drinks are sent to the men in uniform and their dates. We will learn that this man is Oskar Schindler, businessman from Zwittau, in the Sudetenland, that part of Czechoslovakia annexed by Hitler because its population was "ethnically German." The men he is courting are SS-*Hauptscharfuhrer* Wilhelm Kunde (Jochen Nickel), SS-*Obersturmfuhrer* Rolf Czurda (Friedrich von Thun) and SS-*Oberfuhrer* Julian Scherner (Anderzej Seweryn), all highly placed in the military government of Krakow. Flashbulbs pop, and the good times being had by the entrepreneur and the brass are recorded for posterity.

Random conversation among the Nazi officers centers on the fact that the Jews of Krakow are wearing their mandated Star of David armbands "…as if it's the mantle of a riding club." That's when Kunde makes a pertinent observation:

KUNDE

It's human nature: "We do this to avoid that." That's what they have done since thousands of years. It's what they do. They weather the storm. But this storm is different. This is not the Romans, this storm is the SS.

As Nazi troops occupy the capital, harassment of the local Jewish population increases. Orthodox Jews are stopped on the street, their beards and ritual locks clipped. All Jews, of whatever denomination from totally orthodox to nearly assimilated, are subject to a bewildering array of edicts and regulations deigned not only to restrict and disempower them — but to confuse, disorient, and humiliate. At this stage, there is still somewhere they can turn:

> "The Judenrat. The Jewish council comprised of twenty-four elected Jews personally responsible for carrying out the orders of the regime in Krakow, such as drawing up lists for work details, food and housing. A place to lodge complaints."

Of course, once those complaints are lodged, they may not be resolved in any way. Into this beehive of unhappy humanity strides the bear-like businessman, Oskar Schindler, looking for Itzhak Stern, a dapper little fellow with the bearing of a Talmudic scholar, which he is. Oskar takes him into a private room to question him.

STERN
By law I have to tell you, sir, I'm a Jew.

SCHINDLER
Well, I'm a German, so there we are.

While talking, Schindler pours himself a drink from a flask, downs it, and offers one to Stern, who pointedly ignores it. This will become a pattern with them.

SCHINDLER
There's a company you did the books for, on Lipowa Street. Made what, pots and pans?...Change the machines around, whatever you do you could make other things, couldn't you? Field kits, mess kits, Army contracts. Once the war ends, forget it, but for now it's great, you could make a fortune, don't you think?...I can get the signatures I need. That's the easy part. Finding the money to buy the company; that's hard. You know anybody? Jews, yeah. Investors. You must have contacts in the Jewish business community, working here.

STERN
What community? Jews can no longer own businesses. That's why this one's in receivership.

SCHINDLER
Well, they wouldn't own it, I'd own it. I'd pay them back in product, pots, and pans. Something they can use, something they can feel in their hands. They can trade it on the black market, do whatever they want, everybody's happy. If you want, you could run the company for me.

STERN
Let me understand. They'd put up all the money. I'd do all the work. What, if you don't mind my asking, would you do?

SCHINDLER
I'd make sure it's known the company's in business. I'd see that it had a certain panache. That's what I'm good at. Not the work, not the work — the presentation!

STERN
I'm sure I don't know anybody who'd be interested in that.

SCHINDLER
Well, they should be, Itzhak Stern. Tell them they should be.

There is absolutely no reason for the austere Jewish accountant to trust the beefy German carpetbagger, but they have one thing in common: like Schindler, Stern knows an opportunity when it drops into his lap.

Next, we see a tall, good-looking young man in suit and tie on the street. He is wearing the Star of David armband, but when no one's watching, he takes it off, proving that he has the boldness to do such a thing and the Aryan looks to get away with it.

This is our introduction to Poldek Pfefferberg (Jonathan Sagall), and it's a shame the film hasn't time to tell us more about him. He was an incredibly audacious and resourceful young man (and remained so to his death). Prior to the events of the film, he was a high school teacher, then rose to captain in the Polish Army at the Bydgosch Academy, overcoming a good deal of anti-Semitic sentiment to do so. After the defeat of the Polish Army, he was being transported to a P.O.W. camp when the train stopped in his hometown of Krakow, a few short blocks from his home. With awesome *chutzpah*, he showed the guard a very official-looking pass, covered in stamps, that had allowed him passage through a hospital — and the guard, not speaking German but unwilling to admit it, let him out the door, where he caught the trolley for home and a watchful return to civilian life.

After the events of the film, on the boat to America, he had the equivalent of $10 in his pocket. By playing bridge with the captain and the ship's officers, he increased that to $105. In the USA, he Americanized his name to Leopold Page, and eventually earned success running a leather-goods store, the Handbag Studio, in Beverly Hills. That's where he told the story of Oskar Schindler to every writer or producer who crossed his threshold. In 1980, he piqued the curiosity of an Australian writer named Thomas Keneally, who wrote the book that originally caught the attention of Steven Spielberg. For the eleven years it took for Spielberg to consider himself ready to tackle the project, Poldek Page pestered him with weekly phone calls. After *Gremlins*, Page was reported to have said, "Enough with the furry animals!" So, in a very real sense, we would not have Schindler's story to read or to watch without Poldek: "He gave me my life, and I tried to give him immortality." (He swore the film would earn "an Oscar for Oskar." So it did.)

Poldek and Mila Pfefferberg (Jonathan Sagall and Adi Nitzan). It was Poldek who persuaded Keneally to write the book and Spielberg to make the movie. "It is not a story for Jews but for everyone. A story of humanity man to man," he said.

In the film, he's first shown black-marketeering with other Jews inside the Church of the Virgin Mary in the market square of Krakow. (Embarrassed by this invented scene, the real Poldek insisted "I would never black-marketeer in that beautiful church.") In walks Oskar, who compliments Poldek on his shirt and asks where he can get one like it, implying he has the cash to cover it: "Nice things cost money." Poldek takes out his note pad. One crook recognizes another, and Oskar has his contact in the Krakow black market.

"March 20, 1941: Deadline for entering the ghetto. Edict 44/91 establishes a closed Jewish district south of the Vistula River. Residency in the walled ghetto is compulsory. All Jews from Krakow and surrounding areas are forced from their homes and required to crowd into an area of sixteen square blocks"

We see Jews trundling their belongings, whatever they can carry, into the ghetto, and one family in particular, the Nussbaums, being ejected from their fashionable apartment, as they make their way down the street to the cruel taunts of "Good-bye, Jews! Good-bye, Jews!" from a teenage girl. We see Oskar Schindler arriving; his Nazi friends have appropriated the apartment for him. Scenes of Schindler stretching out on the bed are intercut with shots of the Nussbaums (Michael Gordon and Aldona Grochal) entering their newly-assigned ghetto hovel:

SCHINDLER
It could not be better.

ROSALIA NUSSBAUM
It could be worse.

WILHELM NUSSBAUM
How? How could it possibly be worse?!?

Then, as a line of *other* new residents of these wretched quarters come filing in politely, he sees *exactly* how it can be worse.

From the ghetto gate, Itzhak Stern prompts two older men into Oskar Schindler's luxurious automobile: these are Jews who still have cash money on hand. He recaps the offer he had described to Stern: the investment will be repaid in product. "Not good enough," the investors declare.

SCHINDLER
Not good enough? Look where you're living. Look where you've been put. "Not good enough." A couple of months ago, you'd be right. Not anymore... You want a contract? To be upheld by what court? I said what I'd do, that's our contract.

(Incidentally, in his first feature, *Duel,* Steven Spielberg inadvertently immortalized himself, momentarily capturing his own reflection in the glass of a phone booth from which Dennis Weaver is calling for help. Here he does it again: in the windows of Schindler's car, we briefly glimpse the director, especially the emblem on his cap.)

As the potential investors confer in hushed tones, Schindler knows he's won, because it's the best deal available to them, in this time and place. He pours a drink from his flask and proffers it to Stern, who, true to form, stares ahead stonily. We soon see the investors favoring Schindler with briefcases full of zloty, and the deal has been struck. As they prepare their offices, Stern fills Schindler in on the realities of employment practices in occupied Krakow:

STERN
The standard SS rate for Jewish skilled laborers is seven marks a day, five for unskilled and women. This is what you pay the Reich Economic Office, the Jews themselves receive nothing. Poles you pay wages. Generally, they get a little more... The Jewish worker's salary, you pay it directly to the SS, not to the worker. He gets nothing.

SCHINDLER
But it's less. It's less than what I would pay a Pole. That's the point I'm trying to make. Poles cost more. Why should I hire Poles?

That's all Stern needs to hear. Soon, he's moving through the Jewish ghetto: "An enamelware factory, over at, uh, Lipowa Street...It's owned by a German, but it's outside the ghetto, so you can barter for extra goods — for eggs, I don't know what you need — with the Polish workers, you can't get it here."

Quiet, nondescript, almost mousy in demeanor, Itzhak Stern is, in fact, just as much a wheeler and dealer as Oskar Schindler. What he's doing is, in fact, singling out the writers, the artists, the educators, those who are most likely to be considered expendable by their German masters, and passing them off as skilled metalworkers and craftsmen, eligible for the holy of holies: the *Blauschein*, the stamped document testifying that the bearer is "essential" to the war effort. A typical example is Chaim Nowak (Uri Avrahami), who looks like exactly what he is — a professor — and is therefore denied a *Blauschein*.

CHAIM NOWAK
Not essential? I think you misunderstand the meaning of the word. I teach history and literature, since when is not essential?

Stern enlists the aid of a forger to produce a document testifying that Nowak is, in fact, a metal polisher. Stern then takes the pristine document and wads it up, pours coffee on it, and bites the corners. "It's too new!" With a change from suit and tie to workers' garb, Nowak presents his "distressed" document and obtains the Blauschein. Stern works similar magic again and again, credentialing Jewish workers for the factory.

Schindler, meantime, is holding auditions for a secretary. Applicant after applicant is gorgeous, but can't type for beans. Hilariously, he shows one how to return the carriage! The final candidate is a cigarette-smoking battle-ax, who types with effortless efficiency. He voices his dilemma to Stern: "They're all so — *qualified*." In the next shot, we see that he has hired them all!

Workers are trained, machines are fired up, and Schindler is in business. "It is my distinct pleasure to announce the fully operational status of Deutsche Email Fabrik, manufacturers of superior enamel crockery, expressly designed and crafted for military use. Anticipating the enclosed bids will meet with your approval, and looking forward to a long and mutually prosperous association, I extend to you in advance my sincerest gratitude and very best regards. Oskar Schindler."

As this sales pitch is read in voice-over, we see that it is invariably accompanied by huge hampers of black market goods — liquor, chocolates, Cuban cigars, all procured by the ever-resourceful Poldek. Practically every one of the prospective "customers" has a framed photograph on his desk of himself in a party setting with *Herr Direktor* Schindler. The contracts are signed and stamped, and D.E.F. is a going concern, to the extent that Schindler summons Stern to his office for congratulations.

SCHINDLER
My father was fond of saying you need three things in life — a good doctor, a forgiving priest, and a clever accountant. The first two, I've never had much use for. But, the third — !

With that, he raises his glass to the accountant. Stern, as always, just stares at him, his own glass untouched. With a long-suffering sigh, Schindler plunges gamely ahead, never acknowledging the gap that separates the two men, the gap Stern can never forget:

SCHINDLER

Just pretend, for Christ's sake…I'm trying to thank you. I'm saying I couldn't have done this without you. The usual thing would be to acknowledge my gratitude. It would also, by the way, be the courteous thing.

STERN

You're welcome.

Stern hoists his glass, hesitantly, and sets it back down again. Schindler, as usual, downs both drinks.

Early morning in Schindler's new apartment. His Polish mistress, Wiktoria Klonowska (Malgoscha Gebel), wearing a man's silk robe, answers the front door, and confronts a pretty, nicely-dressed woman. Klonowska's face falls as she realizes she's looking at Mrs. Schindler (Caroline Goodall). Oskar's wife, too, knows just who and what she's looking at.

This is another element of the puzzle that was Oskar Schindler: never would he show embarrassment over his female companions. Emilie, however, is constantly reminded of her status. When she and Oskar leave the apartment, the doorman is about to address her as "Miss," which Oskar quickly corrects to "*Mrs.* Schindler."

The same thing happens with the maitre d' at the elegant restaurant they enter. Despite herself, Emilie is impressed with the material success of her ne'er-do-well husband, and he basks in her approbation:

SCHINDLER

They won't soon forget the name Schindler here, I can tell you that. "Oskar Schindler," they'll say. "Everybody remembers him. He did something extraordinary. He did something no one else did. He came here with nothing — a suitcase — and built a bankrupt company into a major manufactory. And left with a steamer trunk — two steamer trunks full of money — all the riches of the world. There's no way I could have known this before, but there was always something missing. In every business I tried, I see now it wasn't me that failed. Something was missing. Even if I'd known what it was, there's nothing I could have done about it, because you can't create this thing. And it makes all the difference in the world between success and failure... War!

Later, as the two lay in bed like spoons, Emilie asks pointedly whether she should stay, or return to their home in Czechoslovakia. When her husband is non-committal, Emilie sets a condition:

EMILIE
Promise me no doorman or maitre d' will presume I am anyone other than Mrs. Schindler — and I'll stay.

And, bang! In a cut so abrupt it borders on slapstick, we see Emilie waving goodbye to Oskar from the window of a first-class train compartment.

We next find Schindler sitting down to a meal in his office, as Stern hands him a report:

SCHINDLER
I could try to read this, or I could eat my lunch while it's still hot. We're doing well? Better this month than last? Any reason to think next month will be worse?

STERN
The war could end.

— which proves that the dour accountant does indeed have a sense of humor. He has one more item of business for the *Herr Direktor*:

STERN
There's a machinist outside who'd like to thank you personally for giving him a job. Every day he comes. He's very grateful. It'll just take a minute.

With that, Stern opens the door, and invites in Mr. Lowenstein (Henryk Bista), a feisty old man, with one arm.

LOWENSTEIN
I want to thank you, sir, for giving me the opportunity to work. The SS beat me up. They would have killed me, but I'm essential to the war effort, thanks to you. I work hard for you. I'll continue to work hard for you! God bless you, sir. You're a good man.

Stern takes the man's arm, guides him out, away from the mortally embarrassed Schindler. Shortly, Stern is hustling Schindler to his car:

> SCHINDLER
>
> *By the way, don't* ever *do that to me again. Didn't you notice that man only had one arm?*

> STERN
>
> Did *he?*

As the car drives off, Schindler is still shouting, and Stern is still dissembling:

> SCHINDLER
>
> *What's his use?*

> STERN
>
> *Very useful! Success!*

All this time, the senselessness of the Holocaust is growing exponentially. Each morning, Schindler's workers leave the ghetto to trudge to the factory, already aware that they enjoy a level of safety there that is not generally available to them elsewhere. To be safe, they have to arrive at the factory, and one especially cold morning, they don't. Instead, they are stopped by S.S. troops and made to shovel snow, but that's not the worst of it. Old Mr. Lowenstein stands out, because he's trying to shovel with one arm. Although he claims to be "an essential worker…for Oskar Schindler," the S.S. guards aren't buying it: "A one-armed Jew. Twice as useless." The old man is taken aside and shot. The entire scene is played out in tandem with Oskar's later complaint to his friend Rolf Czurda about the incident:

> CZURDA
>
> *You shouldn't think of them as yours, Oskar. You need to understand that some of the officers here don't give a damn about production. To them, it's a matter of, um, national priority that Jews be made to shovel snow. It's got nothing to do with reality, Oskar. You know it and I know it. Jews shoveling snow — it's got a, um, ritual significance.*

SCHINDLER
I lost a day of production, Rolf. I lost a worker. I expect to be compensated.

Now Oskar, who had so recently questioned Lowenstein's usefulness, finds the tables turned on him:

CZURDA
A one-armed machinist, Oskar?

SCHINDLER
He was a metal press operator. Quite skilled.

To his credit, he says it with a straight face. But, more and more, Oskar is coming face-to-face with the savage absurdity of the Third Reich's "Final Solution." Even as they are beginning to lose the war, they have no compunctions about diverting men and material, essential resources, from the struggle, in order to indulge their compulsive campaign against European Jewry. Many scholars suggest that this is what sets the Holocaust apart from all other genocides: that it was pursued even when it was politically — and practically — pointless.

Another example of this is not long in coming, when Poldek knocks on the *Herr Direktor's* door to inform him that the plant manager, Stern, has been seized on the way to work and placed on the latest cattle-car transport. (In reality, it was Abraham Bankier who was put on the train. As mentioned earlier, the film has combined many of the experiences of Bankier, Stern, and others into the Stern character.) Oskar loses no time in hustling to the depot, where a clerk (Joachim Paul Assböck) confirms that Stern's on the list:

SCHINDLER
I'm talking to a clerk. What is your name?

TAUBER
Klaus Tauber.

As Oskar writes it down, the clerk has second thoughts and calls to his superior, an SS sergeant (Grzegorz Damiecki):

TAUBER
Hauptscharfuhrer, *this gentleman thinks a mistake's been made.*

> SCHINDLER
>
> *My plant manager is somewhere on this train. If it leaves with him on it, it'll disrupt production and the Armaments Board will want to know why.*
>
> KUNDER
>
> *Well, the list is correct, sir. There's nothing I can do.*
>
> SCHINDLER
>
> *What is your name?*
>
> KUNDER
>
> *My name? My name is Kunder. Hauptscharfuhrer Kunder.*
>
> SCHINDLER
>
> *Gentlemen, thank you very much. I think I can guarantee you you'll both be in southern Russia before the end of the month. Good day.*

And, bang! We next see all three of them — Oskar, the clerk and the sergeant — striding alongside the cars, calling for Stern. The train is already starting to move, when Oskar spots the accountant's face through the slats. The train is stopped, Stern is reprieved, and Oskar is requested to sign and initial the changes in the list.

                              TAUBER
Makes no difference to us, you understand — this one, that one. It's the inconvenience to the list. It's the paperwork.

Stern is apologetic:

                              STERN
I somehow left my work card at home. I tried to explain them it was a mistake, but — I'm sorry, it was stupid!

And Schindler is gruff — he will *not* let his deeper emotions show.

                            SCHINDLER
What if I got here five minutes later? Then where would I be?

Stern has been reprieved, but the others on the train have not, and even as it leaves, the suitcases they left behind on the platform — "It will follow you later!" — are being emptied and sorted for clothing, shoes, utensils, gold, any and all valuables. The owners will not need them where they are going.

Human beings can adjust to almost anything, and the Jews in the ghetto — many of whom are Oskar's workers that we recognize — are becoming almost comfortable in their ancestral squalor: the walls that keep them *in*, keep others *out*, or so they believe.

That's when Evil Incarnate enters their lives, driven into the ghetto in an open-top staff car. A work camp is being constructed just south of the city, and *Untersturmfuhrer* Amon Goeth (Ralph Fiennes) has been brought in to fill it and to command it. The camp is being built on the site of a Jewish cemetery, and in a gesture of calculated disrespect, the gravestones are being torn down and used to pave the camp road. This is not, technically, a death camp like nearby Auschwitz, since it has no crematoria or other facilities for mass murder, but that's not the sort of thing to stop a man like Goeth. His first item of business is to select a maid from among the prisoners already present in the camp: young Helen Hirsch (Embeth Davidtz) will have cause to regret her close proximity to the *Herr Kommandant*.

Helen is a mute witness, as Goeth sets the tone for his administration of the camp. One of his Non-Commissioned Officers (NCO), Hujar (Norbert Weisser), has been driven to distraction by the Jewish prisoner in charge of constructing the barracks (Elina Löwensohn):

> HUJAR
>
> *She says the foundation was poured wrong; she's got to take it down. I told her it's a barracks, not the fucking Hotel Europa!*
>
> DIANA REITER
>
> *Herr Kommandant, the entire foundation has to be torn down and repoured. If not, there will be at least a subsidence at the southern end of the barracks — subsidence, and then collapse.*
>
> GOETH
>
> *You are an engineer?*
>
> DIANA REITER
>
> *Yes. My name is Diana Reiter. I'm a graduate of Civil Engineering from the University of Milan.*
>
> GOETH
>
> *Ah, an educated Jew — like Karl Marx himself. Unterscharfuehrer! Shoot her!*
>
> DIANA REITER
>
> *Herr Kommandant! I'm only trying to do my job!*
>
> GOETH
>
> *Ja, I'm doing mine... We're not going to have arguments with these people. Shoot her! Here! On my authority!*

Hujar shoots the woman, in cold blood, in front of everyone. This is how it will be at Plaszow. Surrealistically, Goeth calmly orders:

> GOETH
>
> *Take it down, repour it, rebuild it. Like she said.*

Savage as it is, the execution of Diana Reiter is but a single murder. Amon Goeth is about to invade the false sanctuary of the Krakow ghetto. For this type of mass outrage, his men cannot simply be ordered in; they must be must be worked up to a fever pitch of righteous exhilaration, the rhapsodic ecstasy of being part of a historic mission. Goeth is the coach in the locker room, but Knute Rockne never gave a pep talk like this:

GOETH
Today is history. Today will be remembered. Years from now the young will ask with wonder about this day. Today is history and you are part of it. Six hundred years ago when elsewhere they were footing the blame for the Black Death, Casimir the Great — so called — told the Jews they could come to Krakow. They came. They trundled their belongings into the city. They settled. They took hold. They prospered in business, science, education, the arts. With nothing they came and with nothing they flourished. For six centuries there has been a Jewish Krakow. By this evening those six centuries will be a rumor. They never happened. Today is history.

The date is March 13, 1943. The liquidation of the Krakow ghetto — how neat and clinical a phrase to sum up an exercise in human savagery seldom equaled in all of history. The dawning of the nuclear age in just two years would usher in whole new vistas in mass killing from a distance, but this is up close and personal, "in your face." These are *men* marching into the homes of other men, women, and children, brutally seizing them, lining them up, shoving them onto trucks, and shooting without hesitation those who show the slightest hint of resistance, move a little too slowly, or incur the wrath of their tormentors in any of a thousand invisible ways. The streets are littered with the discarded and broken luggage of the living, and the discarded and broken bodies of the dead.

To us, these are not strangers. One of the first taken is Itzhak Stern, but others are recognizable to us; we have seen them laughing and joking in the streets, and working in the Emalia factory: Chaim Nowak, and the Schindler investors. Mrs. Dresner (Miri Fabian) attempts to hide her daughter Danka (Anna Mucha) with another family, but eventually has to settle for being escorted into the good line — those who'll be taken away to work — by a young boy who is a member of the Ghetto police force (OD), employed to do the bidding of the Nazi masters. His name is Adam Levy (Adam Siemion), and we will see him again.

MRS. DRESNER
Do you know the saying "an hour of life is still life?" You're not a boy any more. I'm saying a blessing for you.

Meanwhile, Poldek Pfefferberg intends to flee though the sewers, though his wife is resistant to the idea. He goes ahead to check things out, and finds the other end of the sewer route guarded by Nazis with machine-guns. Several others fleeing the same way are shot down. Poldek gets out and finds himself surfacing back in the ghetto in a welter of bloodied bodies and broken suitcases, with Mila already gone. Worse, he's standing in full view of another line of Nazi executioners coming down the street.

This is almost certain death, but we're dealing here with Poldek Pfefferberg, the man who can talk his way out of almost anything. Falling back on his military training, he begins to pick up the suitcases, piling them on either side of the road. Then, as the Nazis reach him, he clicks his heels together and *salutes*.

POLDEK PFEFFERBERG

Herr Kommandant! *I respectfully report I've been given orders to clear the bundles from the road, so there will be no obstructions to the thoroughfare.*

He'll never know why he used the phrase *Herr Kommandant*, but it's the right one: Poldek is staring into the eyes of Amon Goeth himself, who is vastly amused by this approach:

GOETH

Finish and join the line, little Polish clicking soldier!

And to all the morning's savagery, Oskar is a witness. He and his secretary, Ingrid (Beatrice Macola), have picked this, of all mornings, to go horseback riding. From a rise overlooking the ghetto, they have a front-row seat for scenes from the darkest depths of the human psyche. Oskar cannot tear his gaze from a small girl dressed in red. (Spielberg's decision to colorize her red coat, in the midst of black-and-white footage, was hailed as brilliant by some, but was dismissed as self-indulgent by others.) In reality, researchers later identified her as a cousin of the Dresners, a little girl named Genia, who passes gruesome examples of the very worst violence in almost a daze.

In the film, what strikes Schindler to the core is that the Nazi executioners *don't care* what this girl witnesses — they don't expect her to live to testify. They don't expect *any* witnesses to survive.

Little Genia makes her way into an uncle's apartment and hides under the bed. All through the ghetto, people are hiding under beds, in dressers with false drawer fronts, in attics, and under false floorboards, waiting for the storm to pass. This time, the storm will not pass; this time the storm will sweep through again and again, searching out those who have so cleverly hidden themselves. Searchlights, savage dogs, even stethoscopes are brought in to locate the last of the doomed — and many are simply machine-gunned on sight. One man is found hiding in a piano and shot; an SS man then sits down at the keyboard and pounds out Bach — or is it Mozart? — as a macabre, surrealistic accompaniment to the orgy of violence consuming the ghetto.

Oskar, of course, doesn't see these succeeding waves of savagery. What he observes is the silence and stillness on the factory floor the next day. This brings him for the first time to Plaszow, to the villa of Amon Goeth.

SCHINDLER
I go into work the other day. Nobody's there. Nobody tells me about this, I have to find out. I have to go in…everybody's gone.

GOETH
No, no. They're not gone. They're here.

SCHINDLER
They're MINE!

Goeth has summoned the local industrialists Schindler, Bosch, and Madritsch to Plaszow, to make them a proposal: to move their operations inside the Plaszow wire, where their workers will be available to them twenty-four hours a day. Goeth soon senses that Oskar wants to stay right

where he is and keep "his" workers with him, but, he totally misinterprets the reason for this, ascribing his own venal motives to the other man:

GOETH

Scherner told me something else about you: that you know the meaning of the word 'gratitude.' That it's not some vague thing with you like it is with others. You want to stay where you are. You've got things going on the side, things are good. You don't want anybody telling you what to do. I can understand all that. You know, I know you: What you want is your own sub-camp. Do you have any idea what's involved? The paperwork alone? Forget you've got to build the fucking thing, getting the fucking permits is enough to drive you crazy. Then the engineers show up. They stand around, they argue about drainage, foundations, codes, exact specifications, parallel fences four kilometers long, six thousand kilograms of electrified fences…I'm telling you, you'll want to shoot somebody. I've been through it, you know — I know!

Oskar knows, too; he has heard the stories. It is the *Herr Kommandant's* early morning habit to stand on his balcony, naked to his prodigious waist, and take target practice with his high-powered rifle on the prisoners in the courtyard below. (Ralph Fiennes, a naturally thin man, went on a "reverse diet" to produce a bulging belly for these shirtless scenes that would match the contemporary photos of the real Amon Goeth. Another testament to his handling of the role: the Pfefferberg-Pages, Poldek and Misia, traveled to Poland for the filming. Misia was introduced to Fiennes in full SS uniform as Amon Goeth, and began to shake uncontrollably — he was that close to the monster of her memories.)

Plaszow is not a designated death camp, which makes little difference to the individuals who catch Amon's sporting eye. Oskar wants his people out of there, and can talk fast and sweet enough to get them moved to a sub-camp he has built on the factory grounds — all except Itzhak Stern. Goeth has him installed in his own Plaszow office with specific instructions: "Goldberg and Chilowicz make sure I see my cut from the, uh, factory owners in this camp, leaving you to take care of my main account: the Schindler account. He wants his independence; I gave it to him. But independence costs money. This you understand?…Don't forget who you are working for now."

On one of his regular visits to the camp to drink and party with Amon Goeth — who expects it — Oskar is able to confer with Stern, who briefs him on the intricacies of business by bribery:

STERN
Herr Direktor, don't let things fall apart. I've worked too hard.

Stern will continue to work hard, not so much at running the business, but at getting people out of harm's way. The first is a rabbi (Ezra Dagan), who is now employed in the Plaszow metalworks making hinges, and is approached one morning by the *Kommandant:*

GOETH
Ja, I've got some workers coming in tomorrow. I've got to make room. Make me a hinge.

As Goeth times him with a pocket watch, Rabbi Lewartow works at making a hinge as though his life depended on it, which he knows it does. He finishes in less than a minute, but —

GOETH
That's very good. But I'm a bit confused, and perhaps you can help me, What I don't understand is that you've been working since, I think, what, about six this morning — yet such a small pile of hinges?

The rabbi has crafted his own death, and well he knows it. Goeth and two other Nazis drag him outside and shove him on his knees in the dirt. Goeth takes out his Luger for the shot. Once, twice, three times, four times — nothing happens but dry clicks. Goeth pulls a smaller revolver from a pocket. Meanwhile, the rabbi has managed to splutter something in his own defense:

RABBI LEWARTOW
Herr Kommandant, *I beg to report that my heap of hinges was so unsatisfactory because the machines were being recalibrated this morning. I was put on to shoveling coal.*

Goeth, of course, is unmoved, and fires the smaller pistol, once, twice, half a dozen times — it, too, misfires every time! (In reality, some people called this a "hand-of-God" moment.) Enraged, he hits the rabbi over the head with the useless gun — and stalks off in disgust.

The rabbi is alive, but from this point on, he's a marked man. Stern tells the story to Schindler on the *Herr Direktor's* next visit. Schindler sighs, then hands his gold lighter over to Stern. We next see Marcel Goldberg,

Lord of Lists, lighting his cigarette with it and putting Rabbi Lewartow's name on a list of transfers to Oskar's sub-camp.

Next, it is young Adam Levy, the boy who rescued Chaja and Danka Dresner in the ghetto, who falls afoul of the *Kommandant*, when he blames the theft of a chicken on an already dead man, to save the living ones in a lineup from being shot. Again, a prisoner is marked. This time, it is a gold cigarette case that travels from Schindler's pocket to Goldberg's — and the boy from Plaszow to Emalia. We get the feeling this is happening more and more. Word about Schindler has gotten about on the outside, too.

A young, drably dressed woman (Bettina Kupfer) arrives at D.E.F., gives her name as Elsa Krause, asks to see the *Herr Direktor*, and is refused. She then borrows fashionable clothes, a provocative dress, heels, a Parisian hat, and does up her hair and applies makeup. When she arrives back at the factory, the guard, of course, does not recognize her, but this time, she is quickly admitted to Schindler's office, where he offers her a drink. Instead, she blurts out her story:

REGINA PERLMAN
They say that no one dies here. They say your factory is a haven. They say you are good... My name is Regina Perlman, not Elsa Krause. I've been living in Krakow on false papers since the ghetto massacre. My parents are in Plaszow. Their names are Chana and Jakob Perlman. They're older people. They're killing older people now in Plaszow. They bury them up in the forest. Look — I don't have any money. I — I borrowed these clothes. I'm begging you, please — please bring them here.

He whirls on her, savagely, his temper rising as she begins to cry:

SCHINDLER
I don't do that! You've been misled. I ask one thing: whether or not a worker has certain skills. That's what I ask and that's what I care about. Such activities are illegal. You will not entrap me, Miss Krause! Cry and I will have you arrested, I swear to God!

Next, Oskar barges into Stern's office. For the first time, he speaks openly about what has been happening:

SCHINDLER
People die, it's a fact of life. He wants to kill everybody? Great! What am I supposed to do about it, bring everybody over? Is that what you

think? Send them over to Schindler, send them all. His place is a "haven," didn't you know? It's not a factory, it's not an enterprise of any kind, it's a haven for rabbis, and orphans, and people with no skills whatsoever! You think I don't know what you're doing? *You're so quiet all the time? I know, I know!*

STERN

Are you losing money?

SCHINDLER

No, I'm not losing money, that's not the point. It's dangerous. *It's dangerous to me! You have to understand, Goeth is under enormous pressure. You have to think of it in his situation. He's got this whole place to run, he's responsible for everything that goes on here, all these people — he's got a lot of things to worry about. And he's got the war, which brings out the worst in people. Never the good, always the bad. Always the bad. But in normal circumstances, he wouldn't be like this. He'd be all right. There'd just be the good aspects of him, which — he's a wonderful crook. A guy who loves good food, good wine, the ladies, making money.*

STERN

And killing.

SCHINDLER

What do you expect me to do about it?

STERN

Nothing, nothing. We're just talking.

Then the miracle happens. Oskar pulls a piece of paper from his pocket, removes his watch, and hands it to Stern.

SCHINDLER

Perlman, husband and wife. Have Goldberg bring them over.

We next see the watch on Goldberg's wrist, as he pulls Chana and Jakob Perlman out of the ranks at Plaszow. Regina is watching, as they are marched into Emalia.

Almost despite himself, Oskar is becoming a man who makes miracles happen.

One night, at Goeth's villa, he comes downstairs for a bottle of wine, and confronts Goeth's maid, Helen Hirsch. (Just as the character of "Itzhak Stern" combines the experiences of two real men, Stern and Abraham Bankier, the character of "Helen Hirsch" incorporates the experiences of two Goeth maids named Helen: Helen Hirsch and Helen Sternlicht, both astonishingly strong women who survived their experiences with Goeth). At first she is distrustful of the big German, but before long his comforting presence has triggered a confession:

HELEN HIRSCH
My first day here, he beat me because I threw out the bones from dinner. He came down at midnight and asked for them. And I asked him, I don't know how, I could never ask him now, I said, "Why are you beating me?" He said, "The reason I beat you now is because you ask why I beat you." One day, he will shoot me. I see things. We were on the roof on Monday, young Lisiek and I, and we saw the Herr Kommandant come out of the house on the patio right there below us and he drew his gun and shot a woman who was passing by — a woman carrying a bundle — just shot her through the throat. She was just a woman on her way somewhere, she was no faster or slower or fatter or thinner than anyone else, and I couldn't guess what had she done. The more you see of the Herr Kommandant, *the more you see there is no set rules you can live by. You cannot say to yourself, "If I follow these rules, I will be safe."*

Then, Oskar comes under scrutiny. He is arrested for having impulsively kissed a Jewish girl bearing his cake during a birthday party. Oskar's friend, Scherner, soon arrives with a reprieve — and a warning:

JULIAN SCHERNER
We give you Jewish girls at five marks a day, Oskar. You should kiss us, not them. God forbid you ever get a real taste for Jewish skirt, there's no future in it. They don't have a future. That's not just good old fashioned Jew-hating talk. It's policy now.

Not even hell can remain in session forever. One morning in the spring of 1944, Oskar finds ash falling from the sky and covering everything, even his elegant Mercedes. They are not close enough to the death camps to ordinarily experience the rain of human remains. Oskar drives to Plaszow, where on the hill above the camp called Chukowa Gorka, but also profanely known as "Prick Hill," an enormous bonfire has been constructed — into which are being fed human bodies.

> "Chukowa Gorka, April, 1944. Department D orders Goeth to exhume and incinerate the bodies of more than ten thousand Jews killed at Plaszow and the Krakow ghetto massacre."

Goeth, of course, is mindful not of the human tragedy on a grand scale, but his own inconvenience:

GOETH
Can you believe this? As if I don't have enough to do, they come up with this? I have to find every rag buried up here and burn it. The party's over, Oskar. They're closing us down, sending everybody to Auschwitz as soon as I can arrange the shipments, maybe thirty, forty days. That ought to be fun.

Handkerchief over his mouth, it is all Oskar can do to stomach the sight of so many bodies being trundled to the fire of incineration. He is nearly unmanned when he *recognizes* one of them: little Genia in her red coat:

STERN
I know the destination. These are the evacuation orders. I'm to help arrange the shipments, put myself on the last train.

SCHINDLER
That's not what I was going to say. I made Goeth promise me he'd put in a good word for you. Nothing bad is going to happen to you there, you'll receive special treatment.

STERN
The directives coming in from Berlin talk about "special treatment" more and more often. I'd like to think that's not what you mean.

SCHINDLER
Preferential *treatment, all right? Do we have to create a new language?*

STERN
I think so. You're staying, I take it?

> SCHINDLER
> *In Krakow? What on earth for? No, I'm going home. I've done what I came here for. I've got more money than any man could spend in a lifetime. Someday, this is all going to end, you know. I was going to say we'll have a drink then.*

> STERN
> *I think I better have it now.*

And, wonder of wonders, he does. They've come to the end of the road, but the scholarly Jewish accountant has acknowledged the beefy German playboy as a *friend*. Or *is* it the end of the road?

That night, as his latest big-bosomed mistress sleeps soundly, Oskar paces his bedroom, while Billie Holiday's "God Bless the Child" playing on the radio. What had he told Emilie so long ago….? "Oskar Schindler," they'll say. "Everybody remembers him…He did something no one else did. He came here with nothing — a suitcase — and left with a steamer trunk — two steamer trunks full of money — all the riches of the world." There they are: the steamer trunks full of cash.

Both Thomas Keneally in the book and Steven Spielberg in the film tried to avoid the easy, dramatic employment of "moments of epiphany." But this may well be the moment when….

OSKAR SCHINDLER MAKES HIS STAND

He approaches *Kommandant* Goeth with an outrageous proposition that he be allowed to relocate his factory near his hometown of Zwittau in Czechoslovakia, and take his workers with him.

> GOETH
> *I don't understand. I mean, you want these people? Who are you, Moses? Come on, what is this? Where's the money in this? Look, you've got to move them, the equipment, everything to Czechoslovakia, pay for all that and build another camp. It doesn't make any sense.*

> SCHINDLER
> *Look, Amon, it's good for me. I know them; I'm familiar with them; I don't have to train them. It's good for you. I'll compensate you. It's good for the Army. You know what I'm going to make? Artillery shells. Tank shells. They need that. Everybody's happy.*

                    GOETH

Everybody's happy except me! You're probably scamming me somehow. If I'm making a hundred, you've got to be making three. And if you admit to making three, then it's four, actually. But how? Ja, all right, don't tell me. I'll go along with it. It's just irritating. I can't work it out.

                    SCHINDLER

All you have to do is tell me what it's worth to you. What's a person worth to you.

                    GOETH

No, no, no, no. What's one worth to you?

We next see Oskar dictating and Itzhak Stern typing out a list of names for transfer to the new camp in Brinnlitz, both men working from memory. Schindler paces and chain-smokes; Stern is by now comfortable enough with him to venture a small joke:

                    STERN

How many cigarettes have you smoked tonight?

                    SCHINDLER

Too many.

                    STERN

For every one you smoke, I smoke half.

The names climb into the hundreds, nearing a thousand, before the truth begins to dawn on an incredulous Stern:

                    STERN

What did Goeth say about this? You just told him how many people you needed and — you're not buying them. You're buying them? You're paying him for each of these names?

                    SCHINDLER

If you were still working for me, I'd expect you to talk me out of it, it's costing me a fortune.

(The writing of the List is, of course, simplified for the film. The real list went through several different drafts, and many more hands than those of Stern and Schindler, particularly those of the venal Marcel Goldberg.)

As the list nears 1,100, Oskar tells Stern to finish the page, leaving one space at the bottom. When Oskar presents the list to Goeth, the Kommandant immediately spots the omission. Oskar tells him the one name he wants to add: the maid, Helen Hirsch. Goeth balks — and Oskar offers to play "One hand of 21. If I win, the girl goes on my list."

> GOETH
> *I can't wager Helen in a card game... wouldn't be right. No, I want her to come back to Vienna with me. I want her to come to work for me there. I want to grow old with her... That's what I'd like to do. What I can do, if I'm any sort of a man, is the next most merciful thing. I should take her into the woods and shoot her painlessly in the back of the head. What was it you said for a natural 21?*

We don't immediately see the result of the wager. Instead, we cut to the train platform, and the Schindler workers identifying themselves, having their names checked off: the Dresners, the Rosners, the Nussbaums, Chaim Nowak, Rabbi Lewatow, Josef and Rebeka Bau, Mila and Poldek Pfefferberg, Goldberg, Stern — the many we know and the many more we don't.

The last one to register is Helen Hirsch.

The Nazis being the Nazis, the men are segregated onto one train, the women another. The men's train arrives at the railroad siding in Zwittau-Brinnlitz, where a towering figure in a Tyrolean hat welcomes them, inviting them to walk the short distance to the factory, where hot soup and bread is waiting for them. Oskar also promises that their womenfolk will follow them soon.

But the *Schindlerfrauen* are disembarked at a far different destination. Their train has pulled up inside the gates of a nightmare — a nightmare of great-coated SS guards and barking dogs herding them along. The sky is filled with a terrible ash, belching from the towering chimneys of the busy crematoria. Most frightening for Chaja Dresner (Miri Fabian) is the absence of something always taken for granted:

> CHAJA DRESNER
> *Where are the listmakers?*

Her daughter, Danka (Anna Mucha), already senses that they may be in a place beyond lists:

DANKA DRESNER
Mama, where are we?

In Brinnlitz, Schindler storms out the door, telling Stern, "They're in Auschwitz! The train was never routed here!"

But his arrival will be delayed. He cannot stop the chilling scene that happens next: the women's hair is cruelly cropped short, then they are ordered to strip naked and proceed to the showers for delousing. They've seen the smokestacks, felt the ash, and heard the rumors that what will come out of the nozzles isn't water but Zyklon-B gas.

Anxiety escalates to terror as the overhead lights are doused, and each woman, young and old, is stripped to her core, not only physically but mentally and emotionally. Then the nozzles open up —

It's water.

One more hour of life is still life.

The women are clothed in rags and taken to their barracks. The next day, they are subjected to a selection. This time, the medical man evaluating them is the infamous Doctor Josef Mengele (Daniel Del Ponte). The Schindler women make the cut, probably because they've been eating better while working for Schindler than most prisoners. But their health won't hold up long in this hell-hole. As the days lengthen, with no sight of their saviour, despair looms for some:

CLARA STERNBERG
They say that to fall against the fence is a kindness.

CHAJA DRESNER
Don't kill yourself against the fence, Clara! If you do, you'll never know what happened to you!

(Sound like a made-up, Hollywood line? It's absolutely real. This is how survivors survive!)

Eventually, Oskar arrives and goes straight to the top — the notorious Auschwitz commandant, Rudolf Hoess (Hans-Michael Rehberg):

HOESS
You are not the only industrialist who needs labor, Herr Schindler. I remember earlier this year, I.G. Farben ordered a trainload of Hungarians for his chemical factory. The train came in through the archway, and the officer in charge of the selection went immediately to work and sent two thousand of them straightaway to Special Treatment. It is not my task to interfere with the processes that take place down here. Why do you think I can help you if I can't help I.G. Farben?

SCHINDLER
Allow me to express the reason.

Oskar then opens a small bag and spills a small fortune in diamonds on the desk.

SCHINDLER

I'm not making any judgment about you. It's just that I know that in the coming months we're all going to need portable wealth.

HOESS

I do not say I am accepting them. All I say is, I'm not comfortable with them on the table. I have a shipment coming in tomorrow. I'll cut you three hundred units from it. New ones. These are fresh. The train comes, we turn it around, it's yours.

SCHINDLER

I understand. I want these.

HOESS

You shouldn't get stuck on names.

The color drains from Schindler's face, as he wonders if the women are already dead, but Hoess is regurgitating the same tired line spoken by the clerk, Tauber, on the platform in Krakow:

HOESS

That's right, it creates a lot of paperwork.

But the paperwork *is* executed, and the names of the *Schindlerfrauen* ring out in the frosty air. The half-dead women are escorted onto another train, but this one is bound *out* of hell. Schindler's struggle is still not won. SS NCOs are pulling the younger girls out of line, not believing those are "essential" workers.

SCHINDLER

What are you doing? These are mine. These are my workers. They should be on my train. They're skilled ammunition workers. They're essential. Essential girls!

When the NCO is unconvinced, Oskar grabs young Danka Dresner, shoving her hand in the guard's face:

SCHINDLER

Their fingers polish the inside of shell metal casings. How else am I to polish the inside of a 45 millimeter shell casing? You tell me. You tell me!

Of course, it's an absolutely outrageous lie, a typically brazen Schindler lie, but it works. The girls rejoin their mothers. Soon, the male workers of Brinnlitz are treated to the heart-stopping sight of 300 women clad in rags, their hair raggedly cropped, starved to the point of emaciation, coughing, and many bent with the cramps of dysentery, but it's *their* women. They're alive and they're here.

Actually, in the interests of time, the story has been vastly simplified. In reality, both Schindler trains wound up in concentration camps! The difference was that the men spent only a few days in Gross-Rosen and were fairly easily sprung. The rescue of the women from Auschwitz was far more complicated, and far more unlikely, and it's one of the few parts of the Schindler story where accounts vary widely. The details in Steve Zaillian's screenplay are chosen from several contradictory accounts, and in some cases, elements from the Gross-Rosen incident are transferred to Auschwitz. Nevertheless, the miraculous nature of Schindler's accomplishment in retrieving his women from the very bowels of hell itself simply cannot be overstated. Ironically enough, the reason the Schindler women spent so much time in Auschwitz was the arrest of their previous tormentor, Amon Goeth, not on charges of cruelty or brutality to his charges, which were

considered exemplary by his superiors, but because he had been robbing the camp and the Nazi government blind with his black market activities! Oskar, who'd been to prison twice before, was implicated by his old friend Goeth, and spent several weeks in custody answering questions. That time, his powerful friends had to move mountains to gain his release — and all that time, the *Schindlerfrauen* languished in Auschwitz.

In the film, Schindler then calls the SS guards together to tell them the rules — his rules:

> SCHINDLER
>
> *Under Department W provisions, it is unlawful to kill a worker without just cause. Under the Businesses Compensation Fund I am entitled to file damage claims for such deaths. If you shoot without thinking, you go to prison — I get paid. That's how it works. So there will be no summary executions here. There will be no interference of any kind with production. In hopes of ensuring that, guards will no longer be allowed on the factory floor without my authorization. For your cooperation, you have my gratitude.*

Oskar's gratitude is expressed in the usual manner: cases of schnapps are torn open and set out for the troopers. The SS Commandant, *Obersturmfuhrer* Josef Liepold (Ludger Pistor), is visibly agitated, but what can he do?

Oskar has one more fence to mend, being back in his hometown. He finds his wife at worship in a Catholic church:

> SCHINDLER
>
> *No doorman or maitre d' will ever mistake you again. I promise.*

(Maybe no wife in history has greater ground for bitterness than Emilie Schindler, who in reality was repeatedly betrayed and finally abandoned by her husband. Yet she ends her autobiography with the words, "I hope that as you close this book, you will want to make a toast for my husband — and for me, too." Go figure.)

Soon, in the film, Oskar is introducing Emilie around the factory. That's when a very worried Stern takes him aside:

> STERN
>
> *We've received an angry complaint from the Armaments Board. The artillery shells, tank shells, rocket casings — apparently all of them have failed quality-control tests.*

SCHINDLER
Well, that's to be expected. Start-up problems. This isn't pots and pans; this is a precise business. I'll write them a letter.

STERN
They're withholding payment.

SCHINDLER
Sure, so would I, so would you. I wouldn't worry about it. We'll get it right one of these days.

STERN
There's a rumor you've been going around miscalibrating the machines. They could shut us down, send us back to Auschwitz.

SCHINDLER
I'll call around, find out where we can buy shells, pass them off as ours.

STERN
I don't see the difference, whether they're made here or somewhere else.

SCHINDLER
You don't see a difference? I see a difference. Fewer shells will be made. Stern, if this factory ever produces a shell that can actually be fired, I'll be very unhappy.

If Stern is astonished by the new depth of Schindler's commitment, Rabbi Lewartow is even more bemused:

SCHINDLER
How are you doing, Rabbi? The sun is going down.

RABBI LEWARTOW
Yes, it is.

SCHINDLER
What day is it? Friday? It is Friday, isn't it? What's the matter with you? You should be preparing for the Sabbath, shouldn't you? I've got some wine in my office. Come.

As the Sabbath candle is lit, it blazes forth in color, as it did in the beginning of the film. And a title card tells us:

> "For the seven months it was fully operational, Schindler's Brinnlitz munitions factory was a model of non-production. During this same period, he spent millions of reichsmarks to sustain his workers and bribe Reich officials."

If this sounds like a great deal is being glossed over in the film, it is.

The Brinnlitz period was filled with incidents great and small illustrating the efforts not only of Oskar, but of Emilie Schindler, who threw herself wholeheartedly into the struggle to keep the Brinnlitz Jews not only alive, but healthy. Those included, on several occasions, the replacement of broken or ruined eyeglasses (which often involved tracking down the prescriptions in the dusty files of Krakow optometrists), continual bartering for food and medicines, and the most awe-inspiring accomplishment of all, actually written into Zaillian's screenplay, but excised for reasons of time: the rescue of the Golleschau Jews.

Those were more than a hundred inmates of Golleschau, a subcamp of Auschwitz, loaded into sealed cattle cars without food or water, and moved from siding to siding for ten days, covered in ice. When Schindler finally got the three sealed cars transferred to his siding, human cries and scratching were still audible, but the frozen locks had to be opened with axes and torches.

Inside, of the 100 prisoners deprived of food, water, and heat for ten days, thirteen had died; the others were but breathing skeletons, frozen to the metal, none weighing more than seventy pounds. Not only did Oskar, Emilie and the Brinnlitz prisoners clear space for these human wrecks and nurse them back to health — Emilie spooning milk, medicine, and hot farina into them, knowing that anything richer would induce fatal diarrhea — but Oskar carried them on his rolls at the full SS rate for able-bodied workers. For those who had died, he refused Kommandant Liepold's insistence that they be incinerated. Instead, he bought land in the nearby Catholic parish of Deutsch-Bielau and established a unique Jewish cemetery, where those "victims of a great murder," as Oskar put it, were buried in a proper Jewish manner, with Rabbi Lewartow reciting the Kaddish.

One Schindler Jew, Moshe Beijski, who later became a high court judge in Israel, insisted to Steven Spielberg that the Golleschau incident "…represents Schindler's greatest rescue and humanitarian deed, as well as of Mrs. Schindler."

Because it can't recount all of these incidents, the film skips to Itzhak Stern sheepishly entering Oskar's office:

> **STERN**
> *Do you have any money I don't know about? Hidden away someplace?*

> **SCHINDLER**
> *No. Why, am I broke?*

Oskar had said to Stern a few short months before, "I've got more money than any man could spend in a lifetime." No matter, the end is in sight, as Oskar pipes through the factory the distinctive voice of Winston Churchill, announcing the unconditional surrender of the Third Reich. Even though the majority of the workers don't understand English, they recognize this as a voice of authority, imparting momentous tidings.

Oskar calls all the workers together, to address them — and invites the guards, too:

> **SCHINDLER**
> *The unconditional surrender of Germany has just been announced. At midnight tonight, the war is over. Tomorrow, you'll begin the process of looking for survivors of your families. In most cases, you won't find them. After six long years of murder, victims are being mourned throughout the world. We've survived. Many of you have come up to me and thanked me. Thank yourselves. Thank your fearless Stern, and others among you who worried about you and faced death at every moment. I am a member of the Nazi Party. I'm a munitions manufacturer. I'm a profiteer of slave labor. I am a criminal. At midnight, you'll be free and I'll be hunted. I shall remain with you until five minutes after midnight, after which time, and I hope you'll forgive me, I have to flee.*

He then turns to the factory's SS guards:

> **SCHINDLER**
> *I know you have received orders from our commandant, which he has received from his superiors, to dispose of the population of this camp. Now would be the time to do it. Here they are; they're all here. This is your opportunity. Or — you could leave — and return to your families as men instead of murderers.*

There is just a moment of hesitation — then, one by one, the guards turn and leave, until only Kommandant Liepold remains — and he, too, finally exits. (In reality, he'd exited some time before. Oskar had feared that the real Liepold's complaints to his superiors would expose the charade of Brinnlitz, and so he arranged in his usual way for Liepold to get what he craved: a transfer to combat.)

Oskar locks eyes with Stern and exhales. A moment of silence is observed, then, Rabbi Lewartow begins to intone a blessing.

As Oskar and Emilie pack, a worker named Simon Jereth agrees to have his gold teeth pulled. The gold is melted down and a ring is fashioned.

At Midnight, Oskar prepares to leave. He is instructing Stern to distribute horded supplies of cloth, vodka, and cigarettes, so his *Schindlerjuden* will have something with which to begin new lives. They have gifts for him, too:

RABBI LEWARTOW
We've written a letter trying to explain things — in case you're captured. Every worker has signed it.

Stern then presents Oskar with the gold ring, translating the inscription: "It's Hebrew. It's from the Talmud. It says, 'Whoever saves one life, saves the world entire.'"

That's when Oskar is hit by the enormity of what he has done, and what he hasn't done:

SCHINDLER
I could have got more out. I could have got more. I don't know, if I'd just — I could have got more.

STERN
Oskar, there are 1,100 people who are alive because of you. Look at them.

SCHINDLER
If I'd made more money — I threw away so much money, you have no idea! If I'd just —

STERN
There will be generations because of what you did.

SCHINDLER
I didn't do enough! *This car... Goeth would've bought this car... ten people right there. Ten people. Ten more people. This pin... two people. This is gold... two more people. He would have given me two for it, at least one... one more person. A person, Stern... for this. I could have gotten one more person — and I didn't!*

The workers of Brinnlitz come forward to comfort their savior.

The foregoing scene is completely fictitious, and yet, it's filled with truth. In reality, Oskar left the Brinnlitz factory quietly and secretively. There *was* no "breakdown" scene, and yet, Spielberg's movie is nearly done, and he needs, somehow, to communicate the truth of the remaining twenty-nine years of Oskar's life during which the roles were reversed. The *Schindlerjuden* had been dependent on Oskar throughout the war, but from that point on, *he* was dependent on *them*, both materially and spiritually.

Screenwriter Zaillian and director Spielberg crafted a scene of fiction, and into it, they condensed more than a quarter-century of the deepest shared emotion. Itzhak Stern may have captured the incredible depth of this emotion in testimony at Yad Vashem in 1962:

"My brothers, in the Hebrew language, there are three definitions of a human being; first he is born a man; secondly, he grows into a person; and third, he becomes like Adam, a full human being. Now, I think, there should be a last, and additional, stage, and it should be called Oskar Schindler."

Oskar and Emilie then climb into striped prison uniforms (historically accurate) and leave the factory with several of the Jewish workers, the idea being to pass as escaped prisoners until they can reach the American lines (which they eventually did). The next morning, the *Schindlerjuden* are waiting beside the factory as a lone Russian officer (Jan Jurewicz) rides up on a horse, and grandly announces:

RUSSIAN OFFICER
You have been liberated by the Soviet army!

Asked where they should go, he has few options to offer:

RUSSIAN OFFICER
Don't go east, that's for sure. They hate you there. I wouldn't go west either, if I were you.

CHAIM NOWAK

We could use some food.

RUSSIAN OFFICER

Isn't that a town over there?

Well, of course it is, but it requires a major attitude adjustment for these folks to begin thinking and acting as free men and women. As uplifting music plays (an odd choice, "Yerushalayim Shel Zahav," or "Jerusalem of Gold," written at the time of the Six-Day War), we see them walking toward us, toward life, toward the future. Two title cards wrap up unfinished business for us:

"Amon Goeth was arrested while a patient at a sanitarium in Bad Tolz. He was hanged in Krakow for crimes against humanity."

"Oskar Schindler failed at his marriage and several businesses after the war. In 1958, he was declared a righteous person by the council of the Yad Vashem in Jerusalem, and invited to plant a tree in the Avenue of the Righteous. It grows there still."

Then, an amazing transformation takes place. The picture shifts, for the first time, into glorious color, the cloudy sky turns a dazzling blue, and the people marching toward the viewer become "The Schindler Jews today."

Two by two, they march past Oskar's gravestone in Jerusalem's Catholic Cemetery, the real-life Schindler Jews, accompanied by the actors who portrayed them in the film, each laying a pebble on the gravestone in memoriam: Danka Dresner and Olek Rosner, now of course middle-aged adults, Josef and Rebeka Bau, the musicians Henri and Leo Rosner, Helen Hirsch, Mila Pfefferberg, and her husband Leopold/Poldek, who has at last kept his promise to his old friend. With Itshak Stern having died a quarter-century before, Ben Kingsley is accompanied by Stern's widow. Emilie Schindler is pushed in a wheelchair by her portrayer, Caroline Goodall. On and on come the *Schindlerjuden,* laying their stones, while a title card puts it all in perspective:

"There are fewer than four thousand Jews left alive in Poland today. There are more than six thousand descendants of the Schindler Jews."

Thomas Keneally's book ends with the simple words, "He was mourned on every continent."

THE BALANCE SHEET

The message of *MacArthur* and *Schindler's List* is not new to them. It has been conveyed since the earliest films. In *The Grapes of Wrath* (1940), the screen adaptation of John Steinbeck's harrowing account of the "Okies" and how they were dispossessed by the deadly combination of the Dust Bowl and the Depression, this same sentiment finds its voice in the central character of Tom Joad (Henry Fonda), as he prepares to leave his family, probably forever, and his mother asks, Where will you go? Tom's answer represents the culmination of his own grappling with the ideas of life and death, right and wrong, and eternity. Tom has arrived at the conclusion that a man is not isolated unto himself, that "maybe we're all part of one big soul somewhere." And so it's alright, he says, "I'll be around in the dark…I'll be everywhere. Wherever you can look, wherever there's a fight so hungry people can eat, I'll be there. Wherever there's a cop beatin' up a guy, I'll be there. I'll be there in the way guys yell when they're mad. I'll be there in the kids' laugh when they're hungry and they know supper's ready. And when people are eatin' the stuff they raised and livin' in the houses they built, I'll be there, too."

"I'll be there"…Walter Cronkite used to host a program called *You Are There*, and that's the idea. We are there when one human being *helps* another — and we are there when one human being *hurts* another. When an old lady dies in Israel because a terrorist set off a bomb, that's *your* grandmother who's just been killed. When a little boy in Ethiopia stops breathing because he didn't get enough food to sustain him, that's *your* son who just died. When a drunk driver plows head-on into an oncoming car, that's *your* daughter who's just been snuffed out. When a madman orders the systematic destruction of an entire race, those are *your* fathers, *your* mothers, *your* brothers, *your* sisters who are herded into gas chambers, or worked to death in mines, or experimented on to change their eye color — whenever a human being is victimized, *we are there*, and we are there with the victims. We must be. We are required to be. This is not something that would be nice if we did it, this is something that you and I are *required* to do. We are *required* to dispose of our own partialities based on race, based on sex, based on color, based on beliefs — because when we fail to do this, when we fail in our duty to identify with all men, and all women, everywhere, men and women suffer, and they die. Every

enslavement, every rape, every degradation, every lynching, every murder, and especially any attempt at genocide, can be traced to that basic failure to *identify with the other* — be it the other man, the other woman, or the other race. *On this one point hinges the future of the human race*, and if we cannot manage this jump from inhumanity to humanity — we may well not deserve a future.

The question unanswered by Keneally's book, and by Spielberg's film, is: why did Oskar Schindler do what he did? It's been debated for more than half a century. Some say he loved Jews; some say he loved playing the role of father-protector; some say he loved living on the edge and taking risks. There is even a certain cynical element that says Oskar did it to save his own skin, that he saw the handwriting on the wall, and that he set out to ensure that he would not be tried as a war criminal for having used slave labor, but would, rather, be celebrated as a savior.

Possible? Of course. Even some of the *Schindlerjuden* themselves believe this, though they're quick to tell you that it doesn't matter why he did what he did — it matters that he *did* it. Does the idea of Oskar the cynic, an Oskar whose rescue of "his" women from Hell, his wheeling and dealing, risk-taking, and spending into bankruptcy resolves into play-acting, with no real concern for the people he was saving — does that idea hold water?

Not for this writer.

The truth, it is said, is in the details, and certain details that were omitted from the film have the ring of truth. When Itzhak Stern died of a heart attack in 1969, witnesses say that Oskar, when told, cried like a baby and wouldn't be consoled. If this was play-acting, it was certainly unnecessary at that point. Back in Oskar's heyday, when he was running his factories and people were finding relative safety there, he liked to give his workers cigarettes — not much of a gift by today's standards, but profoundly appreciated then. Thing is, he couldn't just give the cigarettes to his workers, not with the Nazis watching — so he'd light a smoke for himself, take one drag, and toss it on the floor where a worker could pick it up a short time later.

Do these images square with the image of *Herr Direktor* Schindler cynically using "his" Jews as instruments of his own deliverance? Not for me, but maybe I don't want them to. In the end, the survivors themselves have it right: it doesn't matter why he did what he did — it matters that he *did* it.

Dr. Stanley Robbin, born Samek Rubinstein in Krakow, worked as a doctor in Oskar's Emalia factory. He didn't make the list, for which Oskar later apologized, but instead, he went on to endure — and ultimately survive — the Mauthausen death camp.

In front of City Hall in Long Beach, Long Island, there stands a monument erected by Dr. Robbin. It honors four men: Raoul Wallenberg, the Swedish diplomat who arranged the deliverance of so many Jews; Father Maximilian Kolbe, a Franciscan friar and a journalist, who substituted himself for a condemned man at Auschwitz; Janusc Korshak, a Polish pediatrician, educator, and radio personality, who went to his death with the children from his orphanage, and Oskar Schindler. The inscription reads, "Their brother's keepers." Whatever else he may have been, Oskar Schindler was, indeed, his brother's keeper.

James T. Kirk's Starship Enterprise, *recreated as a museum ship.*

STUDY VI

Trek El Grande or *Trek* Pure Spirit?

All ten films examined so far were made well before the turn of the century. Does this mean that "they don't make movies like they used to," or that there are no current films that "get it right?"

Hardly. The sheer volume of movies released by both the major studios and the increasingly influential independents invokes the "infinite number of monkeys" theory: now and then, the magic combination will be hit, if only by accident.

Remarkable people are still making remarkable pictures. The one-time Dirty Harry, Clint Eastwood, has been responsible for an astonishing number of exceptionally moving films: *Letters From Iwo Jima, Changeling, Invictus, Million Dollar Baby,* and the powerful *Gran Torino,* in which he fuses his two public images as tough-guy actor and sensitive filmmaker.

The year 2010 was kicked off by two utterly dissimilar films: Sandra Bullock's *The Blind Side,* the true-life story of a poor Black youth who blossoms into a football prodigy and a fine man after being "adopted" by a well-to-do White family, and James Cameron's *Avatar,* decisively demonstrating that a special-effects-heavy, largely computer-generated epic can still be filled with love, compassion, and nobility. Surprisingly, both of these resonated, in their different ways, with huge throngs of eager moviegoers.

Elsewhere, *Milk,* with Sean Penn as the San Francisco City Supervisor who was shot to death, succeeded in presenting its protagonist as an American hero who, gay agenda aside, gave his life for his country and its best values. *I Am Legend,* with a moving performance by Will Smith, came tantalizingly close to giving Richard Matheson's story of New York City's sole survivor of vampirism its proper due, quite amazing in light of the fact that the property has been bastardized in at least four different previous adaptations, including 1964's *The Last Man On Earth* with Vincent Price, and the Charlton Heston version, *The Omega Man*, in 1973.

Still, movies that are both thoughtful and entertaining remain very much the exception as opposed to the rule. Even the very best of the twenty-first century films too often adhere to the new Holy Writ: to connect with a "modern" audience, a picture must unfold at a dizzying pace — *as though the audience's decreasing attention span is something to be catered to, rather than something to be resisted* — and it must be filled to the brim with "attitude," best expressed as "Don't mess with me, sucker!"

Two films from the late 2000s best express the pros and cons of adhering to The New Wisdom. Paramount's pull-out-all-the-stops re-imagining of *Star Trek*, and Renegade Studios' love letter to the fans, *Star Trek: Of Gods and Men*, are both dedicated to Gene Roddenberry, the man with the original vision. Both are exceptionally entertaining films, but no two movies based on the same theme could possibly be more different.

I like to think of them as *Star Trek: El Grande* and *Star Trek: Pure Spirit*.

Gene Roddenberry, the Great Bird of the Galaxy.

STAND ELEVEN: *STAR TREK* (2009)

(4/6/2009: Paramount) Directed by J. J. Abrams; Written by Roberto Orci and Alex Kurtzman; Music by Michael Giacchino; Photographed by Dan Mindel; Edited by Maryann Brandon and Mary Jo Markey.

STAND TWELVE: *STAR TREK: OF GODS AND MEN*

(12/22/2007: Renegade) Directed by Tim Russ; Written by Ethan H. Calk, Sky Douglas Conway and Jack Treviño; Music by Justin R. Durban; Photographed by Douglas Knapp; Edited by Joyce Brand.

"I have no belief that *Star Trek* depicts the actual future. If this is not the way we really are, it seems to me most certainly a way we *ought* to be. During its voyages, the starship *Enterprise* always carried much more than mere respect and tolerance for other life forms and ideas — it carried the more positive force of love for the almost limitless variety within our universe. It is this capacity for *love for all things* which has always seemed to me the first indication that an individual or a race is approaching adulthood. While we humans may still be a considerable distance from understanding *truth*, or even being able to cope with it, I believe we are at last beginning to understand that *love* is somehow integral to *truth*. Perhaps it demarks the path leading there."

— Gene Roddenberry

After the original series, covered in our Stands Five "Arena" and Six "The Doomsday Machine," *Star Trek* underwent a unique and unprecedented metamorphosis, from a failed network television show to a part of the fabric of American culture, all in only a quarter-century. This involved three separate and identifiable, bona-fide miracles.

Star Trek: The Motion Picture (1979): Following the program's cancellation, three concepts rescued it from sliding into obscurity: *Syndication* — playing at earlier times on independent stations (often as an alternative to the 6 p.m news), *Star Trek* found the loyal viewers who had missed its late-night network airings; *Demographics* — after the cancellation, network and studios began to measure audiences in terms of age and income, rather than raw numbers, and began to sense what a gold mine they'd let slip through their fingers; *Conventions* — just beginning to be a viable expression of fan enthusiasm, these started in the 1970s to feature *Star Trek*, and eventually to be dominated by it. When fandom refused to let the show die (it even resurfaced briefly as a Saturday morning kiddies' program), Paramount decided that a new series called *Star Trek: Phase Two* would be the flagship of their proposed Fourth Network. That concept faded about the same time that *Star Wars* enriched the moguls at 20th Century-Fox beyond the dreams of avarice, and Paramount searched about for a concept that would go and do likewise for them. Thus, Kirk and his Federation colleagues found themselves at the center of the most expensive (at the time) picture ever made.

Star Trek: The Wrath of Khan (1982): though it established the U.S.S. *Enterprise* and crew on the big screen, *ST: TMP* had emerged as a slow-moving, pastel-colored "tone poem," completely missing the joyous, tap-dancing spirit of the original. Effectively, the franchise was a beached whale, but Paramount head honcho Charlie Bluhdorn tapped television producer (*The Mod Squad, The Six-Million Dollar Man*) Harve Bennett, with two key questions: could he make a more interesting film than *ST: TMP*, and do it for less than a quarter of its $45 million dollar budget? Bennett did, screening all the television episodes to see what made them tick, and then, hand-in-hand with an up-and-coming writer-director named Nick Meyer, redesigning uniforms (which had looked like pajamas in *ST: TMP*), lighting and tone, and employing Ricardo Montalban to recreate his villainous role from the first-season episode *Space Seed*. The result: *The Wrath of Khan*, simply one of the most entertaining films of *any* genre ever made, and the one that kicked the entire *Star Trek* franchise back into its natural groove. Many consider the trilogy of the second, third and fourth films — *The Wrath of Khan, The Search for Spock*, and *The Voyage Home* — to be the high-water mark of original *Star Trek*. No argument will be offered here.

Star Trek: The Next Generation (1987): rightly or wrongly, Gene Roddenberry had been blamed by Paramount for both the artistic flaccidity and the extravagant cost of *ST: TMP*, and subsequently removed from any of the decision making processes surrounding the future films — his comments were listened to respectfully (or not) and generally ignored. Nevertheless, the studio did employ the Great Bird to achieve perhaps his most awesome accomplishment: *he captured lightning in a bottle a second time!* Nothing did more to verify Roddenberry's vision of a future of peaceful co-existence and joy in diversity than *Star Trek: The Next Generation*, where, once again, superb casting, daring storylines and a stubborn adherence to vision produced superior and meaningful entertainment. True, the new series took well into its third year to "find" itself — that's about the time that Original Series cast members like Jimmy Doohan and Walter Koenig stopped dissing *The Next Generation* and began to praise it — but it eventually settled in as a worthy successor to the initial series, actually surpassing it in some areas, and serving as the first of many incarnations, some fairly true, and some less so, to *le vision Roddenberry*.

STAR TREK IN THE TWENTY-FIRST CENTURY

By the late 2000s, many considered *Star Trek* to be at worst played out, at best stalled out. The tenth and most recent feature film, *Star Trek: Nemesis*, had sputtered at the box office, and perhaps for good reason: Producer Rick Berman, who had succeeded Roddenberry as bearer of the Trekkian torch, and screenwriter John Logan went way off-track, pointlessly marrying First Officer Riker and Counselor Troi, whose romance had decidedly cooled during *The Next Generation's* seven seasons, then turning the cautious Captain Picard into a dune-buggy (!) daredevil, and, finally, asking us to believe that the villainous Shinzon — played by Tom Hardy, who, despite a shaved head, looks and sounds nothing like Patrick Stewart — was an exact clone of Picard!

On the television side, *The Next Generation*, *Deep Space Nine* (in many ways, the most meaningfully *written* of all the incarnations) and *Voyager* had come and gone, each leaving voluntarily after a seven-year run — but, in 2005, the prequel *Enterprise*, after only four seasons, became the first *Star Trek* series since the original to be cancelled, and Berman's tenure as the Prime Trekker suffered a similar fate.

That's about when two entirely separate revival efforts began.

Stand Six, "The Doomsday Machine," details how James Cawley used his earnings as an Elvis impersonator to finance a series of fan-produced films on the Internet. These continued to improve in quality by leaps and bounds, attracting actors from the original series: Supporting players Eddie "Lieutenant Leslie" Paskey and John "Commander Kyle"

Winston, followed by guest stars such as William Windom, BarBara Luna, Malachi Throne and Mary Linda Rapelye and finally three of the principals, Walter Koenig, George Takei and Grace Lee Whitney. (Even Majel Barrett added her voice talents for the "Next on *Star Trek*" promos). Commendably, Cawley continued the *Star Trek* tradition of combating bigotry by introducing a character — a nephew of Kirk's — who is openly

Three Starfleet Captains confront a menace from the past in Star Trek: Of Gods and Men. *The gold-shirted officer at right is producer Sky Conway.*

gay. Paramount gave its "backhanded" approval of the Internet series in a curious manner: Cawley (and others) may produce "off-brand" *Star Trek* product, *as long as they don't profit from it.*

Paramount, of course, was involved in its own effort to resuscitate its staggering cash cow. Believing a major jumpstart to be in order, they approached writer-producer-director J. J. Abrams, riding high on the crest of the television series *Lost* and *Alias*, plus motion pictures, including *Mission Impossible III,* and the truly clever *Cloverfield*, a sort of "Godzilla in the Big Apple" as seen through the hand-held video camera of a participant.

Like most major filmmakers from Eastwood and Spielberg back to John Ford, Abrams has his hard core of repeat collaborators, with whom he sat down to "break" the task of re-creating *Star Trek* for modern audiences. For better or worse, the key question they asked was: how do we make it cool? The answer wasn't entirely original — Harve Bennett had wanted to do something similar as far back as *Star Trek VI: The Undiscovered Country* — cast new (and younger) actors in the roles made famous by Shatner, Nimoy and company in the Original Series, and fashion the new movie as a "prequel" to that series.

The genesis of the "other" film dates back also to *Undiscovered Country*: that's when Nichelle "Uhura" Nichols talked with producer Sky Conway about doing their own *Star Trek* film. This idea was bandied about with other *Star Trek* veterans, from both sides of the camera, from all the different *Star Trek* incarnations, and evolved into the idea of a 40th Anniversary "gift to the fans" that would celebrate the ideas and ideals that Roddenberry had originally envisioned and espoused. Partnering with James Cawley and his existing operation gave the renegade filmmakers, who had appropriately called themselves Renegade Studios, access to his painstakingly-crafted Original Series sets, costumes and props — so incredibly close that Nichols took one look and declared she'd "come home," while Koenig called them better than the originals. So, while Abrams and company evolved their concept of *Star Trek* (2009) — no holds barred, balls-to-the-wall — the Renegades worked up their own project, still an Internet venture, but about halfway between the fan-based projects and a full-fledged, professional production — a labor of love about the human adventure, or *Star Trek: Of Gods and Men*.

Considering the differences in conception and execution, what is amazing is not that the two films should show such wide discrepancies — but that they should demonstrate an astonishing number of *similarities*.

STAR TREK (2009)	STAR TREK: OF GODS AND MEN
Romulan Commander Nero and the crew of the Narada *travel back in time just before the birth of Jim Kirk, and changes history.*	*Charlie Evans, a human with advanced mental abilities, travels back in time just before the birth of Jim Kirk and changes history.*
The ships and equipment of the Original Series era updated to meet the expectations of "modern" audiences.	*The ships and equipment of the Original Series era are painstakingly recreated to match the expectations of longtime fans.*

STAR TREK (2009)	STAR TREK: OF GODS AND MEN
Starfleet uniforms, while resembling those seen in The Original Series, are modified and redesigned.	*Starfleet uniforms, whether from The Original Series or the Kirk-era movies, are precisely duplicated.*
Outside of Leonard Nimoy as the "original" Spock, all familiar roles are recast with new, younger actors.	*Whenever possible, familiar roles are cast with the original actors, from regulars such as Nichelle Nichols and Walter Koenig, to guest stars such as Lawrence Montaigne.*
While some characters, most notably Kirk and McCoy, act like themselves, others undergo inexplicable changes, including a harsher, much more assertive Uhura and a more playful but less responsible Scott.	*Everyone behaves very much "in character" — at least until the sharply altered timeline produces radical changes, especially in Chekov and Harriman.*
Cadet Kirk dallies with a fellow cadet: a beautiful green-skinned Orion girl.	Conqueror *Captain Harriman's Communications Officer is also his slave: a beautiful green-skinned Orion girl.*
Nyota Uhura falls for a Vulcan (Spock).	*Nyota Uhura falls for a Vulcan (Stonn).*
The planet Vulcan is blown up!	*The planet Vulcan is blown up!*
Memories of the "proper" timeline are conveyed by Vulcan Mind Meld (older Spock, or "Spock Prime," to Kirk).	*Memories of the "proper" timeline are conveyed by Vulcan Mind Meld (Uhura to Tuvok, Tuvok to Khitrec/ Chekov — "My life. My choice."*

STAR TREK (2009)

The heroes defeat the machinations of Nero and his renegade Romulans, but the timeline changes are not resolved: Vulcan is not restored, while Kirk and the crew of the Enterprise *have altered pasts — and altered futures!*

STAR TREK: OF GODS AND MEN

The heroes defeat the machinations of Curate Prime and the Galactic Order, restoring the "normal" timeline, although some have learned lessons from the alternate timeline, most especially Captain Uhura, who has discovered how much she loves the Vulcan Stonn.

So, the similarities in the "official" and "unofficial" versions mount up, coincidentally, or not. A fair comparison of the two takes us into the areas of plot, casting, special effects, and adherence to canon — the established history of the *Star Trek* universe.

PLOT — *STAR TREK* (2009)

The future meets the past, with devastating results: a gargantuan Romulan starship from the late twenty-fourth century arrives in the early twenty-third, a quarter-century before the events of the Original Series, attacking and overwhelming the Federation survey ship *Kelvin*. After *Kelvin* Captain Robau is killed, First Officer George Kirk pilots the mortally wounded ship into the Romulan vessel, buying time for the crew and passengers to flee in small shuttlecraft — including Kirk's wife Winona, who has gone into premature labor, and gives early birth to their son James Tiberius, just one of many differences, large and small, from the *Star Trek* universe we know.

The film then traces the childhoods of the rebellious young Kirk, raised in the home of a none-too-sympathetic uncle, and Spock, the son of the Vulcan Sarek and the human Amanda Grayson, who struggles to reconcile his dual heritage.

Both wind up at Starfleet Academy in San Francisco, and Kirk is seen accomplishing what had first been mentioned back in *Star Trek: The Wrath of Khan*, becoming the first cadet to defeat the no-win *Kobayashi Maru* training scenario (page 282), by re-programming the simulator. (It's this film's most meaningful acknowledgement of existing *Star Trek* chronology.) This lands Kirk in hot water with the Academy administration, and with the officer who had programmed the scenario: Spock.

Before Kirk's case can be decided, an emergency on Vulcan causes the senior cadets to be called to duty, except for Kirk, who is under academic suspension, but is nevertheless smuggled aboard the newly commissioned *Enterprise* by his friend, Doctor McCoy. There, Kirk's quick, outside-the-box thinking enables him to deduce that they're heading into an ambush — laid by the *Narada*, the very Romulan ship that destroyed the

Kelvin twenty-five years before. Kirk's timely warning saves his own ship, but Captain Pike is taken prisoner by the Romulans, the other starships are destroyed, and the *Narada* succeeds in destroying the planet Vulcan.

Acting *Enterprise* Captain Spock attempts to rendezvous with the rest of the fleet, while headstrong Kirk challenges that decision, insisting that they pursue the *Narada*, which is on its way to do to Earth what it had done to Vulcan. Spock then maroons Kirk on the nearby ice planet Delta Vega, where Kirk encounters an elderly version of — Spock himself. This is the Spock we know (Leonard Nimoy), the one from "our" universe, who was last seen on *The Next Generation* on the planet Romulus.

It is Old Spock (sounds like an after-shave; the film credits call him Spock Prime) who unravels the mysteries: in the future, he had tried to save the planet Romulus from a super-nova — and failed. *Narada* Captain Nero had blamed the destruction of his home planet on both Spock and the Federation, and when he and Spock were thrown backwards in time, he vowed to destroy Vulcan, Earth and all other Federation planets, thus rendering the universe safe for Romulus and Romulans.

With the help of Spock Prime and extraordinary engineer Montgomery Scott, Kirk is able to return to the *Enterprise*, wrest command from Spock, and save the Earth from Nero — in the process, establishing the unique friendship with Spock that will, in the words of Spock Prime, "define you both."

Alan Ruck as the untested Enterprise-B *Captain John Harriman, in* Star Trek Generations *(1994). The crewman at right is Tim Russ, who directed Ruck twelve years later in* Star Trek: Of Gods and Men.

PLOT — *STAR TREK: OF GODS AND MEN*

What better way to honor Roddenberry's twenty-third century storyline than to pick up where it officially ended? *Star Trek Generations* — the film that officially passed the torch to the Next Generation — set its prologue in the twenty-third century, with Kirk, Scott and Chekov as honored guests on hand for the launch of the newest *Enterprise*, NCC-1701-B, under the command of Captain John Harriman. When the unblooded (and incomplete) ship responds to a distress call from two refugee vessels under attack by a giant "energy ribbon," the vets, of course, take over, but Kirk, saving the day, is supposedly killed.

Kirk will eventually be found by Captain Picard in the next century — as will Scotty, for that matter — but this is where the official movie and television *Star Trek* history of the twenty-third century ends.

Of Gods and Men picks up twelve years later, with three Starfleet captains — Chekov, Uhura, and a much more confident Harriman — attending the dedication of NCC-1701-M, "M" for Museum — an

exact replica of the *Enterprise* from Kirk's first five-year mission. In what Chekov correctly terms "déjà vu all over again," the ship is called away from its ceremonial observations by a distress call.

What they find harkens back to two first-season episodes. The Guardian of Forever, the mysterious time portal from "The City On The Edge of Forever," has been taken over by Charlie Evans, from "Charlie X." As a teenager, he had nearly destroyed the *Enterprise* with his extraordinary mental powers until taken in hand by the extraterrestrial Thasians. Forty years later, he blames the late Kirk for failing to help him, and steps inside the Guardian to wreak his vengeance — thus remaking history.

And what a remake. A much harsher Harriman now commands the G.S.S. *Conqueror*, a rechristened *Enterprise* now in the service of something called the Galactic Order, an evil empire which includes many races of the former Federation *and its enemies:* Terrans, Klingons, Romulans and more. Not everyone has joined the Order: Chekov is part of the inevitable rebellion, an embittered "freedom fighter" calling himself Khitrec, which is Russian for "fox." Uhura is living on Vulcan, where she has married Stonn, Spock's onetime romantic rival (in "Amok Time"), and left Starfleet, along with other officers such as Tuvok from the television series *Voyager* and Spock (unseen here, but referenced).

It is Uhura — who, along with Chekov and Harriman, was present when Charlie changed history — who harbors memories of the "correct" timeline. When these memories are passed to Khitrec/Chekov by a mortally wounded Tuvok, the three who had been Starfleet colleagues, but are bitter enemies in this timeline, must put aside their present enmity to accomplish the greater good: defeat the Galactic Order, and persuade a repentant Charlie to undo the depredations he has wrought by killing Jim Kirk's mother before she could give birth to him. (This had led to the birth of the Order, founded by Curate Prime, who turns out to be Gary Mitchell, Spock's predecessor as *Enterprise* First Officer, who gained superhuman powers — and a huge dose of megalomania — in the series [second] pilot, "Where No Man Has Gone Before." In the manner of *It's A Wonderful Life*, the absence of Kirk — the man who stopped Mitchell — has led to the ghastly consequences of the Order.)

CASTING — *STAR TREK* (2009)

Hands down, the best casting here is Karl Urban as Doctor McCoy: he accepts the challenge of playing not just Bones McCoy, but Bones McCoy as created by DeForest Kelley: this is indeed the Doctor McCoy we've come to know and love. Close on Urban's heels comes Chris Pine as Captain Kirk: by turns cocky, audacious, determined and humorous, he wisely avoids any attempt to copy William Shatner's individualistic and highly imitated delivery, but cleverly allows little flashes of Shatner to peep out now and then, usually in expression or inflection.

From here on, the fealty of the characterizations to their initial models varies. Zachary Quinto's Spock *looks* uncannily like Leonard Nimoy's, but Nimoy always played the part with a bemused, almost facetious air. (Think of McCoy in "I, Mudd," lamenting that a certain crewman will not report for his physical, and Spock's reply: "He is probably terrified of your beads and rattles.") This lightness is utterly missing in Quinto's Spock, and is replaced with an air of barely contained anger; that might be appropriate after Vulcan is destroyed, but Quinto starts *out* that way.

The same hostile attitude seems to be present in Zoe Saldana's Uhura: the Communications Officer was always a strong willed-woman, but she carried herself with an air of regal nobility; Saldana's street-smart toughness hits a jarring note.

Perhaps the filmmakers have slipped into a most un-Roddenberry-like mindset: They seem to have forgotten that Uhura is much more than a black woman, just as Sulu in more than an Asian, Chekov more than a Russian, and Scotty more than a son of the old sod. In the latter case, not only Simon Pegg in this film, but also the actors who played Scotty in Cawley's *New Voyages* seemed to go for the accent first and the character

second. Thus, Pegg's Scotty has a better brogue than Jimmy Doohan ever did, but it's hard envisioning this light-hearted elf commanding the *Enterprise* in Kirk and Spock's absence. Likewise, John Cho's Sulu is a bit off, not because Cho is Korean where George Takei is Japanese — but because Cho is dour where Takei, that most "scrutable" of Asians, is unremittingly joyful.

Other actors recreating established roles are, as the saying goes, close enough for government work: Anton Yelchin as Chekov, Ben Cross and Winona Rider as Spock's parents, and Bruce Greenwood as the ramrod-straight Captain Pike, which was originally rendered in one-note fashion by Jeffrey Hunter. As the villainous Nero, Eric Bana is a bit over-the-top, but the role, as written, allows him little else.

Leonard Nimoy, the only returning original, unless you count Majel Barrett's voice-overs as the ship's computer, carries the part of Spock Prime with a old pro's grace — along with a subtle shift in emphasis that suggests that Spock has, in old age, resolved all conflict over his dual heritage.

CASTING — *STAR TREK: OF GODS AND MEN*

The whole point here is to stick with the originals, and in so doing, to give them the chance to soar.

Walter Koenig and Nichelle Nichols are more than up to the challenge: the story calls for a range and depth of emotions, obvious and

subtle, never required of them before. Both hit the ball out of the park; Nichols, in particular, is the conscience of the film. The third lead, Alan Ruck, revels in his opportunity to add muscle to a character who had been little more than a bewildered greenhorn in *Star Trek Generations*. Interestingly, the leads had been designed for Koenig, Nichols, and George Takei as Sulu; Takei's unavailability opened the door for Ruck to reprise Captain Harriman.

Two other actors were willing but unavailable to re-enact their parts: in place of Gary Lockwood, the villainous Gary Mitchell/Curate Prime is played by voice actor Daamen Krall, who is more than a little over-the-top, but it's plausible that forty years as a "god" might have made him such a sadistic bully.

More successful is William Wellman, Jr. (page 297), who played John Bulkeley, the P.T. boat skipper who rescues the title character from Corregidor in our Stand Nine, *MacArthur* — as the story's prime mover, Charlie Evans. Wellman looks, sounds, *moves* like Robert Walker,

Junior's troubled teenager — or, more to the point, as he would be forty years later.

Much of the charm in *Of Gods and Men* derives from the fact that it is very much a labor of love, featuring actors from the broad spectrum of *Star Trek* incarnations. Director Tim Russ reprises his role as the Vulcan Tuvok from *Voyager*. Other cast members Garrett Wang (Harry Kim)

and Ethan Phillips (Neelix) are on hand as, respectively, the sinister security chief of the *Conqueror*, and a hapless Starfleet data clerk. From *Deep Space Nine* come Cirroc Lofton (The Sisko Kid) as Uhura's son, J.G. Hertzler (Chancellor Martok; he also appeared on *Voyager* and *Enterprise*) as *Conqueror* First Officer Koval, and Chase Masterson (the Dabo girl Leeta), who brings unusual depth to the part of Xela, the Orion slave girl/communications officer. *Enterprise* is represented by Gary Graham as Khitrec's fellow freedom fighter, the shape-changing Ragnar, and Crystal Allen as the *Conqueror* navigator.

Two more Original Series actors are back in the parts they originated. Grace Lee Whitney is once again Janice Rand, who was the captain's yeoman in the first season and appeared in three films, *Voyager*, and a Cawley episode.

As for Lawrence Montaigne *(opposite page and above)*, who published his autobiography, *A Vulcan Odyssey*, after appearing in *Star Trek: Of Gods and Men*, *Star Trek* had never been that big a part of his career at the time, but only in retrospect:

"I worked as an actor for over forty years and made a comfortable living. I did more than twenty-five films; in some of them I played the lead. I did over two hundred guest-star shots on episodic television. But the only things I am remembered for by the fans are the two roles I played on *Star Trek*. Ain't life a bitch?"

His involvement came tantalizingly close to being a lot more: At the end of the first season, Leonard Nimoy wanted out, and Gene Roddenberry tapped Montaigne, based on his strong facial resemblance, to take over the part of Spock, "…but the bottom line is that Nimoy recanted… and re-signed for another season. Nimoy in. Montaigne out!"

His two roles were Decius, a Romulan officer in "Balance of Terror," and Stonn, the Vulcan who challenges Spock for the hand of T'Pring in "Amok Time." It is the second role that he was asked to recreate in *Of Gods and Men*, and it's an intriguing portrayal: the angry young Vulcan has evolved into a wise and respected counselor.

Obviously, his dalliance with T'Pring is a thing of the past, since he is here married to Uhura. But the actress who played T'Pring is on hand, too: Arlene Martel is the Vulcan priestess (who may or may not be T'Pring herself) who marries Stonn and Uhura!

Finally, we had been mildly critical back in Stand Six of the performances of James Cawley and Jeff Quinn as Kirk and Spock in *New Voyages*. Here they are much more effective: Cawley is Jim Kirk's nephew, commanding the *Enterprise-M*, and Quinn plays the *Conqueror's* Romulan helmsman.

SPECIAL EFFECTS (SFX) — *STAR TREK* (2009) AND *STAR TREK: OF GODS AND MEN*

This is where the "official" Paramount film could be expected to dwarf the Internet project: the sfx budget of *Star Trek: Of Gods and Men* would not pay for Spock's ears in *Star Trek* (2009). The difference is not nearly that big, not by a long shot. The sets of the Abrams film are, of course, much more elaborate and much more impressive, but they don't necessarily *tell the story* that much more effectively. If the starship battles in *Of Gods and Men* are smaller in scale, they are also easier for the eye to follow than those in *Star Trek* (2009) — again, storytelling trumps aesthetics. Paramount's sfx are good enough to warrant nominations for several major awards, but *Of Gods and Men* wizards may have accomplished a virtual miracle — by doing so very much with so very little! (Not unlike the original series, hmmm?)

It bears mentioning that the *Of Gods and Men* sfx team — Chris Dawson, Henry Gibbens, Wil Jaspers, Peter Christian, Roland Baron, William Thomas, and others — is responsible for more of the storytelling than one might suspect. For instance, an attentive viewer will note that the flagship of the rebel commander, Captain Galt (Herbert Jefferson), the U.S.S. *Liberty*, is the battered Federation Starship NCC-1017. In "our" reality, this was the U.S.S. *Constellation* — the very ship that destroyed/ was destroyed by "The Doomsday Machine" (Stand Six)!

This creates interesting implications regarding the Planet Killer, as well as V'Ger from *Star Trek: The Motion Picture*, the whale probe in *Star Trek*

IV: Voyage Home, the giant amoeba "The Immunity Syndrome," and other menaces: Jack Treviño and his fellow writers "theorized that Mitchell had disposed of such threats, however, such things drained his powers considerably, leaving Mitchell and the Order to rely mainly on fear as a means to maintain control." Yet the writers had not included the *Constellation* in their story: "Regarding the U.S.S. *Liberty*, we gave the special effects team considerable leeway when designing and building the rebel fleet. Several ships were named to honor military soldiers who fought and gave their lives for our country, including Captain Uhura's ship, the U.S.S. Gunderson. So, other than the *Conqueror* and Mitchell's *Destroyer*, the credit for registration numbers and ship names goes to the effects team."

CANON — *STAR TREK* (2009) AND *STAR TREK: OF GODS AND MEN*

This is where the excrement hits the oscillating blades, if you get our drift — by the very nature of the two projects. *Of Gods and Men* aims to celebrate forty years of *Star Trek*, but *Star Trek* (2009) aims to re-invent. Thus, *Of Gods and Men* is almost slavish, in both visuals and storyline, to what has gone before: In the words of writer Jack Treviño, "a great deal of time and effort went into researching documented *Star Trek* history (using StarTrek.com, *The Star Trek Encyclopedia* and numerous other *Star Trek* web sites for reference) to insure we did not violate established canon." By comparison, the attitude of *Star Trek* (2009) to said canon can best be described as — cavalier. Some of the differences are inconsequential; some are anything but. For instance:

When Kirk came to command the *Enterprise* (in established canon), it already boasted a long and storied history under Captain Christopher Pike, and before him, Captain Robert April (who appeared only in the 1970s animated series; in the *Star Trek Encyclopedia*, he is affectionately given the face of Gene Roddenberry). Yet here, the ship is under construction as Kirk enlists, and just entering service at the time of his pending graduation.

Likewise, Pike had an entire bridge crew, seen in the original pilot and in "The Menagerie," which preceded the Kirk crew: the executive officer known only as "Number One," Senior Medical Officer Philip Boyce, Navigator Jose Tyler — only Science Officer Spock was familiar to us. Where'd these guys disappear to?

Pike commanded a crew of more than two hundred on his *Enterprise*. After a refit, Kirk's crew numbered four hundred thirty. Yet, here Pike tells

Jim Kirk that his father saved "eight hundred lives" when he enabled the crew of the *Kelvin* to escape — and the *Kelvin* was a much smaller survey ship, while the *Enterprise* was a "heavy cruiser." For that matter, George Kirk has a pregnant wife on the ship — but on-ship families would not become a regular feature of Starfleet until the twenty-fourth century, much to the disgust of Captain Picard.

We could go on and on and on — and some *Star Trek* aficionados do — but the point is made. Whether the canonical discrepancies of the larger film represent real damage is debatable — and is debated.

It can be said that *Of Gods and Men*, again by its very nature, is somewhat derivative. The script by Calk, Conway, and Treviño ultimately derives a great deal from two celebrated television episodes: Gary Mitchell's "Galactic Order" strongly resembles the Empire into which Kirk, McCoy, Scotty, and Uhura beam in the Original Series episode "Mirror, Mirror," while in the *Next Generation* episode "Yesterday's *Enterprise*," the "wrongness" of the altered timeline is first sensed by a wise black woman — Guinan (Whoopi Goldberg) — much as Uhura divines the discrepancy in *Of Gods and Men*.

Yet a great many of the best of *Star Trek* is derivative — "Balance of Terror" from *Run Silent, Run Deep*, "The Doomsday Machine" from *Moby Dick* — and many of the later episodes use what has gone before as a springboard. Budget and resource considerations aside, the biggest differences between *Star Trek* (2009) and *Star Trek: Of Gods and Men* reside in the realm of ideas.

STAR TREK (2009) AND STAR TREK: OF GODS AND MEN: THE ESSENTIAL DIFFERENCE

Okay, the obvious difference is that the Paramount film has been seen by billions all over the world in theatres, and billions more via DVD, whereas the Renegade product is available to the relative handful seeking it out on the Internet, and those who order it online. Due to their arrangement with Paramount/CBS, Renegade can't sell the *Of Gods and Men* DVD outright, but they can tack it on as a "free gift" with any other product ordered from their online store.

More to the point, both are reasonably entertaining sci-fi films — but so are *Avatar, Blade Runner, Zardoz* (remember *Zardoz*, with a just un-Bonded Sean Connery running around in "a distracting adult diaper?") and the other big franchises such as *Star Wars* and *Aliens*. What has always set *Star Trek* apart is its ideas of friendship that transcends service discipline, race, and species; the virtues of emotional spontaneity versus those of logic and reason; tolerance of different ideas and different expressions that were best stated by the theme, *Infinite Diversity in Infinite Combinations (IDIC)*, the willingness to question when and where fighting and conflict are necessary or appropriate, and finally, the spirit of self-sacrifice.

J. J. Abrams' *Star Trek* (2009) is very big on the friendship angle. In fact, the entire story turns on the concept at two important junctures. First, Bones McCoy risks his career to smuggle Jim Kirk aboard the newly-commissioned *Enterprise* — without this, the sequence of events that results in Nero's defeat would not be set in motion; second, Spock Prime contrives to conceal knowledge of his existence in the current timeline from his younger self, thus enabling that self and Kirk to forge the friendship that would "define them both."

The chronicling of Kirk and Spock's childhoods ensures that the logic vs. emotion question would be explored as well — although this film seems to come down on the side of "emotional justification" more often than not. Tolerance is more implied than stated by the fact that different sexes, different races and different species are working side-by-side — which, admittedly, is no longer the ground-breaking concept that it was when shown on the Original Series. (And that, as Martha Stewart would say, is a Good Thing.)

If anything is missing here in the realm of ideas, it is the asking of the hard questions. Near the film's end, when Nero and the *Narada* are defeated and at the mercy of the *Enterprise*, Kirk offers to save the Romulans from imminent destruction. Spock objects: the Romulans have killed his mother and destroyed Vulcan; he wants them killed. Kirk explains that the offer of compassion is a practical matter: "Showing them compassion may be the only way to earn peace with Romulus." Nero resolves the dilemma by refusing the olive branch: "I would rather suffer the end of Romulus a thousand times. I would rather die in agony, than accept assistance from you!"

What's wrong with this picture — not with Nero necessarily, but with Kirk and Spock? Remember Jim Kirk in Stand Five, "Arena," refusing to kill the Gorn — "You'll have to get your entertainment somewhere else!" — even though the decision risks the destruction of his ship and crew. He behaves this way because that's how he's wired; he can do no other. In other words, Kirk and Starfleet should offer compassion to Nero and the *Narada* not because of practical considerations, *but because that's who and what they are!*

Of Gods and Men director Tim Russ points out one of the main reasons *Star Trek* was created in the first place: "*Star Trek* is unique by virtue of the fact that Gene Roddenberry wanted to address the issues: social issues, social politics, our biases, our discriminations...attitudes about things. He wanted to address all of these, about people and their cultural...ideals and ideologies by dressing them up in a science fiction concept...and be

able to play these things out, to discuss and to demonstrate what these attitudes and difficulties and conflicts are...to be able to incorporate... some of the elements of things in our world that we're dealing with now, such as terrorism, i.e., people who fight for a reason or a cause and why they do it, and also trading security for freedom...trying to discuss the balance between those two."

This analogy to present events seems to be conspicuous by its near-absence in Abrams' *Star Trek* (2009): the bad guys are extremely bad, and the need to defeat them is an absolute given (although Alan Dean Foster's novelization of the Orci-Kurtzman script includes a scene, omitted from the film, in which the crew of the *Narada* try to dissuade Nero from destroying Earth and the other Federation planets).

In *Of Gods and Men,* by contrast, the alternate timeline seems to have been created specifically to address present-day questions of terrorism and justification, which do not lend themselves to easy answers, nor do the writers attempt any. Consider the first exchange between Captain Harriman and Khitrec:

> KHITREC
>
> *We fight for our freedom!*
>
> CAPTAIN HARRIMAN
>
> *Freedom — what is freedom without security? Nothing. The Galactic Order provides that security.*
>
> KHITREC
>
> *Only through fear and violence! Anyone who trades freedom for security deserves neither.*

(The quote is, of course, from Ben Franklin.)
Or, later, Khitrec and Uhura:

> UHURA
>
> *We know who you are. You kill to achieve your own goals — just like those butchers of the so-called Galactic Order. You're no better, sir.*
>
> KHITREC
>
> *We're nothing like the Galactic Order! If we kill, it is to win our freedom.*
>
> UHURA
>
> *That's empty rhetoric. Killing is killing!*

Further on, when the memories of the "correct" timeline have been revealed, Khitrec still finds it all but impossible to let go of his pain and hatred:

> UHURA
>
> *Somehow Harriman is connected to all of this... we're going to need him to figure out how all of this happened.*
>
> KHITREC
>
> *No! I've been hunting that butcher for twenty years!*
>
> UHURA
>
> *Why, because he's part of the Galactic Order? Well, that's not good enough!*

> KHITREC
>
> *Because he slaughtered my family! I lost everything — my wife, my son — and no Vulcan mind trick is going to erase what he did.*
>
> UHURA
>
> *And you think it's easier for me? The same thing happened, on Vulcan, to my family, yet I know we need him. We need Harriman. I know it — and you know it.*

Ultimately, Khitrec and Harriman must face the ultimate enemy: themselves.

> KHITREC
>
> *You've probably forgotten an insignificant little planet called New Eden. I haven't. My family was there.*
>
> CAPTAIN HARRIMAN
>
> *I thought I was doing my duty. Firing torpedoes from the bridge is so easy. You never see the faces.*
>
> KHITREC
>
> *Was I wrong? Was I too busy playing the rebel?*

What applies to these heroes-turned-villains-turned-heroes-again, Khitrec and Harriman, applies even more to Charlie Evans, who has set these events in motion, and who pays the ultimate price to balance the scales: Only when they have purged their own demons, can men (Women? Humans? Sentient life-forms?) win the battle.

That's what ties them in not only with their predecessors in *Star Trek*, but with all the heroes in this book, from Bick Benedict in *Giant*, through Anton Drager in *Spiral Road*, Charlie Anderson in *Shenandoah*, Frank Towns in *Flight of the Phoenix* — all the way through the real-life MacArthur and Schindler — *first they must overcome themselves*, then they can address their particular challenges.

THE BALANCE SHEET

If Renegade's *Star Trek: Of Gods and Men* does indeed renew the tolerant and boldly questioning spirit of *Star Trek* itself, then Paramount's *Star Trek* (2009) performs the necessary function of relaunching the franchise. The Original Series debuted over forty years ago. DeForest Kelley, Jimmy Doohan, and Mark Lenard have passed on — along with Gene and Majel Roddenberry, and Gene Coon, and Bob Justman, and so many of the original visionaries — while Bill Shatner, Leonard Nimoy and their contemporaries are pushing eighty. And yet, if the *Star Trek* vision is important enough to endure, then Chris Pine, Zachary

Quinto and the other "young Turks" will age and pass in the relative blink of an eye, but the vision will remain, vibrant and shining — *if* properly tended.

Bluntly speaking, *Star Trek: Of Gods and Men* is an exercise in tribute and closure, and does not really lend itself to sequels, while

Star Trek (2009) exists to encourage and enable sequels. Just as the role of Hamlet passes from generation to generation, from Richard Burbage to Edwin Booth to John Barrymore to Laurence Olivier to Kenneth Branagh, the roles of Kirk and Spock are open to the interpretations of actors yet to be born, if they pass the same test as Hamlet: they still have something valid and immediate to say.

On James Cawley's meticulously recreated bridge set: J. D. Hertzler (Koval), Tim Russ (Tuvok/director), Chase Masterson (Xela), Crystal Allen (Yara), Gary Graham (Ragnar), Garrett Wang (Garan), Walter Koenig (Chekov/Khitrec), Alan Ruck (Harriman), and Nichelle Nichols (Uhura), all the main players from Star Trek: Of Gods and Men.

Star Trek can continue to make money if its creators continue to strive for better execution — not necessarily *bigger*, mind you, but always *better*. And there's nothing wrong with making money, either. As Woody Allen says, "Money is better than poverty, if only for financial reasons." Those who perpetuate the franchise have to do so with one eye on the fountainhead, on the ideals of friendship and tolerance and the bold willingness to ask the hard questions — and the other eye on the world as it exists at the given moment: just what *are* the questions that need asking, the injustices that need exposing?

Stand Seven in this collection, *Too Much, Too Soon*, quotes Gene Fowler, the friend and biographer of John Barrymore. Gene Roddenberry's life and career were just gearing up, with *Star Trek* on the near horizon, as Fowler was struggling to complete his last book, *Skyline*. The two may or may not have met., but they shared a certain vision, a vision of what *can be*, tempered by that which *is:*

"Life, human and otherwise, is an ordeal. The way one meets that ordeal marks the size and meaning of a man. Some meet it with pious resignation, others with philosophical stoicism, still others with a desperation which finds the wayfarer somewhere between the poles of terror and heroism, lament and exultation…Though wayward at times, I sought to go with faith, to work and live with a measure of gaiety, as opposed to a show of penitential tears. I have had but one fault to find with life: there are too many good-bys."

FINALE:
THREE PRESCIPTIONS

"Pictures are for entertainment, messages should be delivered by Western Union."

— Samuel Goldwyn

Goldwyn's famous quote has a ring to it, but fortunately for us, filmmakers — Goldwyn included — have seldom considered themselves bound by it. In particular, the twelve films in this collection dare to tell us how we should live: outside the boundaries imposed by society in its various manifestations of race, religion, class — even nation. And, Mr. Goldwyn notwithstanding, it's entirely right and proper for them to do so!

Goldwyn's dictum is superseded by remarks made by the dean of television newsmen, Edward R. Murrow, to the Radio and Television News Directors Association in 1958. The "instrument" he refers to is television, but his observation applies equally, if not more so, to movies: "This instrument can teach, it can illuminate; yes, and it can even inspire, but it can do so only to the extent that humans are determined to use it to those ends. Otherwise, it is merely wires and lights in a box."

The actors, filmmakers and storytellers celebrated herein are not content with "wires and lights in a box." But they knew that outright preaching, especially the preaching of new and unwelcome ideas, is acceptable to very few people, unless it's all tied together as part and parcel of a first-rate entertainment package.

In this manner, a filmmaker *earns* the right to tell other people how they should live, to write prescriptions for living. And his prescriptions may very well penetrate where the windy pronouncements of preachers and politicians do not.

To wrap up our little thesis, consider three such prescriptions, which — if heeded — just might have the power to change the world.

PRESCRIPTION NUMBER ONE: FROM *JUDGMENT AT NUREMBERG* (1961)

Abby Mann's brilliantly written play, subsequently filmed, focuses not on the initial war crimes trial of the most prominent surviving Nazi leaders, but on a fictionalized account of the trial of four judges some time

later, thus enabling Mann to prune and rearrange the ideas expressed at the time for maximum dramatic impact. The level of writing is matched by the top-flight casting of the film: Maximilian Schell as defense attorney Rolfe, a part for which he won a "Best Actor" Oscar, Richard Widmark as the prosecutor, Marlene Dietrich as a proud German widow, Werner Klemperer as an unrepentant defendant, Burt Lancaster as the brilliant jurist haunted by his failures, Judy Garland and Montgomery Clift as heartbreaking victims of the Nazi regime — and topping them all, Spencer Tracy as the presiding judge who refuses to bow to political pressure.

Judge Haywood's delivery of the verdict is as apropos today as it was then, as we question whether "preventive wars" and torture of prisoners are either appropriate or acceptable:

JUDGE HAYWOOD
Simple murders and atrocities do not constitute the gravamen of the charges in this indictment. Rather, the charge is that of conscious

participation in a nationwide, governmen- organized system of cruelty and injustice in violation of every moral and legal principle known to all civilized nations. The Tribunal has carefully studied the record and found therein abundant evidence to support beyond a reasonable doubt the charges against these defendants.

Herr Rolfe, in his very skillful defense, has asserted that there are others who must share the ultimate responsibility for what happened here in Germany. There is truth in this. The real complaining party at the bar in this courtroom is civilization. But the Tribunal does say that the men in the dock are responsible for their actions, men who sat in black robes in judgment on other men, men who took part in the enactment of laws and decrees, the purpose of which was the extermination of human beings, men who in executive positions actively participated in the enforcement of these laws that were illegal even under German law. The principle of criminal law in every civilized society has this in common: any person who sways another to commit murder, any person who furnishes the lethal weapon for the purpose of the crime, any person who is an accessory to the crime — is guilty.

Herr Rolfe further asserts that the defendant, Janning, was an extraordinary jurist and acted in what he thought was the best interest of his country. There is truth in this also. Janning, to be sure, is a tragic figure. We believe he loathed the evil he did. But compassion for the present torture of his soul must not beget forgetfulness of the torture and the death of millions by the Government of which he was a part. Janning's record and his fate illuminate the most shattering truth that has emerged from this trial: If he and all of the other defendants had been degraded perverts, if all of the leaders of the Third Reich had been sadistic monsters and maniacs, then these events would have no more moral significance than an earthquake, or any other natural catastrophe. But this trial has shown that under a national crisis, ordinary — even able and extraordinary — men can delude themselves into the commission of crimes so vast and heinous that they beggar the imagination. No one who has sat through this trial can ever forget them: men sterilized because of political belief; a mockery made of friendship and faith; the murder of children. How easily it can happen.

There are those in our own country, too, who today speak of the "protection of country" — of "survival." A decision must be made in the life of every nation at the very moment when the grasp of the enemy is at its throat. Then, it seems that the only way to survive is to use the means of the enemy, to rest survival upon what is expedient — to look the other way.

Well, the answer to that is "survival as what?" A country isn't a rock. It's not an extension of one's self. It's what it stands for. It's what it stands for when standing for something is the most difficult! Before the people of the world, let it now be noted that here, in our decision, this is what we stand for: justice, truth, and the value of a single human being.

"Survival as what?" Does the society — or the individual — that ceases to ask that question even deserve to survive?

PRESCRIPTION NUMBER TWO: FROM *RAGTIME* (1981)

E. L. Doctorow's kaleidoscopic portrait of early twentieth century America was adapted, not without difficulty, for film by director Milos Forman and screenwriter Michael Weller, who decided to narrow their focus to the story of the proud black pianist Coalhouse Walker, Junior (Howard E. Rollins, Junior), the victim of a sick practical joke played by a repulsive volunteer fire chief (Kenneth MacMillan): incensed that an "uppity Nigra" can own a magnificent Model T, the chief and his men seize the car, fouling it with horse manure and otherwise defacing it.

More infuriating to Walker than the damage to his car is the advice of his friends and associates, Black *and* White, that he swallow the insult and forget it. One prominent Black attorney (Ted Ross) tells him to "… just forget that some damn white man caused you offense… I've spent my whole life forgetting. You're a young man. You better start learning now."

"Learning what?" Walker retorts. "How to be a nigger?"

Eventually, after exhausting all his legal alternatives, Walker turns renegade, seizing J. P. Morgan's treasure-laden museum. It falls to Police Commissioner Rhinelander Waldo (James Cagney, magnificent in the role that brought him out of a twenty-year retirement) to root him out. Waldo opts to try persuasion first, calling upon the most prominent Black statesman of the time, Booker T. Washington (Moses Gunn), to speak to Walker. The fact is, Walker is too far gone down his private path to be moved by Washington's words. They are nonetheless magnificent in their eloquence:

BOOKER T. WASHINGTON

Mister Walker, I have spent a lifetime trying to persuade the White man that he needn't fear us, that all we wanted was a chance to work and prosper beside him, and enjoy with him the fruits of this great land. Now, the example of one thousand honest, industrious Black men cannot undo the harm of one like you. What you have done here has set our race back a distance I can't measure. And you say you admire me.

COALHOUSE WALKER, JUNIOR

I tried everything, sir, every legal means to get satisfaction. And I was humiliated at every turn! The woman who bore my child — my child, Mister Washington, whom I may never see again — she watched my pride being snatched away from me, piece by piece. She believed in justice! Oh, yes! She went to the White man and she begged that I be given the justice entitled to me by law. She died begging for it!

BOOKER T. WASHINGTON

I beg you, Mister Walker, on behalf of our people, your young son, and all the children of our race, I beg you to give yourself up. Bring your men and follow me now. I will intercede on your behalf. Your trial shall be swift and your execution painless.

COALHOUSE WALKER, JUNIOR

If my automobile is restored and delivered to the front of this building, and the fire chief is handed over to my justice, I give you my solemn oath I will come out with my hands raised, and no further harm will come to this place, or to any man.

BOOKER T. WASHINGTON

And you think this revenge will restore your damaged pride? Well, you're wrong, Mister Walker. You are wrong to the depths of your soul! Because vengeance does nothing but perpetuate vengeance and on and on, until some race can find the strength to say, "No! The wrong done to me I will not avenge! I shall stand with dignity and Christian love until my enemies are won over because they honor and respect me." And only when this happens, Mister Walker, shall we have our pride back — all of us.

COALHOUSE WALKER, JUNIOR

You speak like an angel, Mister Washington. It's too bad we're living on the earth.

The echoes of Mohandas Gandhi's *Satyagraha*, or soul force, are obvious in Washington's words. And stripping away the limitations of labeling words — the love need not be "Christian" only, and this particular Stand need not be made by a race, but by a nation, or an individual — the prescription can be applied universally, to anyone with courage enough to bear the consequences.

PRESCRIPTION NUMBER THREE:
FROM *THE MARTIAN CHRONICLES* (1980)

Now, we've come full circle, to the actor with whom we began this treatise: Rock Hudson, who enjoyed one of his best late-career roles in the 1980 television adaptation of Ray Bradbury's *The Martian Chronicles*.

Coming on the heels of *Star Wars* (1979), which revolutionized the standards of science fiction on both the large and small screens, *The*

Martian Chronicles stands out like a sore thumb by virtue of its primitive special effects and penny-pinching production values. These stand in sharp contrast to the poetic and peculiarly haunting ideas of Bradbury, as skillfully adapted for the miniseries by Richard Matheson, and the extraordinary, heartfelt performances of many of the cast members, especially Bernie Casey, Christopher Connelly, Barry Morse, Fritz Weaver, Roddy McDowell, and more than any other, Rock Hudson.

As noted earlier, the life and career of Rock Hudson (seen opposite with Darren McGavin) would be cut tragically short in less than five years, depriving him of the "third act" roles enjoyed by actors who live and work into old age. The role of Colonel Wilder may be the closest he came to an "elder statesman" portrayal, almost luminous at times, aided by the fact that Matheson has taken several scenes from the book that had nothing to do with Wilder and given them to him, for continuity's sake.

In the best of these scenes, Hudson's astronaut commander has finally realized his dream: he is conversing at long last with an actual Martian (Terence Longdon). Somehow, the two have broken the barrier of time to perceive, and converse with, one another. If the ideas propounded by our twelve selected films could be synthesized in one philosophy of living, it would be the statement made across the centuries by the Martian to Colonel Wilder. This achieves what all the windy pronouncements of Man, and Man's religions, have failed to do — *it does away utterly with the concept of Us and Them*:

THE MARTIAN
There is no secret. Anyone with eyes can see the way to live: by watching life — observing nature and cooperating with it — making common cause with the process of existence — by living life for itself, don't you see, deriving pleasure from the gift of pure being. Life is its own answer. Accept it and enjoy it, day by day. Live as well as possible. Expect no more. Destroy nothing. Humble nothing. Look for fault in nothing. Leave unsullied and untouched all that is beautiful. Hold that which lives in all reverence, for life is given by the Sovereign of our universe — given to be savored, to be luxuriated in, to be respected.

Taken together, these three "prescriptions," if followed, could literally revolutionize human life and human history.

Survival is not enough — the question must be asked, "Survival as what?"

Life will continue its endless cycle of offense followed by revenge followed by revenge until someone, somewhere, stands up and says "No! This wrong I will not avenge!"

Life is to be lived for its own sake, hurting and humbling no one and nothing.

A film that genuinely entertains its audience — through outstanding accomplishments in writing, acting, directing, scoring and the associated crafts — is in itself a rare and wonderful accomplishment. A film that does all these things, and embodies such profound and compelling truths as those quoted herein — *that film is as true a miracle as the race of man can aspire to.*

Back to the statement from *The Martian Chronicles* quoted above: Life is to be lived for its own sake, hurting and humbling no one and nothing. After saying this to Colonel Wilder, The Martian then goes on to say: "You're intelligent. You know as well as I what has to be done."

Are we?

Do we?

Will we?

BIBLIOGRAPHY

Asherman, Allan. *The Star Trek Interview Book*. New York: Pocket Books, 1988.

_____. *The Star Trek Compendium*. New York: Simon & Schuster, 1981.

Barrymore, Diana, with Gerold Frank. *Too Much, Too Soon*. New York: Henry Holt and Company, 1957.

*Blair, Clay, Junior. *MacArthur*. New York: Pocket Books, 1977.

Blish, James. *Star Trek 2*. New York: Bantam Books, 1968.

_____. *Star Trek 3*. New York: Bantam Books, 1969.

Brode, Douglas. *The Films of Steven Spielberg*. Secaucus, New Jersey: Citadel Press, 1995.

Byers, Ann. *Oskar Schindler: Saving Jews From the Holocaust*. Berkeley Heights, New Jersey, 2005.

Castell, David. *Richard Attenborough: A Pictorial Film Biography*. London: Bodley Head, 1984.

Considine, Bob. *The Long and Illustrious Career of General Douglas MacArthur*. New York: Gold Medal Books, 1964.

Cross, Robin. *2,000 Movies: The 1950s*. New York: Arlington House, 1988.

Crowe, David M. *Oskar Schindler: The Untold Account of His Life, Wartime Activities, and the True Story Behind The List*. New York: Basic Books, 2004.

*De Hartog, Jan. *The Spiral Road*. New York: Bantam Books, 1958.

Doohan, James, with Peter David. *Beam Me Up, Scotty: Star Trek's "Scotty" in his own words*. New York: Pocket Books, 1996.

Dunn, William J. *Pacific Microphone*. College Station: Texas A&M University Press, 1988.

Dwiggins, Don. *Hollywood Pilot: The Biography of Paul Mantz*. New York: Doubleday and Company, 1967.

Fensch, Thomas, editor. *Oskar Schindler and his List: The Man, The Book, The Film, The Holocaust and Its Survivors*. Forest Dale, Vermont: Paul S. Ericksson, 1995.

*Ferber, Edna. *Giant*. Garden City, New York: Doubleday and Company, 1952.

Published tie-ins to films in this collection.

*Foster, Alan Dean, from screenplay by Roberto Orci and Alex Kurtzman. *Star Trek*. New York: Pocket Books, 2009.

Fowler, Gene. *Good Night. Sweet Prince*. New York: Viking Press, 1944.

_____. *Minutes of the Last Meeting*. New York: Viking Press, 1954.

_____. *Skyline*. New York: Viking Press, 1961.

*Gary, Romain. *The Roots of Heaven*. New York: Pocket Books, 1958.

Godfrey, Lionel. *The Life and Crimes of Errol Flynn*. New York: Saint Martin's Press, 1977.

Griggs, John. *The Films of Gregory Peck*. Secaucus, New Jersey: Citadel Press, 1984.

Hirschhorn, Clive. *The Universal Story*. New York: Crown Publishers, 1983.

Hudson, Rock, and Sara Davidson. *Rock Hudson: His Story*. New York: William Morrow and Company, 1986.

Jones, Ken D. with Arthur F. McClure and Alfred E. Twomey. *The Films of James Stewart*. New York: Castle Books, 1970.

*Keneally, Thomas. *Schindler's List: A Novel*. New York: Simon & Schuster, 1982.

_____. *Searching for Schindler*. New York: Nan A. Talese, 2007.

MacArthur, Douglas. *Reminiscences*. New York: McGraw-Hill, 1964.

Madsen, Axel. *John Huston: A Biography*. Garden City, New York: Doubleday, 1978.

Matthews, Jim. *Old Soldiers Never Die: A Photo History of General MacArthur*. Los Angeles: Special Publications, 1964.

Montaigne, Lawrence. *A Vulcan Odyssey*. Charleston, South Carolina: BookSurge, 2006.

Morris, George. *Errol Flynn: A Pyramid Illustrated History of the Movies*. New York: Pyramid Books, 1975.

Pratley, Gerald. *The Cinema of John Huston*. New York: A.S. Barnes & Company, 1977.

Roddenberry, Gene, from screenplay by Harold Livingston, story by Alan Dean Foster. *Star Trek: The Motion Picture*. New York: Pocket Books, 1979.

Rusesabagina, Paul with Tom Zoellner. *An Ordinary Man*. New York: Viking Press, 2006.

Schindler, Emilie with Erika Rosenberg. *Where Light and Shadow Meet: A Memoir*. New York: W.W. Norton & Company, 1996.

Shatner, William with Chris Kreski. *Star Trek Memories*. New York: HarperCollins, 1993.

Silver, Alain and James Ursini. *What Ever Happened to Robert Aldrich? His Life and His Films*. New York: Proscenium Publishers, 1995.

Smith, Starr. *Jimmy Stewart, Bomber Pilot*. Saint Paul, Minnesota: Zenith Press, 2005.

Spoto, Donald. *Rebel: The Life and Legend of James Dean*. New York: HarperCollins Publishers, Inc. 1996.

Thomas, Tony with Rudy Behlmer and Clifford McCarty. *The Films of Errol Flynn*. Secaucus, New Jersey: Citadel Press, 1969.

Thomas, Tony. *A Wonderful Life: The Films and Career of James Stewart*. Secaucus, New Jersey: Citadel Press, 1988.

_____. *Errol Flynn: The Spy Who Never Was*. Secaucus, New Jersey: Citadel Press, 1990.

Thomas, Tony, editor. *From a Life of Adventure: The Writings of Errol Flynn*. Secaucus, New Jersey: Citadel Press, 1980.

Thomson, David. *Rosebud: The Story of Orson Welles*. New York: Alfred A. Knopf, 1996.

Thompson, Howard. *James Stewart: A Pyramid Illustrated History of the Movies*. New York: Pyramid Books, 1974.

*Trevor, Elleston. *The Flight of the Phoenix*. New York: Avon Books, 1964.

Wukovits, John F. *Oskar Schindler*. Farmington Hills, Michigan: Lucent Books, 2003.

ABOUT THE AUTHOR

Neal Stannard is a career radio broadcaster, currently working as a news anchor and program producer for Treasure and Space Coast Radio in Vero Beach, Florida, best known as one of the "hunker down heroes" who stayed on the air during the hurricanes of 2004. He's also a stage actor (opposite, as "Big Daddy" in *The Glass Mendacity*) and a lay speaker for the Unitarian Universalist Association. *Now and Then, The Movies Get It Right* is his first book.

Bear Manor Media

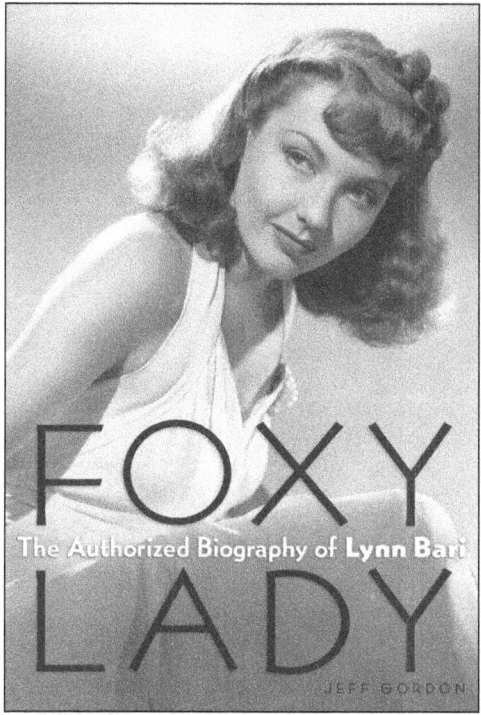

Classic Cinema.
Timeless TV.
Retro Radio.
WWW.BEARMANORMEDIA.COM

www.ingramcontent.com/pod-product-compliance
Lightning Source LLC
Chambersburg PA
CBHW071619170426
43195CB00038B/1472